Science of Selenium

Master Web UI Automation and
Create Your Own Test Automation Framework

---

by

Kalilur Rahman

FIRST EDITION 2020

Copyright © BPB Publications, India

ISBN: 978-93-89423-242

Distributors:

BPB PUBLICATIONS
20, Ansari Road, Darya Ganj
New Delhi-110002
Ph: 23254990/23254991

DECCAN AGENCIES
4-3-329, Bank Street,
Hyderabad-500195
Ph: 24756967/24756400

MICRO MEDIA
Shop No. 5, Mahendra Chambers,
150 DN Rd. Next to Capital Cinema,
V.T. (C.S.T.) Station, MUMBAI-400 001
Ph: 22078296/22078297

BPB BOOK CENTRE
376 Old Lajpat Rai Market,
Delhi-110006
Ph: 23861747

Published by Manish Jain for BPB Publications, 20 Ansari Road, Darya Ganj, New Delhi-110002 and Printed by him at Repro India Ltd, Mumbai

Dedicated to My Family

My wonderful spouse and the two angelic daughters who made me a complete man showered with full of blessings and happiness. It's the cherubic smile of your children and the giant sequoia like support from your spouse and family that motivates simpletons like me to aspire and dream big and take gargantuan tasks of moving mountains. A special dedication to all the great families doing the same and to all the wonderful innovators, authors and leaders who make this world a better place!

About the Author

 **Kalilur Rahman** has a Master's Degree in Business Administration preceded by an Engineering Degree in Computer Science and over 2 decades of experience in software development, testing and management consultancy. Kalilur has been a developer, designer, technical architect, test program manager, delivery unit head, IT Services and Factory Services Head of varying complexity across telecommunications, life sciences, retail and healthcare industries. Kalilur has advised CxO level leaders in market-leading firms for testing, business and technology transformation programs. As a Chapter Chair for Testing Professional organization, SteP-In, Kalilur has helped facilitate two international software conferences on software testing.

Kalilur is a firm Believer in "Knowledge is Power" and is passionate about writing and sharing his knowledge. Kalilur is an active member of various technical and professional forums, and has contributed to internal improvement initiatives in the organizations he worked. Kalilur varied interestsinclude technology, testing in the digital world, artificial intelligence, machine learning, DevOps, continuous delivery, agile, mobility, IoT, and analytics. He is a regular contributor at LinkedIn – a site for professionals – and has over 800,000+ followers. He has published over 150 articles across LinkedIn, DevOps.Com, Qrius, Testing Experience and Artha Magazines.

Kalilur is also an active quizzing enthusiast who participates in and contributes to corporate level quizzing events at competitive and information levels.

About the Reviewer

Maroof Ahmed Khan has 8 years of experience in Automation testing and performance testing using tools like Selenium, Cucumber, RestAssured, Appium, Protractor, Jmeter with programming languages like Java, JavaScript, TypeScript, Python etc. Maroof pursued B.E in Information Technology from Department of Engineering, Barkatullah University, Bhopal. He has worked with companies like UST Global, Tavant Technologies Waste Management US and Xavient Information Systems. He is currently working as Automation Test lead in Pitney Bowes, Noida.

Acknowledgement

I would be missing in my duty if I do not thank all the wonderful people at BPB publications who made this book a reality. This includes the management team (Nrip Jain and others), the Acquisition Editor (Nitin Dass) who persistently reached out to me to get this book going. Priyanka Deshpande who was very methodical, meticulous, friendly and strict to make sure that tasks were done on time and for brilliant inputs to chisel the book for the first draft. My wonderful technical reviewer Maroof Abdul Khan whose technical prowess and attention for detail ensured T's were crossed and I's were dotted in the book. The technical editor Ashi Singh and the copyeditors Ankit Rathore and Rashmi Sawant did a fantastic job in building the final version of the book and entire marketing and management team of BPB including Sourabh Dwivedi, Surbhi Saxena and others who made a wonderful effort to get the best out of this book. I would like to thank my ex-colleague and a testing guru, Paul Mowat for his wonderful foreword.

Lastly, I would like to thank my critics, teachers, and friends who have been pushing me with their inputs. Without their criticism, sagacious inputs, and support I would have never been able to write this book

– Kalilur Rahman

Foreword

Paul Mowat is a Director at Deloitte in Quality and Test with over twenty years of experience in advising global organizations on optimization and transformation of their Software Test Engineering as well as performing lead roles on large-scale delivery. Paul contributes to thought leadership in Software Test Engineering, publishing articles, and blogs in industry magazines as well as sharing his wealth of experience by presenting at conferences and coaching the next generation of Software Test Engineers. Paul was invited by the TMMi to critique the TMMi syllabus before the market launch. He is also part of the TMMi executive board responsible for the TMMi professional work stream and critiqued the DOu certified tester in DevOps certification.

Paul has known Kalilur Rahman as a friend for almost a decade and during this time, he learned about Kalilur's passion for quizzes, technology and his continual pursuit to keep learning. Kalilur has authored articles and been a speaker at conferences, engaging with his followers through sharing of knowledge. Paul and Kalilur have also worked together in shaping a world-class testing service. They have a shared interest in Software Testing Engineering, including management of capabilities across all test phases, innovation, and implementing test automation frameworks, which are the reasons behind this book.

Reflecting upon the changes that have happened in technology in the past thirty years is staggering; it was within this timeframe we experienced the fifth techno-economic revolution, the emergence of a personal computer for all households, who would have predicted that.As the internet and mobile took hold on how people communicated and went about their lives, we see Software is at the centerof organizations today. Open source has taken the industry by storm combined with agile development and DevOps causing organizations to transform. As organizations have transformed, the role of a tester has changed significantly. The skills needed to be successful are no longer the same. There is a huge difference between a tester and an individual who can execute the tests and provide a view on the quality levels compared toa software test engineer.

The software test engineer is high in demand in the market and has the skills to plan, design, and execute the tests while being able to hypothesis and investigate why the software under test does not meet the specification, all within an Agile/DevOps environment. Just having the domain knowledge is not enough; the emergence of the full stack software test engineer is here. Individuals who have experience across the DevOps pipeline, for example, and this is not meant to be an exhausted list of tools but to illustrate the experience needed; JIRA for the product, Sprint and defect backlog, GIT as the source control, Cucumber for business behavior development, Marven as the build tool, SonarQube to analyze the code quality and using a delivery engine like Docker is the key.

Selenium has become one of those open source tools of choice for the software test engineers, especially for automating web applications. If you are thinking about changing roles in the near future, you need to understand Selenium inside out so you can discuss your experience and level of knowledge during the interview phases. This book starts with guiding you through a general overview of test automation related to Selenium covering the history of automation, explaining the framework, for example, Web Driver, IDE, Grid and Remote control, the challenges and the benefits to building upon your understanding of web UI architecture with the various components and elements.For example, Element Locators, Selectors, ID Customization, Event Handling, Asynchronous Interactions, and Simulation of Screen Sizes that make up the web application. The referenced quotes manage to weave themselves into the chapters and resonated with me.

The detailed view of test tools available in the market helps you to appreciate the range of tools available and their primary use. The need to truly understand the architecture and be able to explain it in simple terms and this book enables you to do just that. The easy-to-follow examples cater for the beginner to the more advanced practitioner describing the simple web page object selection, event handling to the more advanced featured such as Page Object Model (POM), Reading and Writing Files, XLS, CSV, Reporting, Use of Object Repository, Integration with Jenkins, GitHub, Maven, Database connectivity using examples in Java and Python which is necessary in understanding how the testing fits within an Agile world using CI/CD pipelines. You are presented with a range of tips and tricks on automation and interview which I am sure you will find most helpful.

Most of the books I have read or friends recommended cover a wide range of topics within test automation which I have found to be too generic, never truly being able to answer the questions I had on understanding how Selenium works. I found myself in an endless loop on the internet, searching for specific pieces of information; this book starts off with the basics of how Selenium was developed, and step-by-step increases your knowledge of architecture, whilebeing a good source of learning to prepare you for those interview questions. I encourage you to continue on...

– Paul Mowat

Preface

Over the past few years, Selenium has been very popular and it has become the first choice of test automation engineers, testers as well as software product engineering companies. It is used for various core aspects of test automation in a very intelligent and simple way. Selenium has opened the doors for making test automation simple by exponentially increasing its open-source nature to automate various types of applications. Complexities such as the need to verify web and mobile applications across a myriad of platforms and devices are addressed by Selenium in an easy manner. With an easy to adapt framework and architecture, Selenium automation offers the capability to write once and run anywhere with the use of ever-expansive and friendly test automation extensions.

Selenium offers several benefits. The primary aim of this book is to create a scholastically simple and easy to use book that spotlights on the core concepts of test automation using Selenium in prominent programming languages. This book can be used to understand the concepts of Selenium in an easy way to prepare the professional reading this book to become ready to face challenging interviews. This book contains many examples showcasing a particular concept, along with key principles that may be useful while addressing potential interview questions. This book will be a good pilot to learn the basic and advanced concepts of test automation using Selenium. It is divided into 12 chapters and provides a detailed description of the core concepts of Selenium.

Chapter 1 introduces the concepts of test automation. It describes how to approach test automation including the challenges and approach. It also explains the importance of using test automation.

Chapter 2 introduces the history and high-level concepts of Selenium. It describes the benefits of using Selenium, core components of Selenium with an introduction to the Selenium architecture.

Chapter 3 covers the Selenium architecture in detail. This chapter focuses on how Selenium WebDriver API connects the dots between programming languages (such as C#, Python, Java, Ruby, Java Script etc.) bound through JSON wire protocols, leveraging the browser driver classes and interfaces to test the applications through real browsers.

Chapter 4 covers the Selenium tools and various aspects of their features such as Selenium Web Driver, Remote Control (RC), IDE and GRID related queries. This chapter covers some examples as well.

Chapter 5 discusses the Web UI automation using Selenium by understanding various options for testing the Web UI. This chapter covers HTML, CSS, DOM, JavaScript and their correlation with Selenium. It also covers various types of browser coverage and options for building a true cross-browser testing experience.

Chapter 6 covers one of the most important features of Selenium, that is, how to automate Web UI using Selenium in Java and Python. It also covers automation at browser, page and element level locator usage using various types of locators such as XPath, CSS, Name, ID etc., and action automation.

Chapter 7 covers how to perform Selenium automation using programming languages such as Ruby and JavaScript.

Chapter 8 explores the strategy, which one needs to keep in mind at the time of deciding a test automation framework. This chapter explores various aspects of test automation approaches. This chapter focuses more on the theoretical and concept-based understanding of test automation.

Chapter 9 addresses the concepts that are required to handle Page Object Models (POM), file and database handling, report creation for test automation using Python and Java programming examples using the Selenium framework.

Chapter 10 introduces the concept of cross-browser testing and importance of test automation. This chapter covers the concept of cross-browser testing using Selenium Grid and commercial cross-browser testing options.

Chapter 11 focuses on tips to follow while doing a test automation project. Chapter 11 also gives an introduction to various types of options to explore, and the myths one needs to be aware of.

Chapter 12 introduces the readers to a set of tips to p repare an approach for interview, practice questions and follow up questions that can be asked during the interview and follow-up approaches post the interview to create better outcomes.

Downloading the code bundle and coloured images:

Please follow the link to download the
Code Bundle and the *Coloured Images* of the book:

https://rebrand.ly/e5590

Errata

We take immense pride in our work at BPB Publications and follow best practices to ensure the accuracy of our content to provide with an indulging reading experience to our subscribers. Our readers are our mirrors, and we use their inputs to reflect and improve upon human errors if any, occurred during the publishing processes involved. To let us maintain the quality and help us reach out to any readers who might be having difficulties due to any unforeseen errors, please write to us at :

errata@bpbonline.com

Your support, suggestions and feedbacks are highly appreciated by the BPB Publications' Family.

Table of Contents

CHAPTER 1
Introduction to Test Automation

> *"Debugging is twice as hard as writing the code in the first place. Therefore, if you write the code as cleverly as possible, you are, by definition, not smart enough to debug it."*
>
> —*Brian W. Kernighan*
> *(Inventor of UNIX Operating System & Author of*
> *"The C Programming Language")*

Automation has been a productivity enhancer for humankind. With the advent of exponential growth in technology, how can we automate testing of the millions of lines of code churned every hour? This is where test automation plays a vital role – automating the testing of the automation tools to enhance the productivity of humankind. Test automation will be an essential part of the productivity growth of humanity. Without test automation, the release of quality code to production will become an activity equivalent to boiling an ocean. To do good quality product development, one should understand the importance of testing. To do rapid, efficient and productive testing, one should understand the importance of test automation. This chapter focuses on why test automation is very important. For a good test automation engineer, the fundamentals of test automation are must-have. He or she ought to know why, which, when and how test automation is essential. This chapter covers an introduction to why do we need test automation, what are the methods and tools we can leverage, when to do with test automation and how to get on with it. If a test automation engineer is thorough with these fundamentals, then the interview will be a smooth ride. This chapter describes key aspects of test automation that would be useful.

Structure

- What is automation?
- Introduction to test automation
- Benefits of test automation
- History of test automation
- Generations of test automation and evolution
- Introduction to different types of test automation
- Test automation framework
- What tests to automate
- Test automation challenges
- Test Automation Interview – Q & A

Objective

After studying this chapter, you should be able to understand some of the key interview questions to answer such as – Why test automation is important. What are the key drivers for test automation? Why should we automate at all? What are the hurdles faced whilst doing test automation? What are the tools available? What are the benefits of test automation? What are the skills needed by the test automation engineers? What is the history of test automation? What are some techniques and frameworks used for test automation? What are some of the challenges to overcome?

What is automation?

The definition of "**Automation**" as per Wikipedia is "***Automation*** *is the technology by which a process or procedure is performed with minimal human assistance.*" Any process or an activity done by a human in a repetitive manner involving motor or cognitive functions is a candidate for automation. From time immemorial, automation propelled every industrial revolution. On the other hand, the success of the industrial revolution was automation. Mechanical automation drove the first industrial revolution, with mechanical engines improving productivity such as steam engines and the use of tools for agricultural and mining production. The automation of mobility with the invention of wheel by Sumerians helped humans to become more agile. The automation of the printing process by *Gutenberg* helped propel the dissemination of knowledge in a rapid manner. The invention of the steam engine by

James Watt and the first industrial train ("**The Rocket**") by *George Stephenson* helped propel the movement of goods in a faster manner during the industrial revolution of the 19th Century. Other automation processes such as telegraph, telephony helped humans communicate better and efficiently. The automation of manufacturing with the assembly line process introduced by Henry Ford for Model-T car paved way for producing good, rapid and cheaper motorcars. The use of robotics with a focus on concepts of quality management like just in time, Kanban etc., helped produce products with precision and consistency and good quality. Thus, automation of production and assembly line aided by the electricity, just in time assembly and other innovations helped the second industrial revolution. The third industrial revolution is all about automation through computer systems. The advances in electronics, identification of transistors, chips and rapid processors helped humans automate and fast track computing, thereby propelling all of the industries to leapfrog. Finally, the fourth industrial revolution is all about the use of AI, robotics and other means to automate the automation process itself. Hence, automation has been and will be critical in the evolution of humankind.

Introduction to test automation

The question then arises, how to automate the testing and verification of systems. Can we boil the ocean with millions of testers spending months to rollout a feature or a product? It will be like the 15th century. How can we change that? Automating the testing process and use of efficient testing techniques will help achieve rapid, high quality testing at a cheaper rate through continuous testing and delivery. For instance, this will be like Amazon and other technology leaders releasing code to production in a matter of seconds to minutes and not in years.

Software Test Automation is a software, code or a process built using a software or a programming language to test a software or application under test to validate tests. This helps in validating checks against expected results and actual results attained by running the automation scripts/software. Test Automation software focuses primarily on automating the repetitive, monotonous and manual tasks. Some of the advanced test automation software could fully automate validation of end-to-end process flows of a software application. Software Test Automation can be leveraged across SDLC phases – right from Unit Testing (when the code is written initially) – to production deployment (where the deployed code can be checked for working functionality). Test automation can also be carried out at various layers, such as Graphical User Layer, **Application Programming Interface (API)** Layer and at the database layer, to validate functionalities, interfaces to ensure the application software under development meets the requirements.

Software Test Automation has been around ever since mainframe computers became a common enterprise automation tool. Even mainframes used **Restructured Extended Executor (ReXX)**, JCL and other tools for automation of the testing process, resulting in productivity improvements. For client-server and GUI applications (with Windows/Mac revolution), it started with a simple codeless record and playback moving towards a code-driven test automation. With the players such as Mercury (which has since become Micro Focus tool after an interim stint with HP), Segue offering leading automation tools of the time, test automation was widely pursued as a means to fast-track testing, reduce cycle times and improve product quality by delivering business value faster. All these resulted in the rapid growth of the software industry.

Benefits of test automation

Some of the benefits of test automation include reduction of time and errors, avoiding repeatability, ability to execute testing around the clock in multiple systems and platforms, and ability to test same functionality with different or multiple data set, platforms at the same time. With the advent of DevOps and continuous integration, test automation has removed the need for manual touchpoints and verifications by automating the end-to-end software processes with zero manual involvement. End-to-end software process could be a validation of a process flow enabled by a software right from the beginning of the process to the end of the process. This could be a combination of use-cases that outline the functionalities of a software application. Almost everything meaningfully automated could be run anytime and anywhere; however, many times we need to rely on a trigger such as an event-based or a database based. Test automation, when done right, along with processes such as test-driven development, model-specific language for testing and behaviour-driven testing etc., can improve the efficiency, coverage and quality of the work product quickly. Additionally, with good quality test automation, the ability to build reusable libraries and modularization of the code is another benefit that can save a lot of time and money across the board, at the module level, project level or enterprise level.

Some of the key benefits of test automation include (but not limited to):

- **Cost Savings**
  - o Cost Savings in terms of:
    - Manual test effort reduction
    - Removal of defects quickly
  - o Cost avoidance in terms of:
    - Reduction in regression defects
    - Removal of wastages

- **Reusability**
  - o Ability to write once and reuse multiple time through:
    - Modular design
    - Efficiency in configuration and clonability

- **Faster time to market**
  - o Efficient automation helps to reduce test execution time, as test cases can be run in parallel, in an unattended fashion and across platforms
  - o Tests can be triggered automatically without dependency on humans

- **Better test coverage**
  - o With test automation, a testing team can have a better test coverage for stability. However, important code branches, business functionalities need to automate by leveraging manual testing experts. Automation can help the skilled manual testers to focus on areas needing high business and functional knowledge on rapidly changing business-critical code branches of an application.

- **Early defect finding**
  - o Having an automated test suite for regression allows us to find defects early and fixing them as well.

- **Efficient testing**
  - o Test automation gives the testing team to run the test cycle efficiently and plan overall test strategy in the optimal manner for efficient outcomes.

- **Repeatability**
  - o It can be repeated in the same format as the automation is coded to run in the same way without the variations shown by human testers.
  - o Repeating, in the same manner, gives a clear view of application behaviour.

- **Avoidance of manual errors**
  - o As the test automation scripts follow a logic, manual errors, such as mistyping, clicking wrong buttons or other types of errors, can be avoided using test automation.

- **Reuse of Skilled Testers**
  - o Skilled testers can be leveraged to run high value-adding testing tasks instead of running low-risk, low-value adding, monotonous test scripts.

- **Ability to run in parallel**
  - o Test automation gives the test team with an ability to run in parallel with multiple data sets, devices and platforms.

History of test automation

To understand the history of test automation, we need to first understand some of the key progress made in terms of software testing and then in test automation. Let us study them:

- 1958 – First independent testing consultants incorporated in the PROJECT MERCURY program.

- In 1961 – *Leeds* and *Weinberg* published the first chapter on Program testing in the book *"Computer Programming Fundamentals"*.

- 1962 – Automatic Program Testing by IBM's Renfe becomes the first full-fledged testing book.

- In the 1970's, test automation picked up steam, TRW and IBM published first papers on test automation. The first seminal book on software testing was published in the early 70s – Program Test Methods.

- Even IBM Mainframe computers had automation tools such as SIMON or OLIVER that helped automate user interfaces or batch program execution. Test automation picked up steam in the most established computing systems of the time – Mainframes.

- NASA's Johnson Space Centre built an automated tool called Automated Test Data Generator in 1976 for testing purposes. (**https://dl.acm.org/citation.cfm?id=805646**). This was the first proven use of test data generation for testing and test automation.

- Test automation picked up steam with the growth of personal computers and desktop software. By late 1980s, software testing tool companies such as Segue, Mercury came into limelight.

- 1995 – First test automation book – *"Automated Testing Handbook"* by *Linda G Hayes* was published. *Linda Hayes* started a software company that has become a popular test management software – **Worksoft Certify.**

- 1999 – Software Test Automation by *Mark Fewster* and *Dorothy Graham – Strategy, Tactics and Issues* became the defacto guide for test automation and test engineers.

Generations of test automation

In this section, we will try to understand all the six generations of test automation:

- **First generation (record and playback)**
  - **Record and playback using a simple screen capturing of actions–**
    - This is a tool-based feature that records the screens and plays back

for validation. It is recommended for validating non-data centric scenarios such as features/menus and navigation validations.

- **Second generation (modularity/data-driven)**
  - o **Data-driven framework uses modular design and use of data lookup through the use of tables, files etc.–**
    - ▪ Modular scripting helps the test automation engineer build a strong library than can be reused across applications, projects and businesses, as some of the key actions and processes could be a tool agnostic or a person agnostic automation. Record-and-play back style automation breaks apart the moment a feature, object or interaction changes. If you have many record and playback scripts, all need to be re-automated. When it comes to modular scripting, you just need to change one script; and the effort reduction for maintenance is significant.
    - ▪ In a data-driven framework, data read from an external file, such as a flat file, excel, databases or a comma-separated file, is used for driving the test automation logic. In a data-driven test automation, the data and test automation logic are separate. The test data in the data file is used for executing test cases by running different test functions or methods based on the value or the test data. As the name says, the data drives the test automation logic.

- **Third generation (keyword-driven, reusable libraries)**
  - o **Keyword-driven frameworks using libraries–**
    - ▪ A keyword-driven test automation framework is a table or an action-word (also known as keyword) based test automation. In a keyword-driven test automation, an action phrase/verb/word known as a keyword defines a set of actions that need to be performed on a test object in a system under test. This contains logic on how a test is executed as defined by an automation analyst. The action phrase would contain the arguments potential values to be used for conducting the test.

- **Fourth generation (hybrid frameworks & behaviour-driven)**
  - o **Hybrid frameworks–**
    - ▪ A hybrid automation framework is a combination of test automation frameworks, such as data-driven and keyword-driven framework being used in combination. As an example, hybrid test automation framework combines the best of both keyword- and data-driven frameworks. A hybrid framework gives the flexibility to choose the best test automation approach for testing a test case or an application by the test automation engineer. One way a hybrid automation framework can be

implemented would be to keep both the test actions and test data in an external file and used in a hybrid manner for test automation execution.

- **Behaviour-driven test automation –**
  - o For a behaviour-driven automation, a simple user behaviour-based approach is used. Scripts and tools, such as Gherkin and Cucumber, are used for behaviour-based automation.

- **Fifth generation (programmable, driver-based frameworks such as Selenium, TestNGetc.)**
  - o Use of modular, multi-platform, programmable, and driver-based frameworks.
  - o Use of Selenium, TestNG, Junit and other mobile test automation tools.

- **Sixth generation (AI-driven full-stack test automation frameworks (self-healing, auto-generating))**
  - o AI-driven test automation leverages AI-driven full-stack test automation frameworks, self-healing test automation scripts, self-maintaining test automation scripts, auto-generating test automation scripts and script-less test automation.

NOTE

Test automation has progressed a long way since the 1970s through the real innovation which took place in the last 2-3 decades, with the evolution of tools, techniques and infrastructure, enable us to design, script and test faster. Current generation is tailor-made for the evolution of an AI revolution. The question is then, how can we test faster with the tools and techniques that allow us to do faster work? The need of the hour is for the enterprises to leverage tools that allow continuous building, integration, testing and deployment and reduction in the overall SDLC time. This is where AI-driven test automation tools come to the core. Even the traditional players, such as Microfocus Unified Functional Tester (erstwhile Mercury QTP) and IBM Rational Robot, are coming up with features to deliver this testing, using machine learning, big data analytics methods such as predictive analytics. The next ask for automation will be to automate testing of Quantum computing techniques, internet of things and multi-faceted robotics system. Use of manual testing will be like boiling the ocean and the sixth generation of test automation will help us overcome these challenges.

An AI application is not a final application at any given point and is a constantly evolving one. The challenges to tackle are:

- How will you automate an application when the scope, program flow and logic isunclear due to always changing business logic driven by Artificial Intelligence?

- How will you handle a situation where the results can be unpredictable and wrong? How will you fail the test?
- How will you test an application that is constantly learning and evolving? What will you be testing?
- What will be your testing objectives?
- How will you handle AI bias?

Given the challenges of AI Testing, it becomes even more complex to automate an AI application. This is an evolutionary concept that will mature over some time.

When to do test automation?

Testing and test automation are not the same. Test automation is largely checking of features and facts. 100% test automation is a myth, just like 100% test coverage. As testing needs to validate the functionality and changes, as against checking of features and facts, there will always be an element of testing that needs validation by human users as understanding of functional knowledge is key. In addition, test automation should produce a meaningful outcome and benefit. 100% test automation is also not feasible as the cost of test automation versus benefits it offers may not be favourable. For example, automating few hundred scripts that are likely to be executed only once by a skilled SME or tester can be exorbitantly costly. Having said that, the test automation coverage will increase in the future with the new age test automation and test design tools. However, it will never reach 100%, as it will be like boiling the ocean.

As an example, one can target to automate the following types of test scripts:

- Functional regression test scripts
- Sanity test scripts
- Post-deployment/build verification test scripts
- Any script that is executed multiple times during a testing release cycle as the benefits of test automation is in execution.
- New functionality scripts that will become core features to be tested, as a regression script in the future with a multiple execution need.
- Load testing scripts
- Cross-platform functional regression test scripts

On similar lines, some of the recommended test cases to avoid for test automation are:

- One-time, rapid test cases that is needed for urgent bug fixes or deployment
- One time, ad-hoc test cases that may never get executed again

- Test cases that take lesser time to execute manually than using automation
- User experience and validation tests that need a user to validate
- Scripts that are getting executed in an unstable, development environment.
- Scripts that produce unpredictable results
- Scripts of an application that change very frequently – high maintenance and enhancement costs and lesser **Return on Investment (RoI)** for test automation

We can use test automation for product build verification testing, continuous integration checks, dry run and sanity testing of products and features. An automation engineer would be using them for validating the regression features to ensure nothing is broken. One needs to check for product stability before using test automation as well.

Testing team can have various options to automate a complex application across the layers. They include:

a) User interface layer – end-to-end testing
b) Database layer
c) Services layer
d) API/integration layer
e) Unit test layer

Among the list mentioned above, inverted test pyramid recommends using test automation heavily for Unit test layer/ API & integration layer followed by Services Layer including DB and finally UI layer in that order, when it comes to amount of testing and test automation. The recommendation is to automate the tests at earlier phases. This is because as the cost of testing and identification of bugs gets higher, you move up the phases. It also takes a longer time to finish testing as well. Having a solid automation framework in earlier phases allows the team to test continuously and rapidly. Hence, the benefits of heavy automation can be realized better, if we have a solid automation suite for earlier phases. The real benefit of test automation arises when automation is done extensively in the earlier phases of testing (starting from the unit test phase).

Based on the system under test, the automation approach can vary. Leveraging the test automation generations, test automation can be as simple as the first generation – such as record and playback that could be used for simple features for login or partial automation. Recommendations for feature-rich applications will be to leverage either a keyword-driven or a data-driven automation approach with a modular programming. However, with the current landscape, it is preferred to leverage the advanced features provided by the tool to automate using a hybrid approach or use the script-less automation features and behaviour-driven automation capabilities provided by the tool. Automation for the sake of automation is not a good choice to pursue, as it could be detrimental and a wasted effort in terms of effort, money and time.

It is not recommended to do full-fledged automation until an end-state architecture/ platform is ready along with stable code. However, one can aim to build test automation frameworks and common infrastructure whilst the development of the application takes place, to ensure automation of scripts is done as soon as the application is ready and stable. As a practice, spending too much time in a parallel test automation can create a futile automation approach and should be adopted only where end user base of your application is very large and execution time of your automated scripts on different devices and platforms can be reduced.

If one needs test automation of an application such as Google Maps, the application testing can be automated by using Google Maps Libraries and by leveraging tools such as Selenium (and Appium in case of mobile apps) to automate actions performed on Google Maps. The Document Object Model of the Google Maps, along with the APIs available to interact can be leveraged by either Selenium or any other automation tool (such as Appium) to create test automation scripts. Testing can be done at the API level to avoid too many UI validation scripts and risk-based key UI scripts can be automated using Selenium or Appium to validate UI features.

Myths of Test Automation

IT Management teams, business stakeholders and testers to an extent have some beliefs that are largely myth than a fact. Some of the myths are:

Myth	Reality/Recommendation
100% automation is possible	It is not possible and not recommended. Test automation removes the checking part of testing. A Manual Test verification is needed for assuring that the functionalities emulate the business logic accurately and hence SME verification of test process is needed.
Test automation saves a lot of time	It depends on the test automation strategy, how it is implemented and the effectiveness of automation. Many test automation projects have resulted in unnecessary costs due to poor implementation.
Test automation scripts are faster than manual testing	Not always, true. Most of the scripts have embedded wait times for SUT to respond and the sum of all these waits can be more than the total end-to-end effort for a manual testing. In addition, the efficiency of short cuts used by skilled testers may not be available in automated scripts. The benefits of timesaving are seen in the reaction time and data entry time of automated scripts. This does not apply to all scripts.

Test automation eliminates needs for manual effort	Not True. A test automation script's execution results need validation with a periodic audit. The scripts need maintenance. Scripts need control and configuration. Test automation is an addendum and not a replacement.
Test automation generates more defects than manual testing	Not True. Test automation is for the areas that are likely to be very stable and for scenarios where it is difficult to find any rare defects. If test automation scripts fail, it is largely due to data configurations and environmental issues and automation scripts are good for sanity testing. Manual testing captures most of the valuable functional defects needing business domain knowledge. The new tools leveraging machine-learning models may change this a bit.
Automation is scripting repeating test actions	Not true. All applications undergo a life cycle of change and keep on changing. The testing of active, complex application is a dynamic process and automated testing for a dynamic application will not be a fully repetitive process. However, automation helps in reducing effort of monotonous tasks through full or partial automation for the regression tests.

Test automation as a tool for test data generation

One of the major benefits of test automation is to generate test data in a synthetic manner. When a system is automated in a stable environment, the test automation scripts can be run to create data configurations in various states and be kept ready for test execution – be it manual or automated. This would save a lot of time for specialist users. The ideal approach would be to get the key regression set automated before testing moves to the user acceptance phase and the test data for the end users running functional tests to validate new functionality is generated. Same set of automated test cases can be run in subsequent phases to generate synthetic test data for various testing purposes.

For example, At the time of generating test data for a change, disconnecting, or a billing of a new activated telecom customer, an automated create customer script can be run before using data for a change or modification of service. The same data can be used for a bill-run, accounting purpose or for disconnection of services.

An efficient automation team with good data management engineers can utilize test automation to run testing operations in a very efficient manner.

Some good test automation tools

Some good tools for test automation include the following:

- **Selenium:** An open-source test automation framework that allows test automation coding using multiple languages (Java, Python, C#, JavaScript, Ruby, PHP and PERL). It is primarily used for web apps.

- **Microfocus Unified Functional Testing:** Test automation using VBScript. Most widely used test automation tool by corporates. Used for automation of web apps testing of UIs and APIs, mobile and desktop apps and packaged applications.

- **Smartbear TestComplete/SOAPUI:** TestComplete is a popular test automation tool from Smartbear. This tool allows test automation of web, mobile and desktop apps. Smartbear has a good number of corporate clients. SOAPUI is an open-source tool from SmartBear for web application testing.

- **Tricentis Tosca:** Another popular test automation tool with advanced features. This tool has features for script-less automation, drag, and drop style test automation capabilities.

- **IBM Rational Functional Tester:** A very good test automation tool from IBM.

- **Ranorex Studio:** Is another good test automation tool that has been around for some time.

- **Apache Junit/JMeter:** Open source-testing tool for unit and load test automation.

- **Postman:** An API test automation tool.

- **Visual Studio Test Professional:** A Microsoft tool for testing.

- **Robotium:** A test automation framework for Android mobile apps.

- **FitNesse:** A test automation tool where tests are written in a Wiki.

- **Telerik Test Studio:** Another commercial test automation tool.

- **Watir:** An open-source test automation tool primarily used for Ruby Programming Language.

- **Appium:** Test automation tool for mobile apps.

- **Worksoft Certify:** Another good test automation tool from a solid test product vendor - Worksoft.

Test automation success criteria/measures

Some of the key measures that can determine the success of a good automation project are:

- **Defect count:** Number of defects detected using test automation suite.

- **Test misses:** Number of defects leaked to later phases because of misses reported by test automation suite – The lower, the better. It should be zero all the times.

- **Manual effort saving:** Total effort saved because of test automation execution.

- **Reduction in costs:** This is the net savings calculated as (overall testing costs before test automation) – (overall testing costs after test automation which includes manual testing costs +test automation implementation costs + maintenance costs).

- **Reduction in test cycle time:** Number of days reduced in the overall testing cycle as a result of automation.

- **Test automation ratio:** This is a number of tests run in an automated fashion/ Total number of tests executed – the higher the number, the better it is.

- **Testing effort at end-to-end level vs. unit test level:** This is overall test effort and costs at end-to-end integration and sum of unit test costs at earlier phases. This should reduce.

- **Compatibility across platforms:** This is the ability of test automation scripts to run across platforms, operating systems and browsers.

Other benefits exist as well. However, a strong baselining exercise is needed for efficient benefit realization tracking.

Test automation framework design

Test automaton framework is a software-based framework that gives a platform to test automation engineers for building efficient test automation scripts. Automation framework gives a set of features and guidelines for the test automation engineers to follow and implement.

Some of the stages include -> Identification of a need for automation -> Determining Scope -> Running a POC/Pilot for a tool selection -> Building an automations strategy/roadmap -> Design automation suite -> Develop automation suite -> Data Management Strategy -> Execution of Test Automation suite ->

Acceptance and freezing of automation suite -> Continuous build and maintenance strategy -> Benefits realization tracking -> Automation Suite/Tool Replenishment.

Some of the elements to consider in an automation framework include:

- Set of reusable functions in the form of libraries to automate faster

- An error handling library

- Logging frameworks

- Reporting libraries

- Templates for test automation data configurations
- Clean-up functions for post-execution closure
- Testing Resource management functions
- Driver scripts and associated
- Environment configuration functions
- Data handling mechanisms
- Object handlers and repository management
- Coding guidelines including documentation
- Common Framework and Configurations across platforms, tools and languages, etc.

A good test automation framework's design supports modularity, easily maintainability, and reusability of test automation scripts.

Conclusion

Test automation has come a long way and will be an integral part of rapid delivery software products and services across the business domain. Without the capability to test and release changes rapidly, an organization could face an existential crisis. The leaders of the digital economy will be those who are the swiftest to adapt to the changing landscape; and not the biggest firms. In order to succeed, technology leaders need to adapt to efficient test automation processes. Based on the introduction, the key question will be how Selenium is relevant for test automation. The next few chapters will introduce what Selenium is its features and discuss the tools that are required to leverage on top of Selenium for achieving the maximum in terms of test automation.

Questions

1. Will you recommend 100% test automation, that is, automation of all testing activities? Where will you use 100% test automation?

2. What are the types of test cases one should avoid from automation scope?

3. Would you suggest test automation for product build verification, dry run, and sanity testing of applications? If so, how will you use them?

4. What kind of tests would you automate?

5. What is the benefit of modular scripts over the record-and-playback type of test automation?

6. What are some of the key elements to consider while defining a test automation framework?

7. What are some of the different generations of test automation framework?

8. What is a data-driven test automation framework?

9. What is a keyword-driven test automation framework?

10. What is a hybrid test automation framework?

11. Can you outline some of the stages in a test automation lifecycle?

12. What are some of the automation approaches you can choose for test automation?

13. What are some of the key measures of test automation success?

14. How can you use test automation for data generation?

15. What are some of the myths you heard about test automation? What is your take?

16. Assume you are asked to automate testing of a massively used application such as Google Maps. Can this be done? What will be your approach?

17. What are some of the famous test automation tools?

18. Will you start test automation before development starts?

19. How will you automate the testing of AI applications?

CHAPTER 2
Introduction to Selenium

The first rule of any technology used in a business is that automation applied to an efficient operation will magnify the efficiency. The second is that automation applied to an inefficient operation will magnify the inefficiency.

– Bill Gates

Test automation has been evolving over the past three decades in full steam. Ever since the emergence of **world-wide-web (WWW)** and the emergence of Internet-based websites and applications, the growth in the computer industry has been humongous. With the availability of web sites and apps across several platforms, browsers and devices, testing of the web application has become a challenging and an arduous task. Nevertheless, the emergence of Selenium and its features have helped the software testers propel the testing process to deliver faster turnaround time through purpose-driven automation framework and flexibility of the Selenium framework. Being an open-source application with outstanding community support, Selenium has emerged as the de-facto tool of choice for all web application automation specialists. This chapter gives an insight into Selenium covering the essentials an automation specialist needs to know.

Structure

- What is the history of Selenium and the reason for its development?
- Features of Selenium – Web Driver, Remote Control (RC), Grid and IDE
- Why should we use Selenium?
- What are the benefits of Selenium?
- What are the limitations and challenges of using Selenium?
- How can Selenium help build solid test automation capabilities using Selenium Architecture?
- What are the complexities of web application automation by using Selenium WebDriver?
- What are the platform and browser combination challenges?

Objective

After studying this chapter, you should be able to understand the preparatory info on Selenium automation and be able to correlate the history of Selenium, the challenges facing Web Application Testing, the platform and browser combination challenges, the reason for Selenium development, reasons for why we should use Selenium, the benefits of Selenium, the features of Selenium, the complexities of using Selenium and how Selenium can help build solid Test Automation capabilities.

History of Selenium

Necessity is the mother of invention. A software development urban legend has even said that a Microsoft software engineer invented the most famous "**Print Preview**" option as a means of automating the choice to avoid walking a long distance to fetch the printed document to validate the features of the tool. It was a brilliant innovation and automation that has been a productivity enhancer and ecologically sustainable choice.

A creative software engineer, *Jason Huggins*, built an internal tool named **JavaScriptTestRunner** in 2004 for his employer *Thought Works to* automate mundane, repeatable tasks for a web application, that is, time and expenses system. The tool got popularity internally and a lot of colleagues joined his project to add features. JavaScriptTestRunner was later renamed as Selenium Core and loaded with libraries to automate repeated tasks on web applications. Jason is considered as the co-creator of Selenium Core, Selenium **Internet Communications Extension (ICE)** and he continues to commit code.

> **NOTE**
>
> It is quoted that the name Selenium was chosen as a result of an email joke sent by Jason himself aimed at a competitor tool (Mercury QTP), that mercury poisoning can be cured by taking Selenium supplements.

However, one creative challenge existed which needed both the test program and server program (web application) to exist in the same local machines due to the "Same Origin Policy" issue. Same Origin Policy refers to the traffic from the browser and the server coming from the same host or IP Address. To resolve this, Jason was joined by *Paul Hammant* who came up with a clever idea of using a proxy-server to trick the browser to believe the request came from the same domain. The team went on to develop the first popular version of "**Selenium Remote Control (RC)**". Post the success of Selenium RC, the project team decided to open source to add more features to the tool and make it a public tool for free use. There was a need for a Selenium server to be running to run the automated execution of Selenium scripts, in the early days of Selenium.

To summarize the progress of the Selenium, let us see it in a visual manner using the image below:

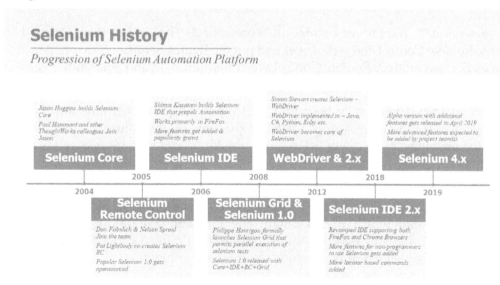

Figure 2.1: *Selenium History*

In 2005, two more key software engineers *Dan Fabulich* and *Nelson Sproul* from BEA Systems (now Oracle), contributed to a driver/server architecture of Selenium. Another Engineer named Pat *Lightbody* worked on an earlier version idea that would lay foundations for what will be known as **Selenium Remote Control** and **Selenium Grid**. *Pat Lightbody* is also known as the co-creator of Selenium Remote

Control. *Patrick's* idea of grid-based and distributed automation testing helped in reducing the overall testing duration.

In 2006, a Japanese software engineer –*Shinya Kasatani* built an IDE for Selenium and shared the features with the Selenium Open source Project. This helped automated code generation of record and playback and made rapid coding features possible. It used a very simple concept of recording a video and playing back. *Shinya Kasatani* is also known as the co-creator of Selenium IDE.

In 2008, *Philippe Hanrigou* formally launched Selenium Grid for popular use to allow parallel execution of multiple Selenium Scripts to be run concurrently across multiple systems – be it local or remote. Philippe is also known as the creator of Selenium Grid. Thus, version 1 of Selenium consisted of a combination of Selenium IDE, Selenium Remote Control and Selenium Grid.

Jason shifted to Google and the popularity of the Selenium tool picked up at the Software giant. A creative engineer *Jennifer Bevan* started to make a lot of impactful changes around the Selenium Project. In 2012, another Googler – *Simon Stewart* delivered the most powerful feature of Selenium – namely WebDriver that enabled the execution of automated scripts across browsers. Selenium WebDriver is implemented across key languages such as Java, C#, Python and Ruby. Simon is also known as the creator of Selenium WebDriver.

For Selenium 2, WebDriver became the core aspect. The project team decided to merge Remote Control and web driver and put the Remote Control on a maintenance phase. For Selenium 3, Remote Control was fully removed and Selenium 3 version consisted of IDE, Grid and WebDriver.

A new revamped version of Selenium IDE supporting both Chrome and Firefox browser was released in August 2018. At present, the Selenium Project team is working on a newer version of Selenium 4 and Alpha version was released in April 2019.

In addition to the core features, a lot of open source and commercial tools started building on top of the Selenium platform to provide additional features to the users. This includes Watir, which offers **Domain-Specific Language (DSL)** - based testing, Cucumber (a behaviour-driven testing tool) and Appium (a tool for mobile test automation using selenium framework among many others).

What are the features available in Selenium?

We've been discussing components of Selenium such as Selenium Core, Remote Control, IDE, WebDriver and Grid in a high-level manner. Let's see it in a pictorial manner (see *Figure 2.2*).

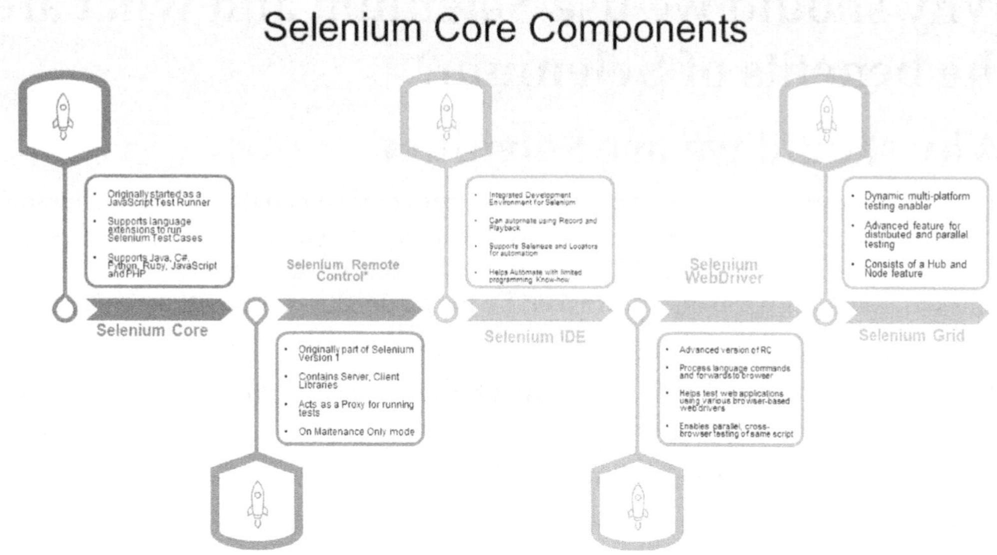

Selenium Core Components

Figure 2.2: Selenium Core Components

Selenium has 4 (considering Remote Control and WebDriver to be of the same category) major components for consideration. We shall be covering all these components in detail with examples in the upcoming chapters. For the purpose of this chapter, the key components of Selenium, to be aware of, as depicted in Figure 2.2, are listed below:

- **Selenium Core:** Core Library providing language support and functions for automation of applications.

- **Selenium Remote Control*:** Older version of a proxy-server-based automation enabler run through a server and a driver concept –

    o *Remote Control was used in earlier versions and is no longer used in newer versions of Selenium and is replaced by Web Driver.

- **Selenium Web Driver:** More structured web-browser/platform-centric web driver enabling automated testing across browsers, platforms in a truly distributed manner.

- **Selenium IDE:** An IDE, which permits non-programmer to automate web applications and also maps web application locators for initial validation purposes using Selenese commands.

- **Selenium Grid:** An advanced feature that enables parallel test execution in a grid (hub and node) fashion to get voluminous automation testing done in a very short time. Selenium Grid is a key enabler for propelling Selenium's popularity amongst technologists.

Why should we use Selenium and what are the benefits of Selenium?

Why should we use Selenium?

There are many questions asked by the top management when it comes to technology investment. Like any project, a cost-benefit analysis will be done and a project delivering positive net present value will be chosen for implementation. When it comes to Selenium, a top question asked by the leadership team will be *"Why should we use Selenium"*?

There are many technical reasons we can offer on why we can use Selenium. Some of them include the following:

It's ease of implementation and usage –

- Selenium is very easy to implement
- Selenium tool is very easy to use
- Selenium has a very nice user interface
- Selenium programming can be easily integrated with other popular IDEs such as Eclipse IDE, Spyder, Atom, NetBeans, and Microsoft Visual Studio etc.

It's free, open-source and very popular –

- All open-source software come at no cost to the organizations and are free to use. It can be freely downloaded and is supported by a very big supporting community.
- Selenium is a very popular and well-run open-source project almost in the same leagues as how Java was run.
- Selenium is also very well maintained and supported

Reusable and extensible framework –

- If you look at the history of Selenium, you can see that it was extended progressively. Selenium Core->Selenium RC->Selenium Grid->Selenium WebDriver. Post the release of the stable extensible framework, a lot of new frameworks and tools leveraged the extensible and modular feature of Selenium Architecture to deliver enhanced and powerful features. Just like Linux, a lot of professional and commercial tools are available for big corporates who are not ready to invest in open-source technology.
- Being an open-source platform, talented developers contribute to developing solid features in the Selenium framework.
- The framework itself is highly reusable and largely compatible across platforms.

- Selenium is easy to integrate with various CI/CD and DevOps tools and gives the flexibility to pick and choose the tools the team wants to integrate automation with.

Easy to learn and use –

- Selenium is a good tool for automation testers. It uses basic features of popular languages and offers a library of functions that are easy to understand and use.

- With tools such as Cucumber and **behaviour-drivendevelopment (BDD)** approaches, such as Gherkin, even business analysts can write a simplified testing use cases that can then be automated easily.

- Selenium IDE gives an easy playground to record the navigations and exports them to scripts in various languages which could then be extended and customized by automation testers.

- Selenium does not use very complex functions and concepts such as pointers in C, lambda functions in Python etc., which make learning a challenge for beginners. Good programmers, however, can mature into writing complex algorithms and code.

Smaller infrastructure footprint/needs –

- Selenium does not require a heavy server footprint or a client machine configuration. All it needs is a set of jar files that serves the purpose of the tester.

- Its considerable optimization efforts have been undertaken by the Selenium Open Source community.

- For a proof of concept or a pilot, an organization does not need to spend a lot of money for an infrastructure to test Selenium.

- Even in production-grade setups for live automation use, selenium uses relatively smaller infrastructure compared to other automation tools.

- All these come at zero cost for licensing.

Concurrent execution rapid time to market –

- With the development of Selenium Grid and WebDriver, an automation developer can develop once and run multiple selenium scripts in parallel across platforms, across browsers and across devices to finish testing quickly.
  - o At the end of the day, automation primarily checks for regression (or existing features). Concurrent execution helps in reducing the overall testing time which then enables the organizations to deploy products/packages/programs in the live environment quickly.
  - o With concurrent, unattended automated execution, the full power of automation is realized and Selenium helps to enable the same.

Refactoring flexibility–

- Since Selenium has a good IDE, it is capable of generating the first level of code that can be refactored into a solid, modular function that could leverage any type of automation such as data-driven, keyword-driven or hybrid automation.

- Availability of various editors, frameworks and libraries permits the automation developers to refactor the code to optimize performance profusely.

- Lot of reporting, unit testing and validation available permits the automation developers to analyse comprehensively to optimize performance.

Multi-platform/multi-device support–

- Just like Java, Selenium toolkit is available for usage across OS platforms. The script written once in one OS can be used across OS platforms.

- Selenium can be run across Windows, Unix, Macintosh OS, as well as Linux.

- Selenium can be run across devices as well. Some of the devices can be tested using extensions of selenium such as Appium, Selendroid etc.

Multi-browser support–

- With the creation of the WebDriver tool, Selenium is powered with features that allow web application testing across 2000+ combinations of *Browser + OS + Devices*.

- With continuing development and support, thriving platforms, such as Crossbrowsertesting.com, enable rapid testing of applications across the globe possible in a matter of hours and minutes as against weeks and months.

- Newer versions of browsers get supported easily with the active open-source community delivering changes on an ongoing basis.

Own scripting language–

- Selenium IDE has its own scripting language for simple automation and playback.

- **Selenese** – has a good number of simple keywords to remember and program through the powerful Selenium IDE.

- This feature allows Selenium automation scripts created using Selenium IDE in *Selenese* to be exported to popular languages such as Java, Python, and JavaScript etc. for further enhancements.

Powerful record and playback IDE:

- Selenium IDE (current version supports both Chrome and Firefox against Firefox till Firefox version 58) is one of the powerful record and playback IDE capable of generating solid automation scripts.

- Selenium IDE is easy to use.
- Selenium IDE permits the users to perform customization or real-time configurations using a very easy to use interface.

What are the benefits of Selenium?

The second question to answer to management after *"why"* is a *"what"*. What are the benefits of using Selenium? If you refer to *Chapter 1*, the benefits highlighted are relevant for Selenium. To recap, some of the benefits are as follows:

- Overall, it is cost saving in terms of testing and managing SDLC cost –
    - o Cost-saving in terms of:
        - Manual test effort reduction
        - Removal of defects quickly
    - o Cost avoidance in terms of:
        - Reduction in regression defects
        - Removal of wastages
    - o Reusability of code and frameworks:
        - Ability to write once and reuse multiple time through –
            - ❖ The benefits of modular design
            - ❖ Efficiency in configuration and clonability
    - o Faster time to market with parallel test execution –
        - Efficient automation helps test execution time to reduce, as test cases can be run in parallel, in an unattended fashion and across platforms.
        - Tests can be triggered automatically without dependency on humans.
    - o Better test coverage – Does more testing with fewer resources and in parallel:
        - With test automation, the testing team can have better test coverage by using test automation for stable but important code branches and leveraging manual testing experts to focus on areas needing high focus on rapidly changing business-critical code branches of an application.
    - o Early defect finding –
        - Having an automated test suite for regression allows us to find defects early and fix them as well.
    - o Efficient Testing –
        - Test automation gives the testing team to run the test cycle

efficiently and optimally plan the overall test strategy for efficient outcomes.

o Repeatability –

- Can be repeated in the same format as the automation is coded to run in the same way without the variations shown by human testers
- Gives a clear view ofapplication behaviour

o Avoidance of Manual Errors –

- As the test automation scripts follow logic, manual errors such as mistyping, clicking wrong buttons or other types of errors can be avoided using test automation.

o Motivated and skilled testers who can become automation engineers –

- Automation specialists are used efficiently while writing highly value-added test scripts.
- Skilled testers can be leveraged to run high value-adding testing tasks instead of running low-risk, low-value adding, monotonous test scripts.

o Ability to run in parallel –

- Test automation gives the test team with an ability to run in parallel with multiple data sets, devices and platforms

    ❖ Ability to run head-less testing

        ○ We can run testing without the need to have actual browsers and infrastructures in place.

Now, let's see some of the challenges and limitations of using Selenium.

What are the limitations and challenges of using Selenium?

While Selenium is a good tool for automation, there are challenges one needs to overcome before using Selenium for enterprise automation.

- It's an open-source tool and a doubt about lack of guaranteed support puts doubt in enterprises though Selenium's open-source community is well endowed with solid sponsors.
- Selenium as a tool was built primarily to support web application.
    o It is not extensible across software landscape – such as desktop software in different operating systems, including Windows, Linux etc., packaged applications, mobile applications, batch processes etc.

o It is possible to use extensions and run automation on some of these applications.

- Needs automation specialist with solid programming skills to do *"meaningful and purposeful automation"*.

- Since it is scripted, the cost of automation maintenance could be high, if not coded efficiently.

- No inbuilt test management integration capabilities like some of the most popular software.

    o Plug-ins and extensions exist to address these challenges

- Automation could take more time if skilled developers are not available for automation compared to commercial tools that fast track automation with script-less and process-driven automation.

- Very limited support for visual regression testing such as image comparison etc. Sikuli or similar tools may be an option to do image-based test automation with Selenium.

- Lack of inbuilt reporting capabilities compared to other commercial tools

- For asynchronous pages taking time to load based on various actions (such as AJAX-based pages), it may be very challenging to write automation scripts in Selenium.

- CAPTCHA, reCAPTCHA and bar-code readers can't be automated using Selenium and need extensions to make it work.

- Unlike the commercial tools, it neither has any built-in object repository, nor in-build features to read data from external sources like .xls, .csv etc.

How can Selenium help build a solid test automation framework?

Selenium follows a layered and extensible architectural framework. This means that as an automation developer, the test automation team can build a test automation framework that is easy to build, maintain and enhance, to deliver the desired business capabilities.

Given that selenium is extensible and possible to get implemented using various languages and constructs, some of the key focus elements for the automation team will be:

- Decide on platform, languages, tools and frameworks.

- Platforms and languages to use –

    o What is the platform in which the applications to be automated built-in?

- What would be the ideal platform for test automation?
  - o What are the programming languages that could be considered?
- Can this be automated using languages supported by Selenium (Java, C#, Python, JavaScript, Ruby etc.).
- Is there a need for a BDD approach to test automation?
- Is there a need to write automation using specification by examples using tools such as Spec Flow (C#), Gherkin language by Cucumber (Ruby), BeHat (PHP), Concordion (Java), Jasmine (JavaScript) or any other tools?
- What are the add-ins, plug-ins and additional tools needed?
  - o Unit testing frameworks
    - ▪ Such as JUnit, NUnit, xUnit, TestNG, PyTest etc.
  - o Frameworks to address the need to test on web applications (mobile etc.) and performance testing.
  - o Appium, Robotium, JMeter, Google Robot Framework.
- Choose your unit testing, logging and reporting approach –
  - o Select the packages, frameworks and extensions to be used for automation.
- Decide on the end-to-end automation framework.
- Build the core components /objects/design patterns for the Selenium automation framework including page object model, locators, setup, teardown, exception handling and graceful shutdown to name a few.
- Build the reusable libraries for various automation purposes that are specific to your application under test and not available readily.
- Build the testing components for validating your automation including the page object model, locator validation, exception handling, logging and reporting to name a few.
- Build-in a case of an Agile, DevOps-based delivery model, and the framework should include an approach to take care of continuous build, integration, deployment and testing or a CI/CD pipeline. The framework should be able to integrate with the end-to-end CI/CD pipeline.

Once the approach is decided, a Selenium-based automation framework can be implemented and evaluated.

What are the complexities of web application automation by using Selenium WebDriver?

While Selenium WebDriver is a very good tool for automation and to build a framework, there are some challenges one needs to overcome before using Selenium for enterprise automation.

Some of the challenges one needs to keep in mind while using Selenium Web Driver automation include:

- First, it is challenging to handle dynamic identifiers created for dynamic content by some content-rich sites. The ids are so dynamic that a brand new, complex id is created every time a page is loaded onto a browser from the server. Automation of dynamic ids and performing parsing becomes very complex, even if one uses a strong regular expression. Therefore, an extension or a professional toll may be needed to automate such web sites. Sites such as Google Gmail or Yahoo or LinkedIn use such dynamic id generators.
  - o One way to handle this situation is to leverage Regular Expressions in Absolute or Relative XPath locators and searching with contains in the relative XPath.
- Second, different websites respond with different latency and timing depending on the server performance, network performance, content delivery network and the client-side speed and can get impacted by latency. If an asynchronous mode of interaction such as AJAX is implemented, the responsiveness could vary. Testing this through selenium could be a challenge as the testers typically implement   a waiting mechanism. This wait could also impact the overall performance of testing by adding incremental time end-to-end for test execution.
- Third, automation maintenance is cumbersome and very time consuming and repetitive. One of the key challenges of using just the Selenium framework is the need for avoidance of a costly and time-consuming maintenance code changes for test automation. Use of a Page Object Model is also not helpful and it needs to be changed as well, every time the website changes.
- Fourth, Selenium is not built to provide advanced features to perform data-driven testing. Every connectivity needs to be managed manually through the code and to run a truly dynamic end-to-end test automation which could be a cumbersome challenge as a lot of code needs to be written. (Not to leave out the complex test automation script maintenance aspect as well.)
- Fifth, the functionalities present in Selenium prevent it from testing complex web application packages with features such as Adobe Flash, CAPTCHA etc. Additional challenges include testing across frames in a higher frame driven web application, handling of content across tables in various frames that get compounded by asynchronous actions.

What are the platform and browser combination challenges?

Some of the challenges faced while using selenium for automation acrossvarious cross-browser (platform and browser) combinations include:

- Challenges in handling different modal windows and pop-ups –
  - o Special code needs to be written to handle various types of modal windows and popups.
- Locators behaving differently in different browsers –
  - o Code to handle browser behaviour using Selenium XPath Locators may behave differently in different browsers or versions. This needs to be handled delicately and may need extra-coding. To avoid this, one can consider using additional plug-ins and extensions to avoid writing complex code that may need maintenance as well, if the application changes dynamically often.
- Integration with frameworks and tools –
  - o While the frameworks and tools help in productivity and aid in rapid automation, the very task can be very tricky and time-consuming. A simple task of writing and running a Selenium script in Java using Eclipse IDE can take a lot of time if not configured properly.
- DevOps and CI/CD pipeline driven automation –
  - o Selenium can be an excellent tool for CI/CD pipeline driven automation. However, given the very nature of code-driven automation and the amount of maintenance and changes with code , one needs to make to keep automation in a runnable state, as Selenium on its own may not deliver the needs, but may need additional features given by tools such as Protractor, Ranorex, Experitest, Smarttest, SahiPro etc.
- Challenges in handling native vs. non-native applications –
  - o The key construct of write-once run-anywhere/run-multiple times test automation may be lost if the code needs to be written to address various types of applications.
  - o Rather than using manual/hand-written code for automation using Selenium, it is advisable to leverage advanced tools for mobile test automation. Appium, Selendroid or tools, such as Perfecto Mobile, SeeTest, Mobile Center, can be leveraged.

There are plenty of tools available in the market for test automation specializedin various aspects of test automation. Some are extensions of frameworks such as Selenium and some are full-scale commercial tools. Most of the popular ones are commercial ones due to the features and support provided.

Some of the well-known tools that can be considered are:

Selenium

- Microfocus Unified Functional Tester (UFT) - It was used to be called as Mercury QTP (Quick Test Professional) and HP QTP earlier
- Microsoft Visual Studio Test Professional
- Appium for Mobile Test Automation

- EggPlant Functional Tester
- TestCraft – Uses Selenium as a base
- LamdbaTest – Cloud-based test automation platform
- Silk Test
- SoapUI
- Neotys NeoLoad for Performance Test Automation
- Applitools – Visual Test Automation Platform
- Watir
- Smartbear TestComplete
- Apache JMeter – Performance Test Automation Tool
- SahiPro

Tricentis Tosca

- Worksoft Certify
- IBM Rational Functional Tester
- Cucumber for behaviour-driven testing automation
- Ranorex Studio
- Testim.IO – Uses AI for test automation
- Smartbear Zephyr
- Katalon Studio
- Postman – API Test Automation Tool
- Parasoft SOATest
- Telerik Test Studio
- Mabl
- Parasoft Virtualize
- PerfectoMobile for mobile test automation
- Provar

Putting all these together, the benefits of Selenium can be compared through a simple comparison table against some additional tools available in the market.

Capability/ Feature	Selenium	Micro FocusUnified Functional Tester (UFT) – a.k.a Mercury/ HP QTP in earlier versions	IBM RFT	Other Tools – Ranorex, SahiPro, Provar, Appium, Perfecto Mobile, Tricentis Tosca etc.
Software Cost/License Fees	Zero/None	License and Annual Maintenance fees	License and Annual Maintenance fees	License and Annual Maintenance fees – depending on the tool and choice of implementation
Applications that can be tested	Primarily Web-Based Mobile Apps can be tested with extensions	Web-Based and Desktop-based Mobile Center tool is available for mobile app automation	Web and Desktop Applications	Web and Desktop Applications, Packaged Applications
Programming Language Support	Multiple Languages – Java /C# / Ruby/ Python/ Perl/ PHP/ JavaScript	VB Script	VB Script & JavaScript	Multiple language Support – depending on the tool
Object Identification Tasks	No library available to identify objects. Need custom code	Built-in mechanism for automatic identification of objects and repository	Built-in mechanism for automatic identification of objects and repository	Built-in mechanism for automatic identification of objects and repository depending on the tool capability
IDE for Scripting	Multiple Choices – Eclipse, Spyder, Atom, IDEA IntelliJ, Netbeans etc.	Only via UFT IDE	IBM Rational Platform, Visual Studio .Net Dev environment	Internal IDEs based on tool
Reporting	With extensions can generate Excel, HTML and PDF reports	Built-in reporting mechanism and dashboards	Built-in reporting mechanism and dashboards	Varies based on tools – Built-in reporting mechanism and dashboards

CI/CD/ DevOps Support	Possible through integration with DevOps Tools such as Jenkins/ Hudson/ Bamboo etc.	Possible through integration with Quality Center/ALM or Jenkins Tools	Possible through integration with DevOps Tools such as Jenkins/ Hudson/ Bamboo / Rational Quality Manager etc.	Possible through integration with DevOps Tools such as Jenkins/ Hudson/Bamboo etc.
Multi-browser Support	Supports almost all browsers through WebDrivers – Chrome, Internet Explorer, Edge, Firefox, Opera etc.	Chrome, Internet Explorer, Edge, Firefox	Chrome, Internet Explorer, Edge, Firefox	Supports almost all browsers – Chrome, Internet Explorer, Edge, Firefox, Opera etc.
Platform/OS/ Environment Support	Windows, Linux, Unix	Only Windows	Windows, Linux, Unix	Windows, Linux, Unix depending on the tool
Mobile App testing support	Almost all devices through extensions such as Appium, Selendroid	Through a separate commercial product – MicroFocus UFT Mobile Center	Not well-known support	Depends on the tool
Hardware and resource consumption	Low	High	High	Medium – High depending on the tool
Product Support	Open-source	Through Commercial Support arrangements/ Forums	Through Commercial Support arrangements/ Forums	Through Commercial Support arrangements/ Forums based on the tool

Table 2.1: Comparison of Selenium with other automation tools

In summary, every choice has its own benefits and drawbacks. Selenium definitely gives a lot of ammunition to propel the automation vision of a firm.

Conclusion

The emergence of Selenium and its features helped the software testers propel the testing process to deliver faster turnaround time through a purpose-driven automation framework and the flexibility of Selenium framework. Being an open-source application with outstanding community support, Selenium has emerged as the de-facto tool of choice for all web application automation specialists. This chapter gives an insight into Selenium covering the essentials, which an automation specialist needs to know. The next few chapters will provide a detailed overview of the Selenium Architecture, the tools available for automation, an introduction to Web UI and elements for automation, with an introduction to coding your first Selenium scripts using different languages.

Questions

1. When was Selenium started? What was the original purpose for Selenium?

2. What are different components of Selenium?

3. What is the difference between Selenium RC and Web Driver?

4. What does a Selenium Remote Control Contain?

5. What are the benefits of Selenium IDE?

6. What are the benefits of using Selenium Grid?

7. How does Web driver help in cross-browser testing of web applications?

8. What are the key benefits of Selenium?

9. Why should a project use Selenium?

10. What are the drawbacks of using Selenium?

11. What are some aspects in which Selenium helps in terms of flexibility of languages, platforms and browsers?

12. Where will you not use Selenium for test automation?

13. What are some drawbacks of using Selenium in web applications using dynamic id and dynamic content creation?

14. What are some challenges preventing big enterprises to adopt Selenium as a tool of choice?

15. Can you explain how features of Selenium are extended by some of the commercial tools for better productivity?

CHAPTER 3
Understanding Selenium Architecture

"You can be a great tester if you have programming skills.
You can also be a great tester if you have no programming skills at all.
And, you can be a lousy tester with or without programming skills.
A great tester will learn what skills she needs to continue to be great, in her own style."

— *Jerry Weinberg*

Now that we have gone through the history, benefits, and challenges of Selenium tool in the previous chapters and known a bit about the process of test automation, we shall get into a bit of more detail. To understand Selenium better, we need to understand the Selenium components that deliver the productivity it is popular for. Each component serves a special purpose for the larger picture of automation. What are the fundamental components of Selenium? How does the architecture glue these components together? How does selenium automation work? What are some of the tips to keep in mind while designing frameworks or test cases? This chapter will address these salient points.

Structure

- Selenium Architecture
- Selenium **Remote Control (RC)** Architecture
- Selenium WebDriver Architecture
- Selenium language bindings and client libraries
- Selenium browser drivers and supported browsers

Objective

This section covers the Selenium Architecture in detail. This chapter focuses on how Selenium WebDriver API connects the dots between programming languages (such as C#, Python, Java, Ruby, Java Script etc.) bound through JSON wire protocol, leveraging the browser driver classes and interfaces to test the applications through real browsers. This builds on Chapter 2 that introduced Selenium to get into a more detailed overview of the Selenium Architecture and components. We shall be using some coding examples in Selenium through Java and Python to understand how Selenium automation is done.

Selenium Architecture

As highlighted in *Chapter 2*, Selenium has four (considering RC and WebDriver to be of the same category) major components for consideration, that is, **Selenium Core, WebDriver/Remote Control, IDE,** and **GRID**. On similar lines, the core architecture components of Selenium include four aspects. We shall cover them later in detail. Four core components of Selenium Architecture include:

- **Selenium client/Core libraries:** Programming language/bindings for Selenium. We have libraries for languages such as Java, JavaScript, C#, Python, Ruby, PHP.
- **JSON wire protocol over HTTP:** This allows the RC or automation of web applications through web drivers.
- **Browser WebDrivers:** While WebDrivers do not apply to Selenium RC, they are the driving force for automating the web applications and help implement cross-browser testing as well.
- **Browsers:** Where the web application under test gets executed and controlled via the automation programs using the libraries, protocols and drivers.

Let's see the core architecture components of Selenium in a pictorial manner, as shown in *Figure 3.1*.

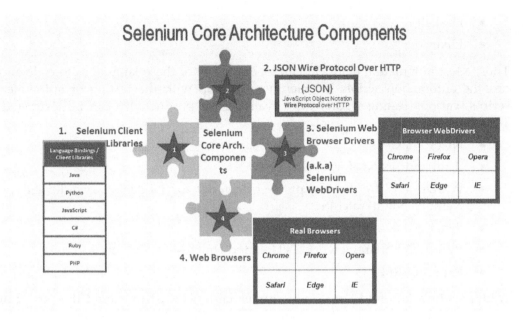

Figure 3.1: *Selenium Core Architecture Components*

Selenium client/core libraries

For writing the automation scripts that interact with Selenium server (through Selenium RC in pre-Selenium 2.0 world), or through Selenium WebDriver, we can use the available language-oriented client libraries to do the coding. As per the Selenium working group, core languages supported are:

- Java
- C#
- Ruby
- Python
- JavaScript

However, third-party language bindings (not developed by Selenium HQ) are available for coding as well. Some of these languages include:

- Perl
- PHP
- Objective-C
- R
- Dart
- Tcl

- Haskell
- Elixir

Thus, a test automation engineer can leverage any of these languages to code and test the automation scripts in Selenium. To help with the testing of automated scripts, various testing frameworks available for productivity can be leveraged. These include:

- NUnit for C#
- JUnit and TestNG for Java
- WebDriverJS for JavaScript, WebDriverIO for Node.JS based JavaScript, NemoJS, NightWatchJS
- Behat+Mink for PHP
- PyTest, Robot Framework, PyUnit and UnitTest for Python
- RSpec for Ruby

Additionally, a lot of add-ons and commercial tools exist to extend the power of Selenium. Some of these include **Sauce Labs** (for Cross-Platform/Browser Testing), **Browser Stack & Cross Browser Testing, Ranorex & Selocity** extensions for Chrome and Firefox, **Katalon** tool for recording and script generation. For the development of scripts, plenty of IDEs and tools exist. We shall cover these in subsequent chapters.

JSON wire protocol over HTTP

In Selenium, **JSON (JavaScript Object Notifications)** wire protocol acts as a conduit that connects the WebDriver implementations. WebDriver is a W3C standard remote-control interface that helps the calling program to control the agents and web elements in the end application. Through JSON wire protocol, the WebDriver provides a simpler model for a platform- and language- agnostic protocol to control automation and behaviour of web browsers to enable automation of web applications.

A Selenium program uses JSON to transfer data between a client and the server. JSON wire protocol uses the **Representational State Transfer (REST) Application Programming Interface (API)** interface, also known as RestAPI style to interact with various states of a browser-based web application asynchronously. In a simpler definition, the JSON wire protocol uses a simple request/response model of handling the commands and responses managed through a language-agnostic way using Selenium Client Libraries (through Java, JavaScript, Ruby, C#, PHP, Python programs). Each Browser Driver invoked using a Selenium client library (or a Selenium program in simple terms) uses its HTTP server implementation to take care of the "Request/Response" of data/action/control exchange between a Selenium program and the browser in which the web application is under test. When we are mentioning that JSON Wire Protocol helps Selenium code interacts with browsers, it's better to also mention that any action that we perform on the browser like clicking button, entering text in a text box etc., are POST request, while fetching info from the browser like getting the title of a web page, getting text from a page are basically GET requests.

Some of the common codes returned are mentioned in *Table 3.1*.

Code	Status
0	Success
7	No Such Element
8	No Such Frame
10	Stale Element Reference
11	Element Not Visible
15	Element Is Not Selectable

Table 3.1: List of JSON Wire Protocol Return Codes

The WebDriver has a set of interfaces to identify, manage and modify the **Document Object Model (DOM)** of a web page and manage the user interactions. Some of the key commands that can be managed through WebDriver using JSON wire protocol are mentioned in Table 3.2.(Full list can be looked up at **https://w3c.github.io/webdriver/.)**

List of Web Driver Endpoints			
New Session	**Delete Session**	**Status**	**Get Timeouts**
Set Timeouts	Navigate To	Get Current URL	Back
Forward	Refresh	Get Title	Get Window Handle
Close Window	Switch To Window	Get Window Handles	New Window
Switch To Frame	Switch To Parent Frame	Get Window Rect	Set Window Rect
Maximize Window	Minimize Window	Fullscreen Window	Get Active Element
Find Element	Find Elements	Find Element from Element	Find Elements from Element
Is Element Selected	Get Element Attribute	Get Element Property	Get Element CSS Value
Get Element Text	Get Element Tag Name	Get Element Rect	Is Element Enabled
Element Click	Element Clear	Element Send Keys	Get Page Source

Execute Script	Execute Async Script	Get All Cookies	Get Named Cookie
Add Cookie	Delete Cookie	Delete All Cookies	Perform Actions
Release Actions	Dismiss Alert	Accept Alert	Get Alert Text
Send Alert Text	Take Screenshot	Take Element Screenshot	

Table 3.2: *List of WebDriver End Points*

The WebDriver implementation across browsers has variations in implementation of end-points. WebDriver also has request/response for various Client Library (also known as languages such as Java, C#, Python etc.) centric actions. The language- and platform- agnostic libraries developed for Selenium permit the programmer to write simple automation programs. These automation programs are browser- and platform- agnostic, if written in a sophisticated manner.

Browser drivers

As mentioned earlier, browser driver is used for interaction with the end browsers where the automated application is tested. The usefulness of the Browser Driver is that it encapsulates and keeps the "browser implementation" details in an abstract manner. This way, the programmer doesn't have to worry about the implementation of the browser itself. With the level of abstraction given by the Browser Driver, it becomes easier to have common functions and commands that can be used by programmers to automate using the language of their own choice.

Selenium'sopen-source community maintains a *browser driver* for every available browser. In one case, there is *browser driver* for a browser-less testing using **"HTMLUnitDriver"** as well! Availability of various browsers across platforms and choice of languages to program allows us to do a real platform-agnostic cross-browser testing as well that propelled the popularity of Selenium.

Browser

A Browser is an application or a software program used for viewing and exploring content on the world wide web. Some of the explorations include interactions involving user actions such as typing, clicking, scrolling, downloading etc.

Most popular browsers include Google Chrome, Mozilla Firefox, Opera, Microsoft Internet Explorer, Apple Safari, Microsoft Edge, Amazon Silk etc. Almost all of these browsers have simplified browser versions for mobile applications as well.

Selenium Remote-Control (RC) Architecture

One of the early success stories of Selenium was how Selenium RC helped testers automate web applications quickly. Selenium RC had two major components that made up the Selenium server to run the automated scripts on various browsers and application under test. These components include:

- Selenium client libraries/language bindings
- Selenium server/Core Selenium RC components –
  - o **Selenium server:** Core HTML and JavaScript components
  - o **Proxy server:** to emulate the request and to avoid same-origin conflicts
- Real browsers for testing
- Application under test

Now, let's see the architecture diagram (see *Figure 3.2*) of WebDriver in a simpler manner, covering its components.

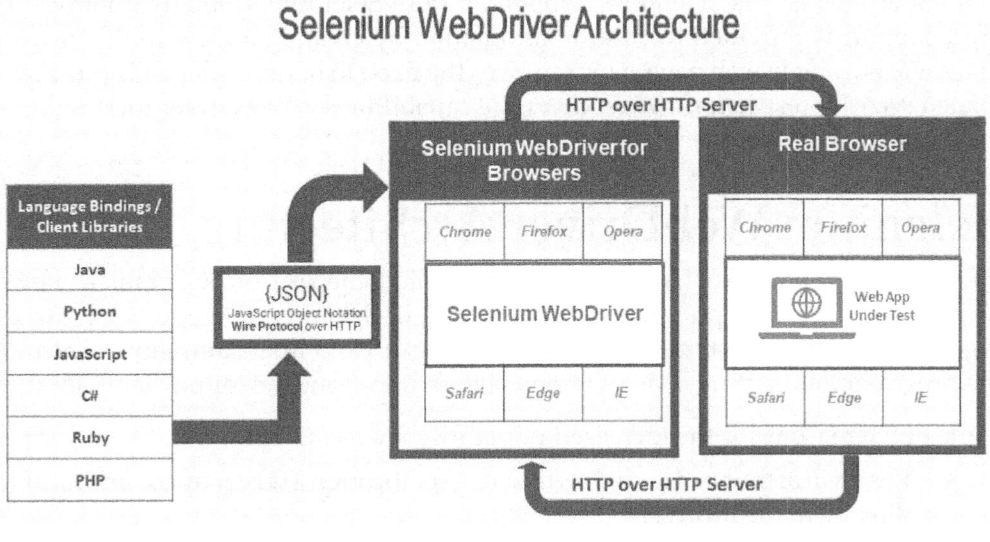

Figure 3.2: *Selenium WebDriver Architecture*

In this, the key purpose of the Selenium server is to launch the browser, run the commands to operate the browser state, remote-control the behaviour and close the browsers when actions are carried out. One of the challenges faced by the automation testers due to a restriction in DOM is Same-Origin-Policy (SOP).This is because access to a DOM is not permitted from an origin that is different from the origin, which tries to access the document. Origin means a combination of the DOM

Scheme, IP address/server name of the host and the port of the URI being accessed. Introduction of Selenium RC via Selenium server &proxy helped solve this issue.

NOTE

- Suppose if you have a script named Books.js on the landing page of **https://bpbonline.com**, as per same-origin, only pages within **bpbonline.com** will be accessible for the "**Books.js**" script.

- This means pages such as **https://bpbonline.com/blogs/programming** or **https://bpbonline.com/collection** will be accessible and pages such as **https://www.ulektz.com/p/BPB-Publications** or **https://bpbcatalogue.netlify.com/**that are linked through the main landing page of **https://bpbonline.com** will not be accessible as per the policy.

- This issue is circumvented through a proxy injection method in which the Selenium server acts as an HTTP proxy configured to the client which obfuscates the application URI undera random-fictitious URI. This round-about approach helps the scripts run without any issues.

With the Selenium server, automation was done smoothly but had certain drawbacks that got addressed via Selenium WebDriver. With Selenium WebDriver native OS-level support is provided to control automation by creating a view to the browser that there is a single web page. This removes the need to handle Single-Origin-Policy related security restrictions. We'll cover the capabilities of WebDriver thoroughly in the subsequent chapters.

Selenium WebDriver Architecture

The introduction of WebDriver in 2006 propelled the use of Selenium to newer heights as the features provided were far ahead of Selenium IDE and Selenium RC together. The direct communication feature was a class apart and gave control to the programmers writing code in various languages using Selenium client libraries.

Some of the reasons for the increased popularity are as follows:

- Removal of the need to control the browser through a server by communicating directly to the browser
- Less server infrastructure needs
- Simpler API commands compared to Selenium RC –
  o Since they are compact and object-oriented, abstraction and encapsulation can be used to hide unnecessary detail, thus keeping it very simple.
- WebDriver has a much simpler architecture –
  o Such as removal of a need to have HTTP proxy to remove the Source-Of-Origin Restriction

- Easy to install and configure
- Browser actions and interactions are almost similar to real user experience
- Faster execution resulting in faster automation experience as a result of native implementations of the WebDriver for various OS and browser types–
  - o WebDriver is faster as the drivers provided by the browsers are used directly to manage and operate the browsers
- WebDriver also gives an option to test rich asynchronous web applications built using AJAX or rich JavaScript constructs (e.g. Gmail, Facebook, Amazon to name a few)
- You can test the application using a headless browser using HtmlUnit Browser tool

WebDriver still has some restrictions that need to be addressed using an extension or extra programming. These include message logs for debugging, run-time, report generation.

Selenium RC Architecture

Selenium Remote Control, as described earlier, uses real browsers accessed and controlled through Selenium server and proxy, unlike the WebDriver. This is represented pictorially in *Figure 3.3*

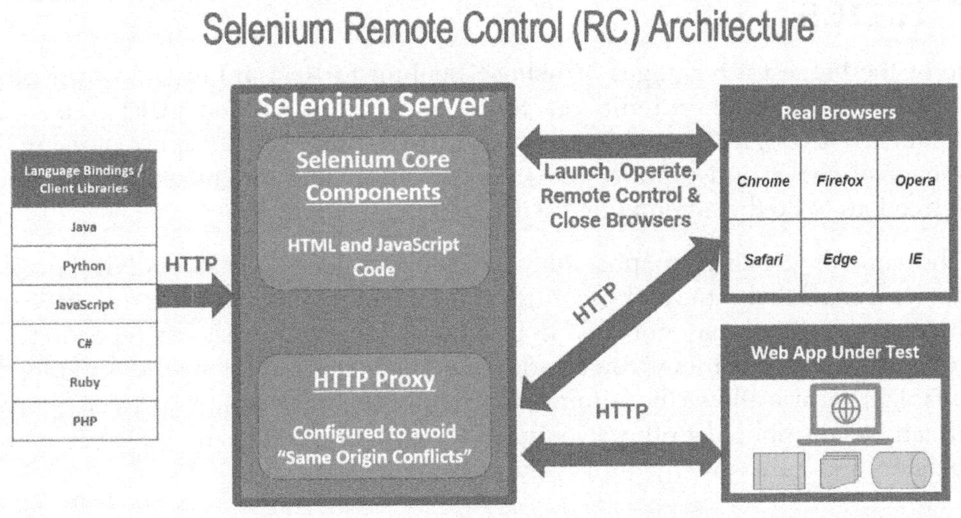

Selenium Remote Control (RC) Architecture

Language Bindings / Client Libraries
Java
Python
JavaScript
C#
Ruby
PHP

Selenium Server
Selenium Core Components
HTML and JavaScript Code
HTTP Proxy
Configured to avoid "Same Origin Conflicts"

HTTP

Launch, Operate, Remote Control & Close Browsers

HTTP

HTTP

Real Browsers

Chrome	Firefox	Opera
Safari	Edge	IE

Web App Under Test

Figure 3.3: Selenium Remote Control (RC) Architecture

In addition to the components outlined in the Selenium RC Architecture section, one additional element to keep in mind is the WebDriver. There are various drivers for different browsers. Some of the popular ones are given in the table below:

Browser	Browser Driver Name
Mozilla Firefox	Mozilla Gecko Driver
Google Chrome	ChromeDriver
Opera	Opera Driver
Microsoft Edge	Microsoft Edge Driver
Internet Explorer	Microsoft Internet Explorer Driver
Safari	SafariDriver
Ghost Driver	PhamtomJS (Deprecated in Selenium 4.0)
HtmlUnit	HtmlUnitDriver

Table 3.3: Browsers and Selenium Browser Drivers

There are more Browser Drivers available, being developed by third-party developers. Some custom libraries are used for mobile browser automation as well such as **QtWebDriver, jBroserDriver, Winium, Blackberry and Windows Phone drivers**. Some of these drivers are not tenable to continue but help us in automating older applications running in different sets of devices and browsers.

Selenium language bindings and client libraries

One of the biggest advantages of using Selenium for test automation over other successful commercial automation tools, such as **MicroFocusUFT** (erstwhile Mercury/HP QTP), is the choice it offers for programming. The choice of using the language of choice and comfort gives the test automation engineers the flexibility and freedom to do the automation easily.

At the same time, being an open-source initiative, Selenium is an evolving project. What it means is that some of the features and functionalities that come out of the box in a commercial tool may not exist in Selenium. Some examples are reporting and logging. These shortcomings can be addressed by using the extensions and plugins available. This also allows the automation engineer using Selenium to build libraries that can be contributed to the Selenium Project. Quite a few successful Selenium superstars and gurus emerged this way though.

Since core languages/bindings supported by the Selenium Project have been outlined in the **Selenium Client/Core Libraries** section earlier in the chapter, let us look at some simple programs for running a WebDriver automation script.

Java program to automate a web action

Let us put this into action. Let's write our first Java program using ChromeDriver for a Selenium test automation. This example will be described in detail in the next chapter.

Ch3_Prog_1_SeleniumChromeJavaExample.java

```
1     package CrackSeleniumInterviewExamples;

2     import org.openqa.selenium.By;

3     import org.openqa.selenium.Keys;

4     import org.openqa.selenium.WebDriver;

5     import org.openqa.selenium.WebElement;

6     import org.openqa.selenium.chrome.ChromeDriver;

7

8     public class Ch3_Prog_1_SeleniumChromeJavaExample{

9     public static void main(String[] args) {

10    // Create a new instance of the Chrome driver - Set the Properties
for the Chrome Driver locations

11            System.setProperty("webdriver.chrome.driver",

12    "C:\\Selenium\\chromedriver.exe");

13            WebElement element;

14            WebDriver driver = new ChromeDriver();

15    // And now use this to visit BPB Publication's website

16            driver.get("https://bpbonline.com/");

17    // Second Method is driver.navigate().to("https://bpbonline.com/");

18

19    // Check the title of the page

20            System.out.println("Page title is: " + driver.getTitle());

21    // Type C to search for book titles with C

22            element = driver.findElement(By.id("bc-product-search")).
sendKeys("C");

23    // Now Press Enter to see the results

24            driver.findElement(By.id("bc-product-search")).
sendKeys(Keys.ENTER);

25    // Check the title of the new page
```

```
26          System.out.println("Page title is: " + driver.getTitle());
27    // Get the text content of the web page
28          System.out.println(driver.findElement(By.tagName("body")).
getText());
29    //Close the browser
30          driver.quit();
31      }
32   }
```

Running the above program will get you the content as a log, covering key print statements included in the program as well. This is mentioned below:

```
"C:\Program Files\Java\jdk-12.0.2\bin\java.exe" -javaagent:C:\Users\
rahma\.IdeaIC2019.2\system\testAgent\intellij-coverage-agent-1.0.508.
jar=C:\Users\rahma\AppData\Local\Temp\coverage8args "-javaagent:C:\
Program Files\JetBrains\IntelliJ IDEA Community Edition 2019.2\lib\
idea_rt.jar=55084:C:\Program Files\JetBrains\IntelliJ IDEA Community
Edition 2019.2\bin" -Dfile.encoding=UTF-8 -classpath C:\Users\
rahma\IdeaProjects\CrackSeleniumInterviewExamples\out\production\
CrackSeleniumInterviewExamples;C:\\Selenium\chromedriver_win32.zip;C:\\
Selenium\htmlunit-driver-2.35.1.jar;C:\\Selenium\selenium-java-3.141.59.
zip;C:\\Selenium\selenium-html-runner-3.141.59.jar;C:\\Selenium\
selenium-server-standalone-3.141.59.jar;C:\\Selenium\ios-server-
0.6.5-jar-with-dependencies.jar;C:\\Selenium\htmlunit-driver-2.35.1-
jar-with-dependencies.jar CrackSeleniumInterviewExamples.Ch3_Prog_1_
SeleniumChromeJavaExample

---- IntelliJ IDEA coverage runner ----

sampling ...

include patterns:

CrackSeleniumInterviewExamples\..*

exclude patterns:

Starting ChromeDriver 75.0.3770.140 (2d9f97485c7b07dc18a74666574f1917673
1995c-refs/branch-heads/3770@{#1155}) on port 46439

Only local connections are allowed.

Please protect ports used by ChromeDriver and related test frameworks to
prevent access by malicious code.
```

[1565451876.527][WARNING]: This version of ChromeDriver has not been tested with Chrome version 76.

[1565451877.186][WARNING]: This version of ChromeDriver has not been tested with Chrome version 76.

[1565451879.628][WARNING]: Timed out connecting to Chrome, retrying...

Aug 10, 2019 9:14:46 PM org.openqa.selenium.remote.ProtocolHandshake createSession

INFO: Detected dialect: W3C

Page title is: Computer & IT Books | Emerging & Trending Technologies 1 E-books - BPB Publications

Page title is: C - BPB Publications

INR

item(s)

Home Videos Computer Books

Computer Books-Hindi

TECH

CAD/CAM

NIELIT

Electronics

Blog Catalogue eBooks

Home C

SEARCH RESULT

10%

Advanced C++

Rs. 180 Rs. 162

11%

Understanding Pointers In C & C++ …5th Revised & Updated Edition

Rs. 297 Rs. 267

10%

Ansi C Programming

Rs. 360 Rs. 324

10%

Learn C# (Includes The C# 3.0 Features) by Sam A. Abolrous

Rs. 150 Rs. 135

10%

The 'C' Odyssey C++ & Graphics The Future Of C by Meeta Gandhi, Tilak Shetty Rajiv Shah, Vijay mukhi

Rs. 250 Rs. 225

11%

Learning RabbitMQ With C#

Rs. 197 Rs. 177

10%

Let us C Hindi

Rs. 450 Rs. 405

10%

101 Challenges In C Programming

Rs. 240 Rs. 216

10%

C internals for coding interviews

Rs. 330 Rs. 297

11%

C Pearls by Yashavant Kanetkar

Rs. 165 Rs. 148

10%

C Projects By Yashavant Kanetkar

Rs. 450 Rs. 405

10%

C# Made Simple by BPB

Rs. 240 Rs. 216

1

2

3

...

12

Next

SUBSCRIBE TO OUR NEWSLETTER

SUBSCRIBE

BPB is Asia's largest publishers of Computer, Electronic Books and CD Roms/ DVDs. For the last 58 years, BPB has been a friend, philosopher and guide for programmers, developers, hardware technicians, IT Professionals who have made things happen in the IT World.

Head Office

20 Ansari Road Darya Ganj New Delhi- 110002

Phone: (+91) 8459388882

Mail: online@bpbonline.com

Connect With Us

Facebook

Twitter

Linkedin

Help

Privacy Policy

Term of Use

Shipping & Delivery

Refund Policy

Payment Policy

Request a specimen

FAQ

About Company

About us

Vision and Mission

Our Book Store

Careers

Contact Us

BPB is Asia's largest publishers of Computer and Electronic Books. For the last 58 years, BPB has been a friend, philosopher and guide for programmers, developers, hardware technicians, IT Professionals who have made things happen in the IT World. Our Chairman Shri G.C. Jain have been honoured with the PADMASHREE award in 2002 by Hon'ble President of India for his contribution in spreading IT Education in India. Welcome to the family of BPB Publications! A family with about 50 million people residing in diverse parts of the Indian subcontinent and even farther than that. A family with computer literate people who have achieved this acumen and expertise by the perpetual quest of excellence by BPB. With such adornments as 2500 publications, about 50 million books sold over the year and about the same number of reader base, it is a matter of no surprise that BPB titles are prescribed as standard courseware at most of the leading schools, institutes and universities in India. BPB has proved its success in the field of computer education and anyone who has graduated in computer & electronics has graduated with BPB books

1958 - 2019 © BPB Publications. All Rights Reserved

Class transformation time: 0.0960139s for 1812 classes or 5.298780353200883E-5s per class

Process finished with exit code 0

A Python program to automate similarly

Let's see an example in Python, which does almost the same thing as the Java program. In this Python Program, we have two variations. First, printing of the HTML page content (as the implementation in Java and Python for getting the page content is different). Second, getting a screenshot of the result.

Ch3_Prog_2_SeleniumChromePythonExample_2.py

```
1    from selenium import webdriver

2    from selenium.common.exceptions import TimeoutException

3    from selenium.webdriver.support.ui import WebDriverWait

4    from selenium.webdriver.support import expected_conditions as EC

5

6    # Create a new instance of the Chrome driver

7    # Pass the location of your WebDriver to executable_path
```

```
8     # parameter while instantiating Chrome Driver
9     driver = webdriver.Chrome(executable_path ="C:\\Selenium\\chromedriver.exe")
10    #Uncomment next line if you have a slow internet connection
11    #WebDriverWait(driver, 10)
12    # go to the BPBOnline home page
13    driver.get("https://bpbonline.com")
14    # the page Uses AJAX - lets check the title
15    print(driver.title)
16    # find the element that's name attribute is Product search
17    inputElement = driver.find_element_by_id('bc-product-search')
18    # type in the search term in the search bar
19 inputElement.send_keys("C")
20    # submit the search
21    inputElement.submit()
22    try:
23    # Wait to check for the title to get loaded
24        WebDriverWait(driver, 10).until(EC.title_contains("C"))
25    # You should see "C in the title Search"
26    print(driver.title)
27    #Print the Page content in HTML format
28    print(driver.page_source)
29    #Save the Screen Shot as a file
30        driver.get_screenshot_as_file("BPBonline_C_Output.png")
31    finally:
32    #Close the Driver
33        driver.quit()
34
```

After editing out more than 100 pages worth HTML/JavaScript output of the logs, the output from the program will be like:

```
runfile('C:/Users/rahma/OneDrive/Desktop/Selenium/Programs/
SeleniumFireFoxPythonExample.py', wdir='C:/Users/rahma/OneDrive/Desktop/
Selenium/Programs')
```

    Computer & IT Books | Emerging & Trending Technologies 1 E-books –
    BPB Publications

    title:C – BPB Publications

Since the final task is to save the screenshot as an image, before quitting the browser
driver, one can use the following command:

    #Save the Screen Shot as a file

        driver.get_screenshot_as_file("BPBonline_C_Output.png")

Executing the program will create BPBOnline_C_Output.png file, as shown in *Figure
3.4.*

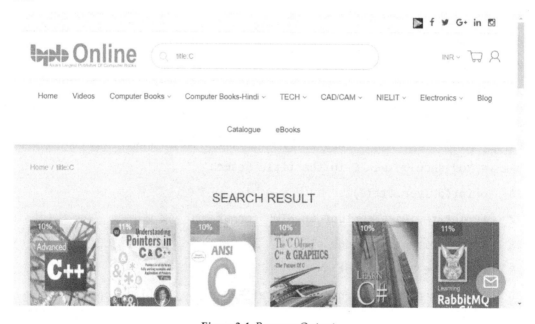

Figure 3.4: Program Output

Selenium WebDrivers

As we saw in the Python example above, the library implementations between
Java and Python are a bit different. This is because the open-source community
maintaining the driver code uses different approaches, albeit the effort put forth by
the steering group to keep it similar. Some of the product backlogs could potentially
be cleared and the libraries may look exactly similar in the future.

As mentioned in the table earlier for various types of WebDrivers, the approaches differ a bit. One way to have a simplified way of handling the permutations and variations is to leveraging the frameworks such as **Sauce Labs, Cross Browser Testing** and **Browser Stack** to name a few.

Let's see some of the features provided by the WebDrivers.

Instantiating a Selenium WebDriver through different languages:

Java:

```
/* Examples to initiate various Drivers */
```
- `WebDriver driver=new FirefoxDriver();`
- `WebDriver driver=new ChromeDriver();`
- `WebDriver driver=new OperaDriver();`
- `WebDriver driver=new EdgeDriver();`
- `WebDriver driver=new InternetExplorerDriver();`
- `WebDriver driver=new SafariDriver();`
- `WebDriver driver=new PhantomJSDriver();`
- `WebDriver driver=new HtmlUnitDriver();`

JavaScript:
- `var driver = require('selenium-webdriver'),By = webdriver.By, until = webdriver.until;  //Standard WebDriver Instantiation`
- `var driver_ff = new webdriver.Builder().forBrowser('firefox').build(); //Firefox Instantiation`
- `var driver_chrome = new webdriver.Builder().forBrowser('chrome').build(); // Chrome Instantiation`

C#:
- `IWebDriver driver = new FirefoxDriver();`
- `IWebDriver driver = new ChromeDriver();`
- `IWebDriver driver = new InternetExplorerDriver();`

Python:
- `from selenium import webdriver`

```
## Examples to initiate various Drivers
```
- `driver = webdriver.Chrome()`
- `driver = webdriver.Firefox()`
- `driver = webdriver.Remote()`

```
## Used for Mobile Apps, Headless Browsers and Browsers not having a
WebDriver server
```

Ruby:

```
driver = Selenium::WebDriver.for :firefox

driver = Selenium::WebDriver.for :ie

driver = Selenium::WebDriver.for :chrome

driver = Selenium::WebDriver.for :internet_explorer

driver = Selenium::WebDriver.for :remote
```

driver = Selenium::WebDriver.for :ff

PHP:

- `$driverhost = 'http://localhost:4444/wd/hub'; // Standard and default. One can change the URL or Port if required`
- `$driver = RemoteWebDriver::create($driverhost, DesiredCapabilities::firefox());// FireFox Example`
- `$driver = RemoteWebDriver::create($driverhost, DesiredCapabilities::chrome()); // Chrome Example`

Some of the key commands that we can look at for WebDriver usage include the following:

WebDriver Function/ API Command	Purpose	Example
driver.get()	For opening a new URL in the browser opened using the Browser Driver	WebDriver driver = new ChromeDriver(); driver.get(https:// bpbonline.com);
driver. getCurrentUrl()	Gets the current URL – can be used for checking the site-map navigation of a website	driver. getCurrentUrl();
driver.getTitle()	Gets the title of the current URL the browser is in	String pageTitle = driver.getTitle();
driver.getText()	Used to get the text of a HTML element specified in a web page	String BodyText = driver.findElement(By. id("body")).getText();
driver. getPageSource()	Used to get the text string of the source of a web page	String PageSource = driver. getPageSource();
driver.getAttribute()	We can get value of any attribute mentioned in the DOM.	driver.findElement(By. id("password").
driver.close()	Closes the browser window	driver.close();
driver.quit()	Quits the current driver instance	driver.quit();

driver.findElement()	Locates a web element in the page. findElement() finds out the first element in the page, if more than one exists.	WebElement element = driver. findElement(By. xpath("/ /");
driver.findElements()	Finds all elements in the page, based on the identifier and method given. It returns a list of items as well	List <WebElement> webelements = driver. findElements(By. xpath("/ /");
driver. getWindowHandles()	Returns a set of window handles of open windows that can be used by the program for navigations	Set<String> windowHandles = driver. getWindowHandles();
driver. getWindowHandle()	Returns a String details of the current window handle the browser is active in that can be used by the program for navigations	String currentWindow = driver. getWindowHandle();

driver.navigate().to()	Similar to driver.get() and navigates to a URL specified as a parameter	driver.navigate(). to("URL");
		
		 driver.navigate(). to("https:/ / bpbonline.com");

driver.navigate(). forward()	Emulates clicking the forward button of a browser. This is useful during navigation of screenshots.	driver.navigate(). forward();
driver.navigate(). back()	Emulates clicking the Back button of a browser. This is useful during navigation of screenshots. Opposite of forward()	driver.navigate(). back();
driver.navigate(). refresh()	Emulates clicking the Refresh button of a browser. This is useful during navigating and capturing the latest updates in an AJAX page.	driver.navigate(). refresh();

driver.switchTo()	A function that permits movement between various windows or frame in a web page.	driver.switchTo(). window("WINDOW NAME OR IDENTIFIER");
		
		 driver.switchTo(). frame("FRAME NAME OR IDENTIFIER");

drageAndDrop(). **perform()**	This allows drag and drop of one web element from a source onto another target web element. This is an action performed by the WebDriver and is implemented through a defined Actions Class.	WebElement sourceElem = driver.findElement(By.name("Source Element")); WebElement destinationElem = driver.findElement(By.name("Destination / Target Element")); (new Actions(driver)).

driver.findElement().
sendKeys()
	This function is used for sending a text, to be typed in a web element (for example, it could be form or a search box).	driver.findElement(By.id("EX_FIRSTNAME")).sendKeys("FIRST NAME");
		
		driver.findElement(By.id("EX_LASTNAME")).sendKeys("LAST NAME");
		
		driver.findElement(By.id("EMAIL")).
		
		driver.findElement(By.id("PASSWORD")).

driver.findElement(). **submit()**	This a function isused to submit the content into a form by clicking the submit button.	driver.findElement(By.id("SUBMIT")).submit();
driver.findElement(). **click()**	This is a function used toClick the button for any web element action. It could be used as submit button click as well, if submit button is clicked using this function.	driver.findElement(By.id("CLICK BUTTON ELEMENT")).click();
driver.findElement(). **isEnabled()**	A function to check if a web element is enabled. It returns a Boolean TRUE/FALSE as a response based on whether the element is enabled or not.	Boolean checkboxEnablement = driver.findElement(By.id("CHECK BOX ELEMENT")).isEnabled();

driver.findElement(). isSelected()	A function to check if a web element is selected. It returns a Boolean TRUE/ FALSE as a response based on whether the element is selected or not.	Boolean checkbox Selection = driver. find Element (By. id("CHECK BOX ELEMENT")). isSelected();
driver.findElement(). isDisplayed()	A function to check if a web element is displayed. It returns a Boolean TRUE/ FALSE as a response based on whether the element is displayed or not.	Boolean checkbox Display = driver. find Element (By. id("CHECK BOX ELEMENT")).is Displayed();

Table 3.4: *Key WebDriver Commands*

We'll discuss additional WebDriver commands as a part of the programs in the subsequent chapters. For instance, the commands that would allow us to write a graceful exit program are "waits, timeouts, visibility, exception handling, cookies, user profile/agent management and headless browser navigations" etc.

One example for handling a pop-up is included herewith:

Ch3_Prog_3_SeleniumChromePythonExample_3.py

```
1    from selenium import webdriver

2    from selenium.common.exceptions import TimeoutException

3    from selenium.webdriver.support.ui import

4    from selenium.webdriver.support import expected_conditions as EC

5    from selenium.webdriver.chrome.options import Options

6

7    # Create a new instance of the Chrome driver

8    # Replace your executable path with the directory where you have the drivers

9    driver = webdriver.Chrome(executable_path ="C:\\Selenium\\chromedriver.exe")

10

11   #A code to disable notifications pop-up. This could be handy

12   options = Options()

13   options.add_argument("--disable-notifications")

14

15   # go to the BPBOnline home page
```

```
16    driver.get("https://bpbonline.com")

17

18    # Lets check the title

19    print(driver.title)

20

21    #Write Code to handle the Pop-up for signing up to Newsletter

22    driver.find_element_by_xpath('/html/body/div[5]/div/div/a').click()

23

24    #Wait for page to load

25    WebDriverWait(driver, 10)

26

27    #Click on Videos link by using Link Text option

28    elem = driver.find_element_by_link_text("Videos")

29    elem.click()

30

31    try:

32    # Wait to check for the title to get loaded

33        WebDriverWait(driver, 30)

34    print(driver.title)

35    #Print the Page content in HTML format

36    print(driver.page_source)

37    #Save the Screen Shot as a file

38        driver.get_screenshot_as_file("OUTPUTFILENAME.png")

39

40    finally:

41    #Close the Driver

42        driver.quit()

43
```

The output is given below "...." refers to the filler text removed from the log.

runfile('C:/Users/SeleniumUser/OneDrive/Desktop/Selenium/Programs/

SeleniumPythonChromeExampleTwo.py', wdir='C:/Users/SeleniumUser/
OneDrive/Desktop/Selenium/Programs')

Computer & IT Books | Emerging & Trending Technologies l E-books – BPB
Publications

Homepage | BPB Online

```
<!DOCTYPE html>

<html>

<head>

….

….

<meta name='apple-mobile-web-app-capable' content='yes' />

<meta charset="UTF-8">

<meta name="csrf-param" content="authenticity_token" />

<meta name="csrf-token"
content="dVX3FIxeWKeX3zoNG5vLRxsT8fiBAAAn10lwZjrN6
eCYPGr4IjID3i0N3GzCSQ1hVrjBLFYtBTIpei7Qc7utKA==" />

….

…


<title>Homepage | BPB Online</title>

<link rel="canonical" href="https://bpbonline.teachable.com/">

<meta property="og:title" content="Homepage">

<meta property="og:type" content="website">

<meta property="og:image" content="https://www.filepicker.io/api/file/
dorzOlITbiw5782dkTz2">

<meta property="og:url" content="https://bpbonline.teachable.com/p/
home">

<meta name="brand_video_player_color" content="#09A59A">

<meta name="site_title" content="BPB Online">

<style>

….

….
```

```
</style>

<script src='//fast.wistia.com/assets/external/E-v1.js'></script>

<script src='https://www.google.com/recaptcha/api.js' async defer></
script>


<meta name="asset_host" content="https://fedora.teachablecdn.com">

<script src="https://fedora.teachablecdn.com/assets/application-a1
63b49b644d840c6b89fc1056fb36e6a95b9994e2a4d3b73c6e49b581817480.js"
data-turbolinks-track="true"></script><script src="https://fedora.
teachablecdn.com/packs/student-2626837ef38c0dc8a508.js"></script>



<script>

…

</script>


<link href="/blog/rss" rel="alternate" title="RSS Feed"
type="application/rss+xml" />

<meta http-equiv="X-UA-Compatible" content="IE=edge">


</head>

<body>

<meta http-content='IE=Edge' http-equiv='X-UA-Compatible'>

…..

…..


</body>

</html>
```

This is the last key statement in the program. Taking screenshots as a piece of evidence is a crucial part of the test validation process and a very handy tool for regulatory heavy industries, such as life sciences and banking services, to get approvals from the regulatory authorities.

```
#Save the Screen Shot as a file
driver.get_screenshot_as_file("OUTPUTFILENAME.png")
```

When the testing is completed, the end screenshot will be captured, as shown in *Figure 3.5.*:

Figure 3.5: *Program Output*

Selenium browser drivers/supported browsers

As covered earlier in the *"Selenium WebDriver Architecture"*, all modern browsers are supported by Selenium for automation. The automation developer needs to leverage the browser drivers built for each of the browsers. Just to give you a flavour of what they are, different types of browsers supported by Selenium are mentioned in *Table 3.5*, with an example to instantiate the browser driver.

Selenium Browser Driver Hierarchy

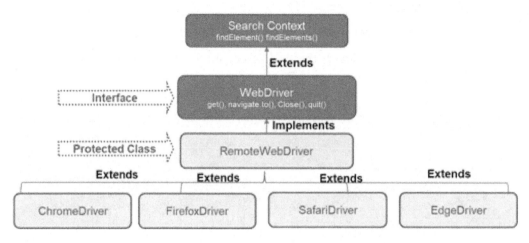

Figure 3.6: *Selenium Browser Driver Class Hierarchy*

Browser	Browser Driver Name	Driver Type	Usage (Java example)
Mozilla Firefox	Mozilla Gecko Driver	WebDriver only - no need for driver server	WebDriverdriver= new FirefoxDriver();
Google Chrome	ChromeDriver	WebDriver server for handling interactions	WebDriver driver=new ChromeDriver();
Opera	Opera Driver	WebDriver server for handling interactions	WebDriver driver=new OperaDriver();
Microsoft Edge	Microsoft Edge Driver	WebDriver server for handling interactions	WebDriver driver=new EdgeDriver();
Internet Explorer	Microsoft Internet Explorer Driver	WebDriver server for handling interactions	WebDriver driver=new
Safari	SafariDriver	WebDriver server for handling interactions	WebDriver driver=new SafariDriver();
Ghost Driver	PhamtomJS	Headless WebDriver – No need for a driver sever	WebDriver driver=new PhantomJSDriver();

HtmlUnit	HtmlUnitDriver	Headless WebDriver – No need for a driver sever	WebDriver driver=new HtmlUnitDriver();

Table 3.5: List of Selenium WebDriver and Usage

For instantiating and using a browser driver using the language of choice for automation, a certain construct needs to be followed. They are typically as follows:

CHROME DRIVER

Language	Usage
JAVA	`WebDriver driver = new ChromeDriver();`
C#	`IWebDriver driver = new ChromeDriver();`
PYTHON	`driver = webdriver.Chrome()`
RUBY	`driver = Selenium::WebDriver.for :chrome`
PERL	`my $driver = Selenium::Remote::Driver->new(browser_name => 'chrome');`

INTERNET EXPLORER DRIVER

Language	Usage
JAVA	`WebDriver driver = new InternetExplorerDriver();`
C#	`IWebDriver driver = new InternetExlorerDriver();`
PYTHON	`driver = webdriver.Ie()`
RUBY	`driver = Selenium::WebDriver.for :ie`
PERL	`my $driver = Selenium::Remote::Driver->new(browser_name => 'internet explorer');`

FIREFOX DRIVER

Language	Usage
JAVA	`WebDriver driver = new FirefoxDriver ();`
C#	`IWebDriver driver = new FirefoxDriver ();`
PYTHON	`driver = webdriver. Firefox ()`
RUBY	`driver = Selenium::WebDriver.for :firefox`
PERL	`my $driver = Selenium::Remote::Driver->new;`

HTMLUNIT DRIVER (For Headless Browser Testing)

Language	Usage
JAVA	WebDriver driver = new HtmlUnitDriver ();
C#	IWebDriver driver = new RemoteWebDriver(new Uri("http://127.0.0.1:4444/wd/hub"), DesiredCapabilities.HtmlUnit());
PYTHON	driver = webdriver.Remote("http://localhost:4444/wd/hub", webdriver. DesiredCapabilities.HTMLUNIT.copy())
RUBY	driver = Selenium::WebDriver.for :remote, :url => "http://localhost:4444/wd/hub", :desired_ capabilities => :htmlunit
PERL	my $driver = Selenium::Remote::Driver->new(browser_name => 'htmlunit', remote_server_ addr => 'localhost', port => '4444');

Now, let's try a program to invoke a Mozilla Firefox browser for automation purposes. The program would use TestNG as a testing framework (more on this will be covered in the subsequent chapter) to run the tests in a modular fashion. The objective of the script will be to log in to a social media site (LinkedIn) by entering a user id and password, thereby getting a screenshot after logging in.

We'll discuss the salient features of the program in the next chapters. However, the program will be as follows:

Ch3_Prog_4_LinkedInTestExampleJavaFireFox.java

```
1    package CrackSeleniumInterviewExamples;

2

3    import java.io.File;

4    import java.util.regex.Pattern;

5    import java.util.concurrent.TimeUnit;

6

7    import org.apache.commons.io.FileUtils;

8    import org.testng.annotations.*;

9    import static org.testng.Assert.*;

10   import org.openqa.selenium.*;

11   import org.openqa.selenium.firefox.FirefoxDriver;
```

```
12    import org.openqa.selenium.support.ui.Select;

13    public class Ch3_Prog_4_LinkedInTestExampleJavaFireFox {

14    private WebDriver driver;

15    private String baseUrl;

16    private boolean acceptNextAlert = true;

17    private StringBuffer verificationErrors = new StringBuffer();

18

19        @BeforeClass(alwaysRun = true)

20    public void setUp() throws Exception {

21            System.setProperty("webdriver.firefox.driver",

22    "C:\\Users\\rahma\\OneDrive\\Desktop\\Selenium\\geckodriver.exe");

23            driver = new FirefoxDriver();

24            baseUrl = "https://www.google.com/";

25            driver.manage().timeouts().implicitlyWait(30, TimeUnit.SECONDS);

26        }

27

28        @Test

29    public void testLinkedIn() throws Exception {

30            driver.get("https://www.linkedin.com/");

31            driver.findElement(By.name("session_key")).click();

32            driver.findElement(By.name("session_key")).click();

33            driver.findElement(By.name("session_key")).clear();

34            driver.findElement(By.name("session_key")).sendKeys("YOUR
LINKED IN ID"); //Replace YOUR LINKED IN ID with login id

35            driver.findElement(By.name("session_password")).clear();

36            driver.findElement(By.name("session_password")).
sendKeys("YOUR LINKED IN PASSWORD");//Replace YOUR LINKED IN PASWORD
with password

37            driver.findElement(By.xpath("(.//*[normalize-space(text()) and
normalize-space(.)='Forgot password?'])[1]/following::button[1]")).click();

38            System.out.println("Page title is: " + driver.getTitle());
```

```
39          System.out.println(driver.findElement(By.tagName("body")).
getText());

40          File ScreenShotFile =((TakesScreenshot) driver).
getScreenshotAs(OutputType.FILE);

41          FileUtils.copyFile(ScreenShotFile, new File("LinkedInFile.
png"));

42          driver.close();

43      }

44

45      @AfterClass(alwaysRun = true)

46  public void tearDown() throws Exception {

47          driver.quit();

48          String verificationErrorString = verificationErrors.
toString();

49  if (!"".equals(verificationErrorString)) {

50              fail(verificationErrorString);

51      }

52      }

53

54  private boolean isElementPresent(By by) {

55  try {

56              driver.findElement(by);

57  return true;

58          } catch (NoSuchElementException e) {

59  return false;

60      }

61      }

62

63  private boolean isAlertPresent() {

64  try {

65              driver.switchTo().alert();
```

```
66    return true;
67            } catch (NoAlertPresentException e) {
68    return false;
69            }
70        }
71
72    private String closeAlertAndGetItsText() {
73    try {
74            Alert alert = driver.switchTo().alert();
75            String alertText = alert.getText();
76    if (acceptNextAlert) {
77                alert.accept();
78            } else {
79                alert.dismiss();
80            }
81    return alertText;
82            } finally {
83                acceptNextAlert = true;
84            }
85        }
86    }
87
```

The program log (edited version) will appear as mentioned below:

```
"C:\Program Files\Java\jdk-12.0.2\bin\java.exe" -ea -javaagent:C:\
Users\SeleniumUser\.IdeaIC2019.2\system\testAgent\intellij-coverage-
agent-1.0.508.jar=C:\Users\SeleniumUser\AppData\Local\Temp\
coverage304args -Didea.test.cyclic.buffer.size=1048576 "-javaagent:C:\
Program Files\JetBrains\IntelliJ IDEA Community Edition 2019.2\
lib\idea_rt.jar=52322:C:\Program Files\JetBrains\IntelliJ IDEA
Community Edition 2019.2\bin" -Dfile.encoding=UTF-8 -classpath "C:\
Program Files\JetBrains\IntelliJ IDEA Community Edition 2019.2\lib\
```

```
idea_rt.jar;C:\Program Files\JetBrains\IntelliJ IDEA Community Edition
2019.2\plugins\testng\lib\testng-plugin.jar;C:\Users\SeleniumUser\
IdeaProjects\CrackSeleniumInterviewExamples\out\production\
CrackSeleniumInterviewExamples;C:\Selenium\chromedriver_win32.zip;C:\
Selenium\htmlunit-driver-2.35.1.jar;C:\Selenium\selenium-java-3.141.59.
zip;C:\Selenium\selenium-html-runner-3.141.59.jar;C:\Selenium\
selenium-server-standalone-3.141.59.jar;C:\Selenium\ios-server-0.6.5-
jar-with-dependencies.jar;C:\Selenium\htmlunit-driver-2.35.1-jar-with-
dependencies.jar;C:\Program Files\JetBrains\IntelliJ IDEA Community
Edition 2019.2\plugins\testng\lib\jcommander-1.27.jar" org.testng.
RemoteTestNGStarter -usedefaultlisteners false -socket52321 @w@C:\Users\
SeleniumUser\AppData\Local\Temp\idea_working_dirs_testng.tmp -temp C:\
Users\SeleniumUser\AppData\Local\Temp\idea_testng.tmp

---- IntelliJ IDEA coverage runner ----

sampling ...

include patterns:

com\.CrackSeleniumInterview\..*

exclude patterns:

===============================================

Default Suite

Total tests run: 1, Failures: 0, Skips: 0

===============================================

Class transformation time: 0.0606566s for 2416 classes or 2.5106208609271523E-
5s per class

Process finished with exit code 0



              Page title is: (13) LinkedIn

LinkedIn

Home

My Network

Jobs

2

2 new messages.

Messaging
```

11

11 new notifications.

Notifications

Me

Work

Learning

Kalilur Rahman

⬚ IT Leader ⬚ Digital Transformation ⬚ Innovation ⬚ Learner ⬚ Futurist ⬚ Author ⬚ All views personal

Who's viewed your profile

13,247

Views of your post

27,575

Your saved articles

93

Access exclusive tools & insights

Reactivate Premium

Recent

hashtag

kudos

Edinburgh Business School

KDnuggets Machine Learning, Data Science, Data Mining, Big Data, AI

hashtag

robots

hashtag

machinelearning

Groups

See all Groups

Edinburgh Business School

KDnuggets Machine Learning, Data Science, Data Mining, Big Data, AI

Future Technology: Artificial Intelligence, Robotics, IoT, Blockchain, Bitcoin | Startups (BIG)

Show more

Show more Groups

Followed Hashtags

See all Followed Hashtags

hashtag

kudos

hashtag

robots

hashtag

machinelearning

Show more

Show more Followed Hashtags

Discover more

Start a post

Upload Image

Upload Video

i18n_document

Write an article on LinkedIn

Sort by:

Top

Feed Updates

***** ***** commented on this

Status is reachable

***** *****

⬚ 1st

Statistics and Data Science Enthusiast| Carnatic and Sufi Rock Musician| Behavioral Economics lover|

1d

Recently, I completed a year at the current, wonderful organisation and in a superb team. Have been fortunate to have amazing colleagues. Some of my biggest personal learnings have been:

1. Throw ego into the trash.

2. Team effort wins delivering any scale projects.

3. Patience, patience and patience.

4. Share knowledge and collaborate with teammates.

5. Learn from everyone. Everyone has a narrative, which is helpful.

6. Perspectives broaden the horizon of thoughts.

7. Amazing work environment brings the best out of people.

8. Freedom to think and present views provide lateral out of the box ideas.

9. Most importantly, enjoying what I do and giving 100% every single day! Happiness and sincere efforts are affirmatively contagious!

⏷see more

36

6 Comments

Like

Comment

Share

Add a comment⏷

Images

5h

Status is reachable

***** *****

1st degree connection

1st

I

***** *****

Congrats to you and the Fab 5 (incl you) on your work anniversary. Proud to have you part of our team

Like

***** *****⬛s comment

⬛

2 Likes

2 Likes on

***** *****a⬛s comment

⬛

1 Reply

1 Comment on

***** *****a⬛s comment

4h

Status is reachable

***** *****

Thanks a lot

***** *****sir. Thank you so much for all the support, encouragement and mentoring. Very happy to work with you

***** *****sir! ⬛

Like *****⬛S comment

Load more comments

Show more comments on *****⬛S post

....

Be the first to comment on this

Today⬛s news and views

The dish India is hungry for ⬛

1d ago ⬛ 482 readers

Flood fury: 33 dead, 180K displaced

1d ago ⬛ 1,750 readers

Successful? Thank your siblings

3d ago ⬛ 16,380 readers

Cognizant alters salary structure

3d ago ▫ 4,910 readers

The truth about salaried jobs

2d ago ▫ 1,369 readers

Show more

LEARNING

Advance Your Career

Intro to network analysis

2:32

Intro to network analysis

From Python for Data Science Essential Training

About Help Center

Privacy & Terms

Advertising

Business Services

Get the LinkedIn app

More

LinkedIn Corporation ▫ 2019

Status is online

Messaging

You are on the messaging overlay. Press enter to open the list of conversations.

2

Compose message

Tap for popup settings

0 notifications total

Finally, your screenshot (edited to protect information) will appear something similar to an image, shown in *Figure 3.6*, based on your LinkedIn's social media feeds or configurations.

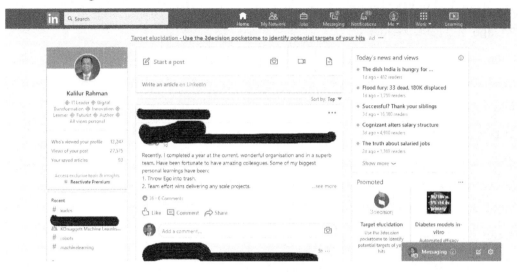

Figure 3.7: Program Output

Conclusion

This chapter aimed to cover the Selenium Architecture to some extent. We were able to focus on how Selenium WebDriver API connects the dots between programming languages (such as C#, Python, Java, Ruby, Java Script etc.) bound through JSON wire protocols, leveraging the browser driver classes and interfaces to test the applications through real browsers. We also built upon the knowledge gained in *Chapter 2* to get into a more detailed overview of the Selenium Architecture and components. We got introduced to some coding examples in Selenium through Java and Python to understand how Selenium automation is done. We also touched upon some API commands available in WebDriver. However, what we covered is somewhat basic, to say the least. In the upcoming chapters, we shall be getting into finer details to build on the knowledge gained to make more complex test automation scripts using Selenium. The next chapter will focus particularly on the Selenium tools and various aspects of their features, including Selenium WebDriver, RC, IDE and GRID, and how to use these with some examples.

Questions

1. Can you explain the components of Selenium architecture?

2. What is SOP? What are the issues caused by SOP when you use Selenium RC server for automation?

3. How does selenium automation work using Selenium RC?

4. What are the advantages of WebDriver API over Selenium RC?

5. What are the drawbacks of WebDriver vs. Selenium RC?

6. What is the benefit of using Selenium IDE?

7. What is Selenese? How will you port Selenese script into a language-based automation script?

8. What are the restrictions of using an IDE-based automation?

9. What are the benefits gained by using IDE for rapid automation?

10. What is a Selenium Grid? How is it used?

11. How will you run parallel testing of automated scripts in Selenium?

12. What are the browsers supported by Selenium automation?

13. What is a Browser Driver? What are the Browser Drivers supported by Selenium?

14. What are the core programming languages supported by the Selenium Project?

15. What are some of the third-party extensions/languages support available?

16. How will you instantiate a Chrome Driver using Python?

17. How will you access various web elements using Selenium? Give some examples.

18. What is the use of `Wait()` function?

19. How will you take a screenshot of a webpage? What function will you use in Java or Python?

20. What are some of the locator methods used in WebDriver?

21. How will you perform a drag and drop action using Selenium?

22. How will you instantiate a Chrome browser using Ruby Language?

23. What are two ways to open a web page using a WebDriver?

24. How will you refresh a web page using Selenium?

25. What is the difference between a `submit()` and a `click()` function?

CHAPTER 4
Understanding Selenium Tools

"If you automate a mess, you get an automated mess."

— Rod Michael

In the earlier chapters, we covered the importance of automation and an introduction to the Selenium Architecture. Understanding all the features of Selenium is important to leverage it skilfully. Selenium WebDriver and Remote Control (RC) need to be understood to become a successful automation tester. Understanding of Selenium Grid gives mastery over parallel test execution and command over cross-browser and cross-platform testing aspects of test automation. Over the next few chapters, we shall be covering all details that a Selenium testing professional needs to haveto become as ought-after test automation professional.

Structure

- Selenium WebDriver
- Selenium IDE
- Selenium Grid
- Selenium RC

Objective

This chapter aims at giving a good amount of details about four core aspects of Selenium Architecture and framework of its tools. Keeping in mind the latest features of Selenium, we shall focus more on the Selenium IDE in this chapter, with an introduction to Selenium Grid and covering details about Selenium RC. Selenium WebDriver, which was covered in detail in *Chapter 3*, will be discussed in detail in anotherchapter. As an objective of this chapter, we shall cover key aspects of all the four tools that make Selenium what it is.

Selenium WebDriver

As discussed in the earlier chapters, WebDriver was developed to overcome the restrictions of RC such as avoidance of Same-Origin-Policy (SOP) and a need to have a server to perform automation etc. The advantage of Selenium WebDriver over Selenium IDE is the fact that it gives freedom to the programmers to use their language of choice to make the code modular, object-oriented and non-hardcoded. This is a restriction for the Selenium IDE where limited browser and language support is available with the code generated needing further modification to make it a professional production quality code for test automation.

Selenium WebDriver is a feature-rich model that permits the programmers to leverage complex web application features enabled by CSS, JavaScript and jQuery, such as AJAX-based asynchronous actions, frame and window navigations, alerts management, multi-user action behaviours, for various form of elements such as checkboxes, dropdowns, multi-select and other features like enabling and disabling web elements etc.

For the benefit of understanding how Selenium WebDriver works, let us analyse the programs we mentioned in *Chapter 3* and understand what each line of the code does. What we covered in those programs was little so far. However, a lot more features and functionalities exist that can be leveraged. These will be discussed in detail in the subsequent chapters.

Let us take the simple program, which we used in *Chapter 3 – Ch3_Prog_1_ SeleniumChromeJavaExample.java first*. This program aims to run a search in the **https://bpbonline.com** site and get the results of the search:

1. First, we will define the package for the Java program. In the example, we are calling it "CrackSeleniumInterviewExamples". Defining a package is optional for a test program. However, for good programming practice to ensure we follow a very good nomenclature, group the relevant programs under a common package to ensure the right code is reused and access mechanisms are taken care of.

```
package CrackSeleniumInterviewExamples;
```

2. We will then import the classes that we used in the main program.

   ```
   import org.openqa.selenium.By;
   ```

   ```
   import org.openqa.selenium.Keys;
   ```

   ```
   import org.openqa.selenium.WebDriver;
   ```

   ```
   import org.openqa.selenium.WebElement;
   ```

   ```
   import org.openqa.selenium.chrome.ChromeDriver;
   ```

   ```
   import org.openqa.selenium.support.ui.ExpectedCondition;
   ```

   ```
   import org.openqa.selenium.support.ui.WebDriverWait;
   ```

3. Add the mainline for defining the Java Class/Object for the test.

   ```
   public class Ch3_Prog_1_SeleniumChromeJavaExample{
   ```

4. We would then define the functions, variables that are private to the class or package. As the program is a very simple Java class with no modularization anduses minimal class objects, variables etc., there is no need to define Object-Oriented Programming (OOP) functions and aspects. For readers with non-Java experienceor non-programming experience, `main()` method is run first whenever a program is run, and it can invoke various functions defined in the program.

   ```
   public static void main(String[] args)
   ```

5. The next two lines would define the property of the driver and its location. In the example, since we are using a Chrome Driver, we will set the system property for "`webdriver.chrome.driver`". The installation of various components of is included inthe Appendix chapter.

   ```
   // Create a new instance of the Chrome driver - Set the Properties
   for the Chrome Driver locations
   ```

   ```
   System.setProperty("webdriver.chrome.driver",
   ```

   ```
   "C:\\Selenium\\chromedriver.exe");
   ```

6. We would now define a variable element of the type `WebElement` to handle various Web Elements in the program.

   ```
   WebElement element;
   ```

7. We would create a WebDriver instance for Chrome, using a new instance of `ChromeDriver()` Object. The hierarchy of classes will be like `WebDriver()` interface being extended by a `RemoteWebDriver()` and then further extended by `ChromeDriver()` or `FireFoxDriver()` or a `SafariDriver()`. For a

headless browser implementation, we shall be using an `HtmlUnitDriver()` class that extends `WebDriver()` class.

```
WebDriver driver = new ChromeDriver();
```

8. Using the WebDriver created, we will navigate to a URL. In this case, let us navigate to **https://bpbonline.com**. There is more than one way to get a page loaded. However, `driver.get()` is the simplest way to do this task.

```
// And now use this to visit BPB Publication's website

driver.get("https://bpbonline.com/");

// Second Method is driver.navigate().to("https://bpbonline.
com/");
```

9. Once we have navigated to the page, we willprint the details of the title page using the `driver.getTitle()` and display in the system output/console.

```
// Check the title of the page

System.out.println("Page title is: " + driver.getTitle());
```

Here, we will get the following output:

Page title is: Computer & IT Books | Emerging & Trending Technologies l E-books – BPB Publications

10. After getting the output, we would then find a web element named "`bc-product-search`" using a findElement function – through an id based locator "`findElement(By.id())`" function – which would return the element matching the parameter "`bc-product-search`". It is wise to add an exception handler to ensure failures are handled smoothly. In this case, we'll get the element and send an emulation by typing "C" into a search bar using `sendKeys()` function. The idea of the program is to search for book titles having "C" in them.

```
// Type C to search for book titles with Cdriver.findElement(By.
id("bc-product-search")).sendKeys("C");
```

11. Once we have entereda search string, we need to press *Enter* key to run the search on the web site. We will do this by sending `Keys.ENTER` defined in the Selenium package.

```
// Now Press Enter to see the results

driver.findElement(By.id("bc-product-search")).sendKeys(Keys.
ENTER);
```

12. As a good programming practice, we need to anticipate unexpected behaviour (such as network connectivity issue, slow response, server overload etc.)

and have exception handling mechanisms and wait-times for graceful state handling. Since we are doing a simple check, we do not have all these good practices in the example. We expect a positive outcome and need to see a page title.

```
// Check the title of the new page

System.out.println("Page title is: " + driver.getTitle());
```

Here, we will get the following output –

Page title is: C – BPB Publications

13. We would then see the page contentappearing in the search result by using another locator element (by Tag Name) searching for content rendered under the HTML tag "body" covered in "<body></body>" section of HTML, using the getText() function.

```
// Get the text content of the web page

System.out.println(driver.findElement(By.tagName("body")).
getText();
```

Here, now, we would get the final output (only a part of itis shown in *Figure 4.1*– full output is shown in *Chapter 3*). Finally, we would complete the program with a smooth closing of the browser and closure of the WebDriver object.

Figure 4.1: Selenium WebDriver Program Output

Finally we close the program with a `driver.quit()` statement

```
//Close the browser

driver.quit();
```

Similarly, if we take the Python program, *Ch3_Prog_2_SeleniumChromePython Example_2.py,* almost all the lines have a similar construct and approach with just two deviations from the Java program.

The first one being console output in an HTML format versus the content itself. This is since the functions available in Java and Python are different. This is a challenge to be known by automation developers who use different languages of their choice.

Following statement prints the page content in an HTML format:

```
#Print the Page content in HTML format

print(driver.page_source)
```

The second change is an addition of a line to save the screenshot as an image using the Python function `get_screenshot_as_file`. A variant of this function exists in Java but the file creation needs to be done using a longer program by taking a screenshot using a `FILE` descriptor and copying it into anopened file stream. This is another example that outlines variation in implementation.

```
#Save the Screen Shot as a file

driver.get_screenshot_as_file("BPBonline_C_Output.png")
```

The same Python code can be implemented in Java as well where `TakeScreenshot` is one of the most widely used functions for validation purposes. As a second option, one can take screenshot using `driver.getScreenShotAs()` method without typecasting it to `TakesScreenshot` interface as well.

```
//Assign the driver output into a Screenshot File
File ScreenShotFile =((TakesScreenshot) driver).
getScreenshotAs(OutputType.FILE);

//Copy the screenshot file into an image file
FileUtils.copyFile(ScreenShotFile, new File("BPBonline_C_Output.png "));
```

In a way, the simplicity of using Python for some of the core functions seen. However, there are other differences such as Python being interpreted and run in a line-by-line fashion versus Java being compiled and run in an operating system and a machine-specific byte-code. There are benefits and disadvantages of both compiled and interpreted languages based on purpose and need. In some cases, interpreted language such as Python can be a lot more powerful than a compiled language such as Java and vice versa. These are some architectural decisions to be made by the team while deciding on the test automation framework.

There are a lot more features that WebDriver offers that allow us to automate various components of Web UI of an application, correlate various Web UI components (CSS, HTML, DOM), perform cross-browser automation with various browsers (Firefox, Chrome, Internet Explorer, Safari) and handle various web element locators, selectors, ID customization, event handling, asynchronous interactions, styling, DOM management, simulation of screen sizes. All these features and examples on how to test Web UI using headless browsers are covered from *Chapter 5* onwards in detail. As of now, let usfocus on the other three topics of this chapter.

Selenium IDE

The main objective of the Selenium IDE was to use the tool to prototypethe automation of web applications quickly. It outperformed the original intent and grew from strength-to-strength to become a solid prototyping tool like an MS Excel Macro-based VBA script to help the users automate web application interactions quickly.

It is an easy to use interface, originally built only for Firefox (now available in Google Chrome as well), and has been enhanced further post an interim stoppage of with more feature builds.

The newer version of Selenium IDE has more advanced features for use than the original release. The website available at **https://www.seleniumhq.org/selenium-ide/**hosts all the selenium IDE information. Key benefits of Selenium IDE include: simple web-ready solution to develop end-to-end automation; reusability of test cases (in a modular manner by calling one test case within another – like a function); rich debugging features and controls including breakpoints and exception handling; and ability to run cross-browser with the command line features available through side-runner options available with Selenium IDE.

However, when it was originally developed as a rapid prototyping tool, too many features did not exist. Some of the core features that were added during the initial releases were:

- Web application action recording – A simple recording feature
- Playback of entire Test Suite – Running a group of test cases
- Playback of a test case/script
- Paus/resume a test case
- Setting/toggling breakpoints – to check the progress of test case and check for status/variables etc.
- Start and stop at any specific point in the test script

Additionally, the version before the current IDE plug-in had a feature to generate test scripts in various languages using language-Specific formatters for C#, Java, Python, Ruby. There was an option to create test scripts in a particular language with an associated testing component such as TestNG, JUnit, RSpec or NUnit, and an ability to run with Selenium RC or WebDriver. This version also had locator builders using ID, link, name, tag, CSS or XPath tags.

The current version of Selenium IDE available in Firefox and Chrome browsers has restrictions in code generation. We can generate code only in Java, Python and JavaScript languages. Tools such as Katalon Recorder or Ranorex have advanced features to automate an application using the Selenium framework, drawing onmultiple languages and combinations. Let us check the feature of the Selenium IDE with some examples.

Selenium IDE can be downloaded as a plug-in for Chrome or Firefox browsers from the Selenium HQ's Selenium IDE micro-portal. The link is **https://www.seleniumhq.org/selenium-ide/**.

- Once the extensions are added to the browser, you can start the IDE by clicking on the icon in your browser.

Figure 4.2: Selenium IDE icon in Chrome Browser

- Once you click on the browser, you will see an IDE landing page, as shown in *Figure 4.3*. You may choose to create a new project by recording a script, opening an existing project to modify and enhance it. Besides, you can also create a new project without recording or closing the IDE.

Figure 4.3: Opening a New Project in Selenium IDE

- For your reference, let us name the project as *"Selenium HQ Tests"* for simplicity.

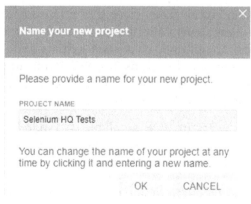

Figure 4.4: Selenium IDE – Naming a Project

- Since we need to set a URL for recording, let us use **https://seleniumhq.org**

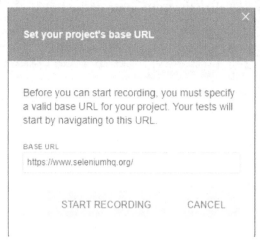

Figure 4.5: Selenium IDE – Setting Project URL

- After entering the master IDE, we will click on the "REC" button available in the panel.

Figure 4.6: Selenium IDE Recording ICON

- Once the recording starts, we willnavigate through SeleniumHQ.ORG in the open browser and click through some of the links.

Figure 4.7: Screenshot for Selenium IDE Recording

We will be seeing a page with a Selenium IDE action popping-up for recording with commands such as "**Selenium IDE is recording...**" "**Recorded Click**" based on the action you perform, as shown in *Figure 4.7* All this will be recorded in the Selenium IDE.

- The recorded commands appearing in the Selenium IDE would be as follows:

https://www.seleniumhq.org

	Command	Target
1	open	/
2	set window size	1050x708
3	click	linkText=edit this page
4	click	id=close
5	click	css=td:nth-child(2) .icon
6	click	css=.inner > span
7	store window handle	root
8	select window	handle=${win1500}
9	close	
10	select window	handle=${root}
11	click	linkText=Plugins

Figure 4.8: Selenium IDE – Recorded Script in IDE

- Once we have recorded the actions, we can use various options available for us to chisel the program:
    - o We can playback the recording to ensure it works fine.
    - o We can run it in a pause & playback mode to understand what is happening.
    - o We can run the recording in various options –
        - ▪ If we have more than one test recorded in the program, we can use *Ctrl+Shift+R* to run them all or use the first icon to run them.
        - ▪ If we want to run the current test highlighted in the IDE, we can use *Ctrl+R* or the second icon in the image to run the script.
        - ▪ If we are running in a debugging mode, the third icon can be used to run one command at a time or use *Ctrl+'*.
        - ▪ If we want to increase or decrease the speed of execution in a browser, we can use the fourth icon (clock symbol) to invoke a slider and change the speed.

Figure 4.9: Selenium IDE – Option to change speed of Execution

- The command panel for the IDE would have four prominent sections namely **Command, Target, Value** and **Description**. All these can be used for various automation script generation purposes.

Figure 4.10: Selenium IDE – Option to add Values and Description to Recording

o Command refers to SELENESE command used by IDE. There are many commands available to choose from. They typically comprise Control statements (If/Else, For, While etc.), Assertions, Locator/Accessors, Actions to be performed.

▪ Some of the commonly used Selenium commands (Full list can be found at **https://www.seleniumhq.org/selenium-ide/docs/en/api/commands/.)** include the following:

add selection	answer on next prompt	assert
assert alert	assert checked	assert confirmation
assert editable	assert element present	assert element not present
assert not checked	assert not editable	assert not selected value
assert not text	assert prompt	assert selected value
assert selected label	assert text	assert title
assert value	check	choose cancel on next confirmation
choose cancel on next prompt	choose ok on next confirmation	Click
click at	close	debugger
Do	double click	double click at
drag and drop to object	echo	edit content
Else	else if	End
execute script	execute async script	for each
If	mouse down	mouse down at
mouse move at	mouse out	mouse over
mouse up	mouse up at	Open
Pause	remove selection	repeat if
Run	run script	select
select frame	select window	send keys
set speed	set window size	Store
store attribute	store JSON	store text
store title	store value	store window handle
store xpath count	submit	Times
Type	uncheck	Verify
verify checked	verify editable	verify element present
verify element not present	verify not checked	verify not editable

verify not selected value	verify not text	verify selected label
verify selected value	verify text	verify title
verify value	wait for element editable	wait for element not editable
wait for element not present	wait for element not visible	wait for element present
wait for element visible	webdriver answer on visible prompt	webdriver choose cancel on visible confirmation
webdriver choose cancel on visible prompt	webdriver choose ok on visible confirmation	while

Table 4.1: Key Selenium IDE Commands

o **Target** refers to the web element identified in the page about the IDE. It could also refer to the URLs if you are opening a URL using OPEN command. The *Target* web elements can also be variables or constants if you are using them in your Selenese-driven program.

o **VALUE** refers to the value assigned to the element or a variable referred to using TARGET. This can be a simple assignment of value (can be hardcoded or passed on through a variable or in case of data-driven testing of a web element).

- One of the most important sections of the Selenium IDE is the test section. This allows the programmer to add test suites, add test cases, search for tests and do renaming, deletion and duplication of test scripts recorded or created using Selenium IDE.

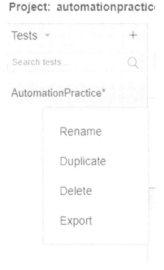

Figure 4.11: Selenium IDE – Project Options

- One of the brilliant features available through the Selenium IDE is the **EXPORT** feature. The current Selenium IDE gives an option of exporting code into three languages (along with comments if needed).

Figure 4.12: Selenium IDE – Export Options

Once you export the code, the base framework can be revamped to make the code much more powerful and robust to meet your automation needs. As mentioned earlier in the chapter, if you want more choices in terms of programming languages and frameworks, you may need to use tools that offer advanced options either in a free/trial manner or a commercial model. Some of these tools include Katalon, Ranorex, TricentisQTest, SahiPro etc.

Let us take an example for Selenium IDE export. What we have done is we navigated **https://www.seleniumhq.org/** site and recorded a few actions. This example script being exported as a Java code can be saved using a standard Windows interface. You can choose the folder where you want to store the output file.

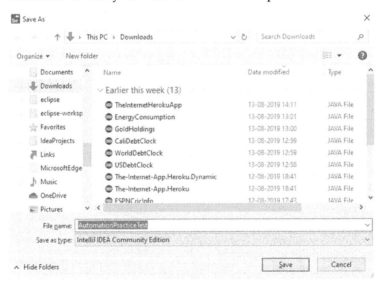

Figure 4.13: Saving a Selenium IDE Project

- Another section of Selenium IDE that is relevant for the users is the option to Create, Open and Save the test suites to ensure the work is saved in time and UI is accessed easily. In addition to **Create**, **Open** and **save** options help is available for the users to get guidance on what is new in IDE, how to run the scripts in a **Continuous Integration (CI)** environment and get general help on the IDE itself.

Figure 4.14: Clicking on Continuous Integration

Overall, the IDE is a power-packed tool for beginners embarking on an automation journey using Selenium. For advanced users, more tools that are comprehensive are recommended for the rapid development of automation scripts.

Putting all things together the Selenium IDE looks like:

Figure 4.15: Overall look of a Selenium IDE Project

Java output from IDE

The sample script in Java created through the "**export**" feature of Selenium IDE against the recording done at the URL **https://www.seleniumhq.org/** will look like the following:

Ch4_Prog_1_SeleniumIDE_SeleniumHQTest.java

```
1     package CrackSeleniumInterviewExamples;

2     // Generated by Selenium IDE

3

4     import org.junit.After;

5     import org.junit.Before;

6     import org.junit.Test;

7     import org.openqa.selenium.By;

8     import org.openqa.selenium.Dimension;

9     import org.openqa.selenium.JavascriptExecutor;

10    import org.openqa.selenium.WebDriver;

11    import org.openqa.selenium.firefox.FirefoxDriver;

12

13    import java.util.HashMap;

14    import java.util.Map;

15

16    public class Ch4_Prog_1_SeleniumIDE_SeleniumHQTest {

17    JavascriptExecutorjs;

18    private WebDriver driver;

19    private Map<String, Object>vars;

20

21        @Before

22    public void setUp() {

23            driver = new FirefoxDriver();

24    js = (JavascriptExecutor) driver;

25    vars = new HashMap<String, Object>();
```

```
26          }

27

28          @After

29   public void tearDown() {

30   driver.quit();

31          }

32

33          @Test

34   public void seleniumhq() {

35   driver.get("https://www.seleniumhq.org/");

36   driver.manage().window().setSize(new Dimension(1050, 708));

37   driver.findElement(By.cssSelector("html")).click();

38   driver.findElement(By.linkText("Download")).click();

39   driver.findElement(By.linkText("Download")).click();

40   driver.findElement(By.cssSelector(".sectionDownload")).click();

41   driver.findElement(By.linkText("Browser Automation")).click();

42   driver.findElement(By.cssSelector("td:nth-child(2) .icon")).click();

43   driver.findElement(By.linkText("Docs")).click();

44   driver.findElement(By.linkText("Code Export")).click();

45   driver.findElement(By.linkText("JavaScript Mocha")).click();

46   driver.findElement(By.linkText("Plugins")).click();

47   driver.findElement(By.linkText("Emitting Code")).click();

48   driver.findElement(By.linkText("Error Handling")).click();

49          }

50   }

51
```

Python output from IDE

The sample script in Python created through the "**export**" feature of Selenium IDE against the recording done at the URL **https://www.seleniumhq.org/** will look like the following:

Ch4_Prog_2_SeleniumIDE_SeleniumHQTest_Python.py

```python
1    # Generated by Selenium IDE
2    import pytest
3    import time
4    import json
5    from selenium import webdriver
6    from selenium.webdriver.common.by import By
7    from selenium.webdriver.common.action_chainsimport ActionChains
8    from selenium.webdriver.supportimport expected_conditions
9    from selenium.webdriver.support.waitimport WebDriverWait
10   from selenium.webdriver.common.keysimport Keys
11
12   class TestSeleniumhq():
13   defsetup_method(self, method):
14   self.driver = webdriver.Firefox()
15   self.vars = {}
16
17   defteardown_method(self, method):
18   self.driver.quit()
19
20   deftest_seleniumhq(self):
21   self.driver.get("https://www.seleniumhq.org/")
22   self.driver.set_window_size(1050, 708)
23   self.driver.find_element(By.CSS_SELECTOR, "html").click()
24   self.driver.find_element(By.LINK_TEXT, "Download").click()
25   self.driver.find_element(By.LINK_TEXT, "Download").click()
26   self.driver.find_element(By.CSS_SELECTOR, ".sectionDownload").click()
27   self.driver.find_element(By.LINK_TEXT, "Browser Automation").click()
28   self.driver.find_element(By.CSS_SELECTOR, "td:nth-child(2) .icon").click()
```

```
29    self.driver.find_element(By.LINK_TEXT, "Docs").click()

30    self.driver.find_element(By.LINK_TEXT, "Code Export").click()

31    self.driver.find_element(By.LINK_TEXT, "JavaScript Mocha").click()

32    self.driver.find_element(By.LINK_TEXT, "Plugins").click()

33    self.driver.find_element(By.LINK_TEXT, "Emitting Code").click()

34    self.driver.find_element(By.LINK_TEXT, "Error Handling").click()

35

36
```

JavaScript output from IDE

The sample script in JavaScript created through the "**export**" feature of Selenium IDE against the recording done at the URL **https://www.seleniumhq.org/**will look like the following:

Ch4_Prog_3_SeleniumIDE_SeleniumHQTest_JS.spec

```
1    // Generated by Selenium IDE

2    const { Builder, By, Key, until } = require('selenium-webdriver')

3    const assert = require('assert')

4

5    describe('seleniumhq', function() {

6    this.timeout(30000)

7      let driver

8      let vars

9    beforeEach(asyncfunction() {

10       driver = await new Builder().forBrowser('firefox').build()

11   vars = {}

12     })

13   afterEach(asyncfunction() {

14       await driver.quit();

15     })

16     it('seleniumhq', asyncfunction() {

17   // Test name: seleniumhq
```

```
18   // Step # | name | target | value | comment
19   // 1 | open | / |  |
20      await driver.get("https://www.seleniumhq.org/")
21   // 2 | setWindowSize | 1050x708 |  |
22      await driver.setRect(1050, 708)
23   // 3 | click | css=html |  |
24      await driver.findElement(By.css("html")).click()
25   // 4 | click | linkText=Download |  |
26      await driver.findElement(By.linkText("Download")).click()
27   // 5 | click | linkText=Download |  |
28      await driver.findElement(By.linkText("Download")).click()
29   // 6 | click | css=.sectionDownload |  |
30      await driver.findElement(By.css(".sectionDownload")).click()
31   // 7 | click | linkText=Browser Automation |  |
32      await driver.findElement(By.linkText("Browser Automation")).click()
33   // 8 | click | css=td:nth-child(2) .icon |  |
34      await driver.findElement(By.css("td:nth-child(2) .icon")).click()
35   // 9 | click | linkText=Docs |  |
36      await driver.findElement(By.linkText("Docs")).click()
37   // 10 | click | linkText=Code Export |  |
38      await driver.findElement(By.linkText("Code Export")).click()
39   // 11 | click | linkText=JavaScript Mocha |  |
40      await driver.findElement(By.linkText("JavaScript Mocha")).click()
41   // 12 | click | linkText=Plugins |  |
42      await driver.findElement(By.linkText("Plugins")).click()
43   // 13 | click | linkText=Emitting Code |  |
44      await driver.findElement(By.linkText("Emitting Code")).click()
45   // 14 | click | linkText=Error Handling |  |
46      await driver.findElement(By.linkText("Error Handling")).click()
47    })
48   })
```

Procedural programming using control statements

One of the advantages of Selenium IDE is the ability to run scripts using control statements, such as IF/ELSE, FOR, WHILE, to control the logic and flow of the program. An example is given in *Figure 4.16* where IF/ELSE and ASSERT commands of Selenium IDE give a view of how Control- and Switch-based logic could be leveraged.

http://the-internet.herokuapp.com

	Command	Target	Value
1	execute script	return "a"	myVar
2	if	${myVar} === "a"	
3	execute script	return "a"	output
4	else if	${myVar} === "b"	
5	execute script	return "b"	output
6	else if	${myVar} === "c"	
7	execute script	return "c"	output
8	end		
9	assert	output	a
10	assert	output	b

Figure 4.16: Selenium IDE – Script Execution Failure

The output of test execution using the Selenium IDE is shown in *Figure 4.17* where the program failed with the final assert statement.

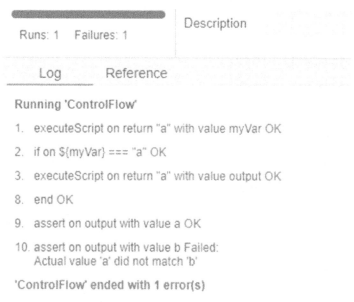

Runs: 1   Failures: 1

Description

Log   Reference

Running 'ControlFlow'

1. executeScript on return "a" with value myVar OK

2. if on ${myVar} === "a" OK

3. executeScript on return "a" with value output OK

8. end OK

9. assert on output with value a OK

10. assert on output with value b Failed:
    Actual value 'a' did not match 'b'

'ControlFlow' ended with 1 error(s)

Figure 4.17: An example of failed Selenium IDE Run

This program will fail the test case due to the non-success of the assertion, and can be handled through an exception handling or response handling to continue the program execution. This program can be controlled by using a GOTO statement by specifying either a LABEL, Break or a conditional logic in a WHILE/ENDWHILE statement.

The IDE exported output (Java sample) is shown below, in which most of the control logic is implemented using JavaScript. This is because the IDE uses the browser-based extension, primarily driven by JavaScript.

Ch4_Prog_4_SeleniumIDE_ControlFlowExample.java

```
1    package CrackSeleniumInterviewExamples;

2

3    // Generated by Selenium IDE

4

5    import org.junit.After;

6    import org.junit.Before;

7    import org.junit.Test;

8    import org.openqa.selenium.JavascriptExecutor;

9    import org.openqa.selenium.WebDriver;

10   import org.openqa.selenium.firefox.FirefoxDriver;

11

12   import java.util.HashMap;

13   import java.util.Map;

14

15   import static org.junit.Assert.assertEquals;

16   public class Ch4_Prog_4_SeleniumIDE_ControlFlowExample {

17   private WebDriver driver;

18   private Map<String, Object>vars;

19   JavascriptExecutorjs;

20       @Before

21   public void setUp() {

22           driver = new FirefoxDriver();
```

```java
23    js = (JavascriptExecutor) driver;
24    vars = new HashMap<String, Object>();
25        }
26        @After
27    public void tearDown() {
28    driver.quit();
29        }
30        @Test
31    public void controlFlow() {
32    // Test name: ControlFlow
33    // Step # | name | target | value | comment
34    // 1 | executeScript | return "a" | myVar |
35    vars.put("myVar", js.executeScript("return \"a\""));
36    // 2 | if | ${myVar} === "a" | |
37     if ((Boolean) js.executeScript("return (arguments[0] === \'a\')",
vars.get("myVar"))) {
38    // 3 | executeScript | return "a" | output |
39    vars.put("output", js.executeScript("return \"a\""));
40    // 4 | else If | ${myVar} === "b" | |
41            } else if ((Boolean) js.executeScript("return (arguments[0]
=== \'b\')", vars.get("myVar"))) {
42    // 5 | executeScript | return "b" | output |
43    vars.put("output", js.executeScript("return \"b\""));
44    // 6 | else If | ${myVar} === "c" | |
45            } else if ((Boolean) js.executeScript("return (arguments[0]
=== \'c\')", vars.get("myVar"))) {
46    // 7 | executeScript | return "c" | output |
47    vars.put("output", js.executeScript("return \"c\""));
48    // 8 | end | | |
49            }
50    // 9 | assert | output | a |
```

```
51    assertEquals(vars.get("output").toString(), "a");
52    // 10 | assert | output | b |
53    assertEquals(vars.get("output").toString(), "b");
54        }
55    }
```

As a good programming practice, it is worthwhile to refactor the code generated through the Selenium IDE export and introduce various leading practices. The reason for the same is due to the following points:

- Selenium IDE primarily follows a linear programming approach as every action is mapped to a piece of code.

- Highly mature programming modularity does not exist by design. Though smaller scripts can be created using Selenium IDE and called implicitly, it is not modular. This needs to be done through a good IDE capable of performing refactoring, and using professional programming skills including **Page Object Model (POM)**. We shall be covering POM in the upcoming chapters.

- Data-driven, keyword-driven or hybrid automation are not possible with the current Selenium IDE. To leverage the benefits of advanced test automation, the use of an advanced tool with enriched features are recommended.

In summary, Selenium IDE is a very good tool to use; it simplifies some of the basic automation tasks. However, for advanced automation needs, IDE is not the recommended tool. We shall cover the reasons in the upcoming chapters as well.

Selenium Grid

Following are benefits of Selenium Grid:

- **Parallel-automated test execution:** Economy of scale and parallelism is achieved by running tests on several machines distributed across.

- **Centralized environment management:** Grid makes test environment management an easy choice with central control. It also gives a mechanism to run tests across operating systems, platforms and browsers (and versions), making cross-browser testing a reality.

- **Simple infra/configuration maintenance:** Selenium Grid permits the automation developer to Write/Configure Once use it many times. With the use of Selenium Grid, it is easy to reduce configuration and maintenance time by building custom plug-ins and hooks to virtual environments. This propels the CI/CD and DevOps related testing. No need for heavy-duty customized coding.

Selenium Grid Architecture

A typical Selenium Grid uses hub and node architecture:

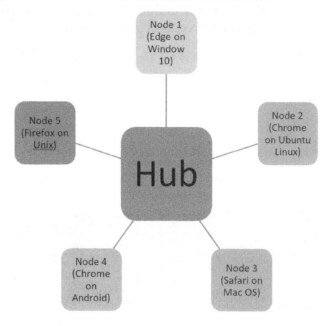

Figure 4.18: Selenium GRID – Hub/Node Architecture

A Selenium Grid follows a hub and spoke architecture. This is similar to a cycle wheel where the hub is at the centre of the wheel and the nodes (spokes) are the connectors to the centre of the wheel - the hub. The hub is like the server and the nodes are the clients consuming a service from the hub. With a Selenium Grid, we can have only one hub per grid but we could have many grids setup and running provided, we have the infrastructure to support the same. A hub can be started using a command-line argument by invoking the Selenium-server.jar library.

In a hub and spoke architecture, the hub knows about all the configurations of the nodes (like the number of browsers and the setup which each node can support, the operating system in which it runs on etc., whether the sessions are available etc.). When a request comes from a node to run a test, the hub knows what to do and how to run the test and responds accordingly. The hub is invoked through instantiation of a `RemoteWebDriver` Class from the node. A hub supports up to five nodes in parallel. However, the hub can support nodes running different operating systems and configurations as it is OS and language-agnostic and the communication happens through a common protocol. In effect, the key benefit of using selenium is the fact that a hub and node can have very different configurations that permit parallel execution to reduce time and browser compatibility to increase test coverage in a myriad of combination.

How to start Selenium Grid

To install the Grid, we can download the *Selenium Standalone Server JAR file* from the Selenium HQ Site, available at **https://docs.seleniumhq.org/download/**. It is advisable to download the latest stable version of the Selenium Server.

The hub for a Selenium Grid can be using the command given below:

```
Java -jar selenium-server-standalone-<version>.jar -role hub

e.g.:

Java -jar selenium-server-standalone-3.141.59.jar -role hub
```

When you will execute the command in your command prompt, a listing would appear, as shown in *Figure 4.19* (Example is on a Windows 10 Machine.).

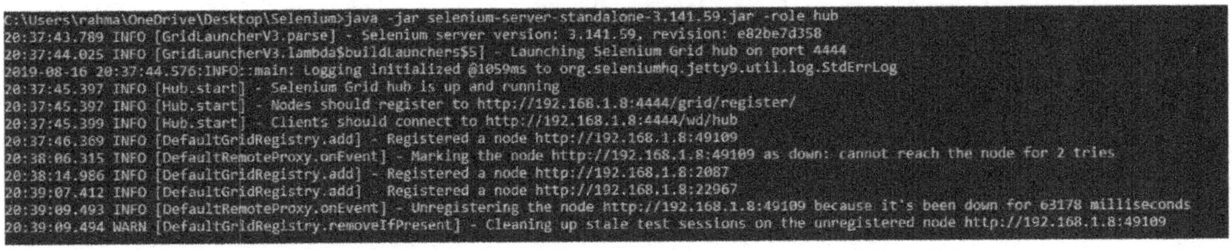

```
C:\Users\rahma\OneDrive\Desktop\Selenium>java -jar selenium-server-standalone-3.141.59.jar -role hub
20:37:43.789 INFO [GridLauncherV3.parse] - Selenium server version: 3.141.59, revision: e82be7d358
20:37:44.025 INFO [GridLauncherV3.lambda$buildLaunchers$5] - Launching Selenium Grid hub on port 4444
2019-08-16 20:37:44.576:INFO::main: Logging initialized @1059ms to org.seleniumhq.jetty9.util.log.StdErrLog
20:37:45.397 INFO [Hub.start] - Selenium Grid hub is up and running
20:37:45.397 INFO [Hub.start] - Nodes should register to http://192.168.1.8:4444/grid/register/
20:37:45.399 INFO [Hub.start] - Clients should connect to http://192.168.1.8:4444/wd/hub
20:37:46.369 INFO [DefaultGridRegistry.add] - Registered a node http://192.168.1.8:49109
20:38:06.315 INFO [DefaultRemoteProxy.onEvent] - Marking the node http://192.168.1.8:49109 as down: cannot reach the node for 2 tries
20:38:14.986 INFO [DefaultGridRegistry.add] - Registered a node http://192.168.1.8:2087
20:39:07.412 INFO [DefaultGridRegistry.add] - Registered a node http://192.168.1.8:22967
20:39:09.493 INFO [DefaultRemoteProxy.onEvent] - Unregistering the node http://192.168.1.8:49109 because it's been down for 63178 milliseconds
20:39:09.494 WARN [DefaultGridRegistry.removeIfPresent] - Cleaning up stale test sessions on the unregistered node http://192.168.1.8:49109
```

Figure 4.19: *Console output for starting a Hub*

Please note that the server was started at **http://192.168.1.8** on Port 4444. Final four lines were for nodes being registered to the node. We shall cover the establishment of hub-node connections in the next paragraph.

The node for a Selenium Grid can be using the command given below:

```
Java -jar selenium-server-standalone-<version>.jar -role node -hub
http://localhost:4444/grid/register

e.g.:

Java -jar selenium-server-standalone-3.141.59.jar -role node -hub
http://localhost:4444/grid/register
```

Based on default configurations, the hub gets started on port 4444. We can change this though through configurations. One of the standard approaches followed is to use a JSON file for configurations. With the JSON files, we can specify the number of browsers configurable for the node (against default 11 browsers with five Chrome, five Firefox and one Internet Explorer) based on the needs, proxy settings and other configurations.

To register a node against a hub, following command syntax can be used:

```
java -jar selenium-server-standalone-3.141.59.jar -role node -hub
HTTP://{REMOTE-HOST-URL/IP-ADDRESS}:{PORT-OF-THE-HUB}/grid/register
```

For example, I have registered two hubs.

When you will execute the command twice, a listing would appear in the command prompt (Example is on a Windows 10 Machine.).

Here, you will see that the node is being created on port 22967:

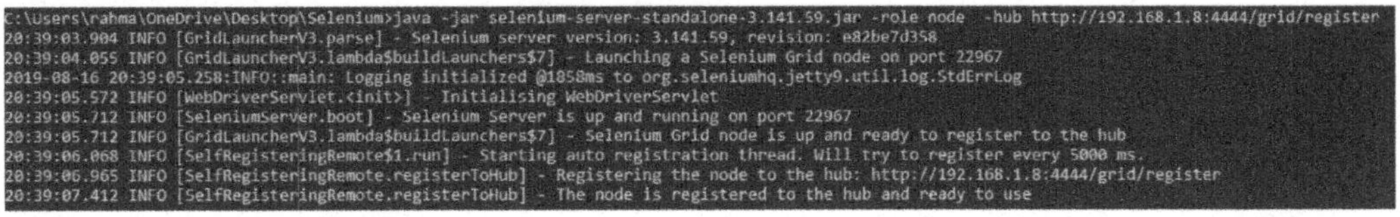

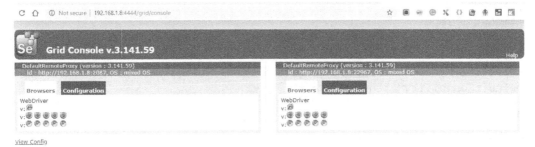

Figure 4.20: Console output for starting of a node

Now, while executing the command for a second time, we will see another node being created on port 2087:

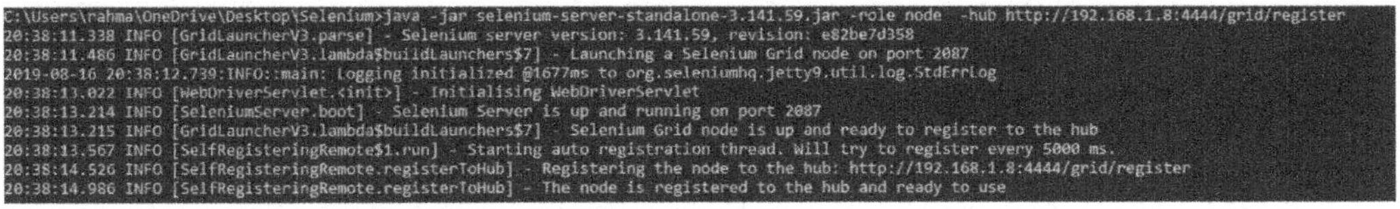

Figure 4.21: Console output for starting of a second node

Once started, the status of the hub will appear from a browser window by accessing the URL: **http://localhost:4444/grid/console** or URL **HTTP://{REMOTE-HOST-URL/IP-ADDRESS}:{PORT-OF-THE-HUB}**/grid/console.

For the example given, the console would look like as shown in *Figure 4.22* by accessing the URL **http://192.168.1.8:4444/grid/console**. The details about the configurations can be seen by clicking on the "**Configuration**" tab.

Figure 4.22: Selenium Grid Console

When you will click on the **Configuration** tab in the console page, the content displayed would be as follows:

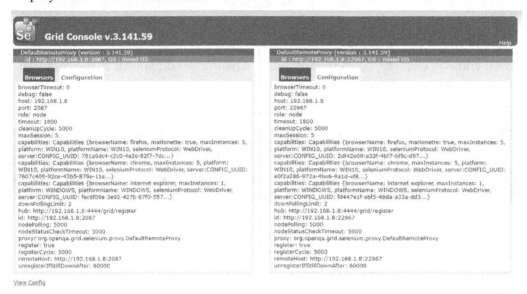

Figure 4.23: Selenium Grid Console - Configuration

The console will also give the configuration details of the hub itself. Some of the content you would see include configuration for the browser timeout interval; debugging options; port and the host the hub runs on; and registry information etc.

Config for the hub :

browserTimeout : 0

debug : false

host : 192.168.1.8

port : 4444

role : hub

timeout : 1800

cleanUpCycle : 5000

capabilityMatcher : org.openqa.grid.internal.utils.
DefaultCapabilityMatcher

newSessionWaitTimeout : -1

throwOnCapabilityNotPresent : true

registry : org.openqa.grid.internal.DefaultGridRegistry

The final configuration comes from:

the default :

browserTimeout : 0

debug : false

host : 0.0.0.0

port : 4444

role : hub

timeout : 1800

cleanUpCycle : 5000

capabilityMatcher : org.openqa.grid.internal.utils.
DefaultCapabilityMatcher

newSessionWaitTimeout : -1

throwOnCapabilityNotPresent : true

registry : org.openqa.grid.internal.DefaultGridRegistry

updated with command line options:

-role hub

Command line parameters and configuration operations

We can also set up parameters and configurations using Command Prompt. If we want to pass the parameters about a Google Chrome browser running in a different port, we can customize the port by giving command line input. The same thing can be done using a JSON file also that we shall cover shortly. Let us take an example of setting up a command-line configuration.

```
Java -Dwebdriver.chrome.driver="<PATH FOR SELENIUM WEB DRIVER
FOLDERS>\chromedriver.exe" -jar selenium-server-standalone-
<version>.jar -role webdriver -hub http://localhost:4444/grid/
register  -port 5678

Java -Dwebdriver.chrome.driver="C:\Selenium\chromedriver.exe"
-jar selenium-server-standalone-3.141.59.jar -role webdriver -hub
http://localhost:4444/grid/register  -port 5678
```

We can also specify the browser name and the versions the node can run tests in using the parameter given below as well. We can cover the setup in detail in the next section while we cover setCapabilities() function.

```
-browser browserName=chrome, version=76.0,maxInstances=3,platform=WINDOWS
```

Running a Selenium Grid test using Selenium RC

We need to remember that Selenium **RC** has been deprecated and the example given below cannot be used with WebDriver 2.0 or WebDriver 3.0. In the case of running a Selenium Grid-based test using Selenium RC, we would need to use Selenium Class to connect to the hub with the Desired Capabilities passed as a parameter. If we want to connect to the Selenium Node running in the localhost on port **4444** and run a test of opening a URL on a Chrome browser, the command will look like the following:

```
Selenium selenium = new DefaultSelenium("localhost", 4444, "*chrome",
"https://bpbonline.com/");
```

Running a Selenium Grid test using WebDriver

For a WebDriver, we use `RemoteWebDriver` and `DesiredCapabilities` objects instead of a **Selenium** object to create the target capabilities that we want to run against. Readers can be informed that `RemoteWebDriver` and `DesiredCapabilities` are used not just for a Grid setup in a local machine but also for execution on remote machines.

`DesiredCapabilities` is also used in in cross browser testing using cloud through service providers like BrowserStack, CrossBrowserTesting, and Saucelabs etc. We will some examples of this in *Chapter 10*.

To run a Selenium test using Web Driver, first, we need to define the required capabilities.

From the example above, we want the browser to be Chrome:

```
DesiredCapabilities capability = DesiredCapabilities.chrome();
```

We can define various capabilities using the functions helping to set the values.

Capability Set Function	Comments
`capability.setBrowserName();`	Can be one of {android, chrome, firefox, htmlunit, internet explorer, iPhone, iPad, opera, safari} browsers
`capability.setPlatform();`	OS Platform - Can be one of {WINDOWS, XP, VISTA, MAC, LINUX, UNIX, ANDROID}

`capability.setVersion()`	Can be the version of browser or empty String such as "76.0" for Chrome or "33.0" for FireFox or "11.0" for Internet Explorer
`capability.setCapability(,);`	Various capabilities that can be written (Read-Write) for RC, WebDriver, Browser, Grid specific capabilities available for various Desired Capabilities

Table 4.1: Key functions for Setting Capabilities for WebDriver

Suppose, if we want to set to capabilities for Chrome browser version 76 running on Windows OS, the command would look like:

`capability.setBrowserName("chrome" );`

`capability.setPlatform(Platform.WINDOWS);`

`capability.setVersion("76.0");`

We will then pass the capability to the driver object instance of `RemoteWebDriver`:

`WebDriver driver = new RemoteWebDriver(new URL("http://localhost:4444/wd/hub"), capability);`

Then, the test using the driver instantiation will be matched with a node based on the Desired Capabilities mentioned.

Hub configuration using a JSON file

```
java -jar selenium-server-standalone-<version>.jar -role hub
-hubConfigJSON_Hub_ConfigFile.json


java -jar selenium-server-standalone-3.141.59.jar -role hub
-hubConfigJSON_Hub_ConfigFile.json
```

A sample JSON file is mentioned below (This is not the default JSON Config.). A very good example of default JSON file configuration can be found at **https://github.com/SeleniumHQ/selenium/tree/selenium-2.53.0/java/server/src/org/openqa/grid/common/defaults.**

```
{   "host": "192.168.1.8",

"port": 4567,

"newSessionWaitTimeout": -1,

"servlets" : [],

"prioritizer": null,

"capabilityMatcher": "org.openqa.grid.internal.utils.
DefaultCapabilityMatcher",
```

```
"throwOnCapabilityNotPresent": true,

"nodePolling": 3000,


"cleanUpCycle": 6000,

"timeout": 200000,

"browserTimeout": 0,

"maxSession": 10,

"jettyMaxThreads":-1

}
```

Node configuration using a JSON file

```
Java-Dwebdriver.chrome.driver="chromedriver.exe" -Dwebdriver.
ie.driver="IEDriverServer.exe" -Dwebdriver.gecko.
driver="geckodriver.exe" -jar selenium-server-standalone-
<version>.jar -role node -nodeConfigJSON_Node_ConfigFile.json

Java-Dwebdriver.chrome.driver="chromedriver.exe" -Dwebdriver.
ie.driver="IEDriverServer.exe" -Dwebdriver.gecko.
driver="geckodriver.exe" -jar selenium-server-standalone-3.141.59.
jar -role node -nodeConfigJSON_Node_ConfigFile.json
```

A Sample JSON file is given below (This is not the default JSON Config.). A very good example of default JSON file configuration can be found at **https://github.com/ SeleniumHQ/selenium/tree/selenium-2.53.0/java/server/src/org/openqa/grid/ common/defaults.**

```
{   "capabilities":

    [

      {

"browserName": "*firefox",

"maxInstances": 4,

"seleniumProtocol": "Selenium"

      },

      {

"browserName": "*googlechrome",

"maxInstances": 4,
```

```
"seleniumProtocol": "Selenium"
        },
        {
"browserName": "*iexplore",
"maxInstances": 3,
"seleniumProtocol": "Selenium"
        },
        {
"browserName": "firefox",
"maxInstances": 4,
"seleniumProtocol": "WebDriver"
        },
        {
"browserName": "chrome",
"maxInstances": 4,
"seleniumProtocol": "WebDriver"
        },
        {
"browserName": "internet explorer",
"maxInstances": 3,
"seleniumProtocol": "WebDriver"
        }
    ],
"configuration":
  {
"proxy": "org.openqa.grid.selenium.proxy.DefaultRemoteProxy",
"maxSession": 5,
"port": 5555,
"host": "192.168.1.8",
```

```
"register": true,

"registerCycle": 5000,

"hubPort": 4567,

"hubHost": "192.168.1.8"

  }

}
```

We will cover a good example of how to use Selenium Grid in *Chapter 10* while covering the Cross-Browser Testing concept.

Command-line help using Selenium Grid

In the case of configuration help for node or hub setup, one can use -h option whilst running the server jar file to get the details.

For example:

```
java -jar selenium-server-standalone-3.141.59.jar -h
```

How to leverage a proxy?

In the case of running behind a proxy server, one can refer to the following points to get around:

1. Selenium Proxy Class - `org.openqa.grid.selenium.proxy.DefaultRemote Proxy` needs to be extended with a Custom class – say `MyGridProxy`

2. Once the `MyGridProxy` jar file is built, it needs to be added to the class path of the hub and node.

3. This can be done using java -cpinstead of java -jar by invoking `org.openqa. grid.selenium.GridLauncher -role hub / org.openqa.grid. selenium.GridLauncher -role node`

4. Additionally, the proxy parameter needs to be passed on along with cp(classpath) and roll through-proxyorg.openqa.grid.MyGridProxy

   For example:

   ```
   java -cp *:. org.openqa.grid.selenium.GridLauncher -role node
   -hub http://localhost:4444/grid/register -proxy org.openqa.
   grid.MyGridProxy
   ```

Selenium RC

As covered in *Chapter 3*, Selenium was a resounding success since Selenium IDE and Selenium RC helped testers automate rapidly. Selenium developers were able to convert the recording done using IDE in Selenese to meaningful automation programs using Selenium RC with the support of client libraries in multiple languages.

To recap Selenium Architecture, let us look at *Figure 4.24*.

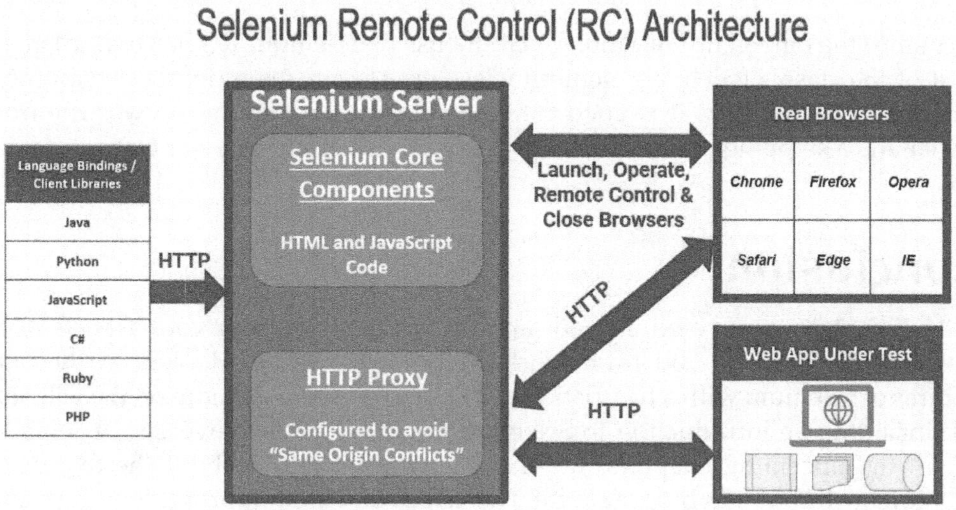

Figure 4.24: *Selenium Remote Control Architecture*

A simple program available at Selenium HQ (**https://www.seleniumhq.org/docs/05_selenium_rc.jsp**) can be tried using a downloaded Selenium Standalone Server, which uses a Firefox browser, runs a Google search of "Selenium RC" and an assertion of the outcome of the search.

```
package com.example.tests;
import com.thoughtworks.selenium.*;
import java.util.regex.Pattern;
public class NewTest extends SeleneseTestCase {


    public voidsetUp() throws Exception {
        setUp("http://www.google.com/", "*firefox");
    }

    public voidtestNew() throws Exception {
```

```
            selenium.open("/");
            selenium.type("q", "Selenium RC");
            selenium.click("btnG");
            selenium.waitForPageToLoad("30000");
            assertTrue(selenium.isTextPresent("Results * for Selenium RC"));
        }
}
```

Ever since the emergence of WebDriver, the use of Selenium RC has dwindled and most of the classes (such as Selenium Class itself) have been deprecated in future versions. For simplicity, it is good to remember that, Selenium RC was the front-runner and a stepping-stone for the emergence of Selenium as a star test automation tool.

Conclusion

In this chapter, we covered a good amount of details on four core aspects of the Selenium Architecture and framework of its tools. We also looked at the latest features of Selenium with a futuristic perspective. We focused more on the Selenium IDE including an introduction to Selenium Grid and a brief coverage of Selenium RC. In the upcoming chapters, we shall delve into details about the features of Selenium including top programming languages that are important for automation using Selenium.

Questions

1. What are the key benefits of using Selenium IDE?

2. How will you leverage RemoteWebDriver for test automation? What are its benefits?

3. What is the use of DesiredCapabilities function in Selenium?

4. What is the benefit of using TakeScreenShot function in Selenium (Python or Java code)?

5. What are the benefits of Selenium Grid such as Parallel Execution?

6. How Selenium Grid addresses "SOP"

7. What are the benefits of Selenium WebDriver over Selenium RC?

8. What are the benefits of using Selenium Grid in terms of Cross-Browser Testing?

9. What were some of the core features added in the initial releases of Selenium IDE?

10. What is the purpose of "export" in a Selenium IDE?

    a. What language options exist whilst doing an export?

    b. What is required to ensure that comments are embedded in the exported script?

11. What are the default configurations of the selenium Grid? How can one setup custom configurations?

12. How can you invoke the Selenium Grid console in a browser? What are the features one has in the console?

13. How can you implement a conditional logic program in Selenium IDE?

14. What are some of the advanced tools available that permit meaning for automation, leveraging features of Selenium?

15. Would you use Selenium RC for any automation currently?

    a. If yes, why and where will you use?

    b. If no, is there a need to understand Selenium RC? Why?

16. How can you leverage Selenium IDE for a DevOps project delivery model using CI/CD (continuous integration/deployment) pipeline?

17. Why do we need Selenese commands instead of the functions we have in Selenium Client Library? What is the benefit of a separate command library?

18. What are language formatterswhen it comes to Selenium IDE? What purpose do they solve?

## CHAPTER 5

Introduction to Web UI Automation Using Selenium

> *"If you automate a mess, you get an automated mess."*
>
> *- Rod Michael*

So far, we learned about the importance of automation, what Selenium can deliver to help us with automation. In this chapter, we will cover the Web UI Automation using Selenium by understanding the various components that make up a web UI and various options for testing the Web UI. This section will cover **Hyper Text Markup Language (HTML)**, **Cascading Style Sheets (CSS)**, the **Document Object Model (DOM)**, and JavaScript and correlation. To do good automation, it is important to know the relationship between UI components, Selenium API, and various types of browsers. This chapter targets to demystify these doubts and give some good examples to leverage the power of the Web UI to perform seamless automation.

Structure

- Components of the Web UI
- Correlation of various Web UI components (CSS, HTML, and the DOM)
- Element Locators, Selectors, ID Customization, Event Handling, Asynchronous Interactions, and Simulation of Screen Sizes

- Web UI Automation with Browsers (Firefox, Chrome, Internet Explorer, and Safari)
- How to test the Web UI using Headless Browsers

Objective

Understanding of the web UI architecture and understanding of various components and elements that make up the web application is an important aspect of web application automation using Selenium.

In this chapter, we will cover thecore aspects to a great extent in detail. They include **HyperText Markup Language (HTML)**, usage of **Cascading Style Sheets (CSS)** and the **Document Object Model (DOM)** that shows how content rendersand interacts within a web application, including actions performed by the user.

For automation using Selenium, an automation specialist needs to understand the Document Object Model that can be mapped to a Page Object Model for object-oriented program-based automation. The automation engineer also needs to have skills to locate various web elements, choose the selectors in the web UI, customize various IDs and elements in a page, designa mechanism to handle events, and take care of asynchronous interactions.

The other aspects the engineerneeds to take care of would be the styling of web elements, management of the DOM and simulation of screen sizes across browsers, desktop or mobile configurations to make sure the application works well. The objective of this chapter is to address all these points as outlined in the preceding Structure.

Components of the Web UI

The user interface design is a very important concept in software design. Good software products have very good user interface designs. Similarly, web pages, sites or applications have user interface elements that permit functional and technical capabilities to be leveraged, a visual representation of the user interface and security elements to be implemented for application features. Typically, any UI design has four major components to be leveraged. They are as follows:

- Input Control Elements
- Navigational Elements
- Informational Elements
- UI Containers

The user interface of a web page, site or a web application uses more or less standard elements outlined by various global bodies. Some of the types of UI elements include the following:

UI Element	Description
Input Controls	
● CheckBox	Checkboxes are controls used to select and confirm input on one or more items.
● Radio Buttons	Controls to choose one from one or more input items.
● Dropdown Lists	A control to select from a list of values.
● List Boxes and Multi Selects	A control to select one or more item from a list of values in a box or a scrollable control.
● Buttons	A control used for selection of a decision – typically to perform an action that could be synchronous or asynchronous.
● Drop Down Buttons	A combination of a control and a drop-down menu to choose an option.
● Switch On/Off or Toggling elements	Typically used as a control to enable/disable an element/value or an action.
● Text Fields - Short andLong	A control for getting inputs in a short or a long format.
● Date Picker	A date selection control.
● Time Picker	A time selection control.
● Forms	A control to get a set of inputs using the input controls specified above. Typically used to pass values from one page to another.
Navigational Elements	
● Search Bars	Self-explanatory. It is used for searching content on the web site/application or on the Internet.
● Navigational Breadcrumbs	Typically used in a multi-page navigational or in a session or order tracking application to show a functional/logical progression made by the user in the site. This can be used for understanding the progress and to track back if a change is needed.
● Paginations	Typically used when multiple records/content exists to ensure the content displayed per page is limited to the number of items configured either by the web site or application.
● Tags	Tags are used for simplified grouping and to search a group of similar web pages together. For example <a> anchor tag is used for referring to resources such as HTML pages or web sites.

• Slider or Progress bars	Typically used in order fulfillment or a task-oriented action such as order booking, training, survey, etc. This gives a view of how much more work is remaining.
• Icons for linking	This is a simple mechanism for providing a visual navigation option for the user. The users can click an icon to navigate to a page/element they want to.
• Carousels - Typically Images	A carousel is a web element that gives a visual and content-centric view on what the page or element is all about.
• Tab Bars	Tab bars are typically multi-page content grouped as per the tab giving a better user experience for the user to choose, view and interact with limited elements.
• Steppers - High and Low Values	Typically used for giving a range of inputs (high and low) to filter the dynamic content rendered in a web page or application.
• Side Bars	Typically, consolidated grouping of elements that appear as a vertical column on either the left or right side of an HTML page.
• Menus	A control that allows users to choose from a list of choices and perform actions (if needed).
Informational Elements	
• Notifications	Notifications are messages displayed in a status bar or as a pop-up or a text message.
• Progress Bars	This shows the progress of an action using text or a graphical unit of progression.
• Tool Tips	This highlights helpful tips or info while hovering over an item.
• Message Boxes	This pop up message boxes is used for confirmation or information purposes.
• Modal/Pop-up windows	A pop-up window or an interstitial pop-up that is used to share information.
Containers	
• Accordions	Accordions are UI elements that contain the content that is shown to know basis post an action by the user. Accordions typically hold content that is exposed when the user clicks the link or a button or any other element associated with the accordion to view content relevant to that web element.

Table 5.1: Different Navigational elements of a Web Page

Structureof a Web Page

A structure of a web page has multiple components. Some of the key components include HTML Content, CSS, and the Document Object Model highlighting the web page.

HTML

HTML is a key founding block of the World Wide Web. It provides a meaning and structure to content represented in the World Wide Web. HTML is a Document Layout Language using Hypertext Mark-up Tags. It does not have programming constructs on its own except in cases of Dynamic HTML enabled by programming languages such as JavaScript, PHP, Python, etc. Hypertexts are links that connect one page to another. HTML also uses CSS for appearance/presentation and JavaScript for functionality/logic/actions and behaviors to provide dynamism to rendering of the web pages.

It has a defined structure as per W3C standards (**https://html.spec.whatwg.org/multipage/#toc-infrastructure**)/**https://html.spec.whatwg.org/print.pdf**. This is a sample page showing some of the key elements and attributes used in an HTML Document. We willcover the details of the Document Object Model (and how to generate a Page Object Model) in subsequent chapters. A sample Document Model is shown as follows:

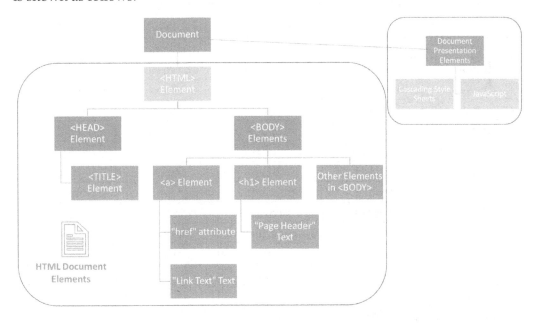

Figure 5.1: Structure of an HTML page

The HTML elements highlighted in the preceding image can be represented as follows:

- Document: This is the root element.

- Each document may have presentation elements in the form of **Cascading Style Sheets (CSS)** or a JavaScript Code.

- Each HTML document will be having the HTML Document Elements in the form of tags starting with an <HTML> element.

- Each HTML element contains a <HTML> element and the <HTML> element will have a <HTML> element as a sub-element in the HTML document.

- Each HTML element will then contain a <BODY> element that can have the following HTML elements:
  - o A link in the form of the <a> element that may have a link reference attribute such as the "<href>" attribute followed by a URL or link path in the form of a "Link Text" Text.
  - o Aheader element with a <h1> tag.
  - o Other Elements in <BODY>.

The list of HTML 5 tags include the following. Some of the tags are obsolete in HTML 5 such as <applet> that arereplaced by <object> and <basefont>, <big>, <center>, <font>, <s>, <strike>, <u> have been replaced by CSS-based styling options. All these tags are important to know while doing automation programs in Selenium:

<a>	<abbr>	<acronym>	<address>	<applet>
<area>	<article>	<aside>	<audio>	<b>
<base>	<basefont>	<bdi>	<bdo>	<big>
<blockquote>	<body>	 	<button>	<canvas>
<caption>	<center>	<cite>	<code>	<col>
<colgroup>	<datalist>	<dd>	<del>	<details>
<dfn>	<dir>	<div>	<dl>	<dt>
<em>	<embed>	<fieldset>	<figcaption>	<figure>
<font>	<footer>	<form>	<frame>	<frameset>
<h1> to <h6>	<head>	<header>	<hgroup>	<hr>
<html>	<i>	<iframe>	<img>	<input>
<ins>	<kbd>	<keygen>	<label>	<legend>
<li>	<link>	<map>	<mark>	<menu>
<meta>	<meter>	<nav>	<noframes>	<noscript>
<object>	<ol>	<optgroup>	<option>	<output>
<p>	<param>	<pre>	<progress>	<q>

`<rp>`	`<rt>`	`<ruby>`	`<s>`	`<samp>`
`<script>`	`<section>`	`<select>`	`<small>`	`<source>`
`<span>`	`<strike>`	`<strong>`	`<style>`	`<sub>`
`<summary>`	`<sup>`	`<table>`	`<tbody>`	`<td>`
`<textarea>`	`<tfoot>`	`<th>`	`<thead>`	`<time>`
`<title>`	`<tr>`	`<track>`	`<tt>`	`<u>`
`<ul>`	`<var>`	`<video>`	`<wbr>`	

***Table 5.2:** Key HTML tags*

All the HTML tags will have a TAG starter and a closer such as **<HTML TAG>&</ HTML TAG>**. For example, an HTML page can have a table body element to group an HTML table's content defined using **<tbody>** and a **</tbody>** tag aligned in the HTML page.

From a grouping of various HTML tags standpoint, HTML elements are grouped under the following categories:

- **Document Metadata:** This typically stores the information of the HTML document/page and is used for categorizing and helps tools such as browsers and search engines to use and present the page when clicked on.
    - o Some of the Metadata elements include `<base>`, `<head>`, `<link>`, `<meta>`, `<style>`, `<title>`

- **Root Content tag:** `<body>` represents content of an HTML document and this is unique per page.

- **Section Content Tags:** These are tags used to group content in a logical order.
    - o Some of the tags include `<address>`, `<article>`, `<aside>`, `<footer>`, `<header>`, `<h1>`, `<h2>`, `<h3>`, `<h4>`, `<h5>`, `<h6>`, `<hgroup>`, `<main>`, `<nav>`, `<section>`.

- **Text Content Tags:** These are tags used for grouping and formatting text content in an HTML page.
    - o Some of the tags include `<blockquote>`, `<dd>`, `<dir>`, `<div>`, `<dl>`, `<dt>`, `<figcaption>`, `<figure>`, `<hr>`, `<li>`, `<main>`, `<ol>`, `<p>`, `<pre>`, `<ul>`.

- **Inline Text formatting Tags:** These tags are used for various HTML text formats either in the main body or in an HTML element such as a table.
    - o Some of the tags include `<a>`, `<abbr>`, `<b>`, `<bdi>`, `<bdo>`, `<br>`, `<cite>`, `<code>`, `<data>`, `<dfn>`, `<em>`, `<i>`, `<kbd>`, `<mark>`, `<q>`, `<rb>`, `<rp>`, `<rt>`, `<rtc>`, `<ruby>`, `<s>`, `<samp>`, `<small>`, span>, `<strong>`, `<sub>`, `<sup>`, `<time>`, `<tt>`, `<u>`, `<var>`, `<wbr>`.

- **Image and Multimedia formatting Tags:** These tags are used for the supporting various image and multimedia types.
  - o Some of the tags include `<area>`, `<audio>`, `<img>`, `<map>`, `<track>`, `<video>`.
- **Embedded content:** This aretypically external programs and objects such as a Java Applet, Flash video, etc.
  - o Some of the tags include `<applet>`, `<embed>`, `<iframe>`, `<noembed>`, `<object>`, `<param>`, `<picture>`, `<source>`.
- **Scripting Content Tags:** These tags are used for inclusion of JavaScript and other scripting elements.
  - o Some of the tags include `<canvas>`, `<noscript>`, `<script>`.
- **Edit demarcation Tags:** These tags are used for highlighting content edit updates using the `<del>`, `<ins>` tags.
- **Table Content Tags:** These tags are used for formatting of the HTML table in a web page.
  - o Some of the tags include `<caption>`, `<col>`, `<colgroup>`, `<table>`, `<tbody>`, `<td>`, `<tfoot>`, `<th>`, `<thead>`, `<tr>`.
- **HTML Form Content Tags:** These tags are used for HTML form elements used in a web page.
  - o Some of the tags include `<button>`, `<datalist>`, `<fieldset>`, `<form>`, `<input>`, `<label>`, `<legend>`, `<meter>`, `<optgroup>`, `<option>`, `<output>`, `<progress>`, `<select>`, `<textarea>`.
- **Interactive UI object Tags:** These tags are used for HTML-5 centric Interactive UI in an HTML page.
  - o Some of the tags include `<details>`, `<dialog>`, `<menu>`, `<menuitem>`, `<summary>`.
- **Web Customization Component Tags:** These tags are used for customization of web components specification in HTML 5.
  - o Some of the tags include `<content>`, `<element>`, `<shadow>`, `<slot>`, `<template>`.

Knowing about various HTML elements is important. These elements will be used by various web sites, applications and pages. These elements are used in various forms and approaches. Different types of locators, tags, and names are used by Selenium commands to do data capturing and functional automation logic execution. We shall be leveraging some of the tags in our examples in the upcoming chapters. For a detailed reference, **World Wide Web Consortium (W3C)** specifications for HTML or Mozilla Developer Network are a couple of useful resources to understand the features of HTML.

Now that we have covered the HTML features briefly, let's move onto another important aspect of the Web UI – **Cascading Style Sheets (CSS)**.

WEB UI - Cascading Style Sheets (CSS)

Cascading Style Sheets is a styling language used for the presentation of an HTML document or other mark-up languages such as (XML, XHTML, etc.). CSS defines the style sheet on how various HTML elements are represented. CSS is also one of the core languages used for Open Web usage across browsers. CSS is also standardized across browsers with a W3C specification. While an HTML page doesn't need to use CSS, it is advised due to the myriad of features CSS offers to build a rich and stylish web page.

A CSS can be added as an external document to an HTML document or as an inline definition. For example, a CSS file defined as `CSSDOC.CS` Scan be referenced using the following code:

```
<link rel="stylesheet" href="CSSDOC.CSS">
```

An example of a CSS could be like the following code `CSSDOC.CSS` that can be included in an HTML Page. As per the preceding code snippet, `CSSDOC.CSS` contains the CSS description for various styling elements.

`CSSDOC.CSS`:

```
h1 {
  color: green;
  font: Calibri;
}


.outeroption {
  border: 4px solid blue;
}


.boxoption {
  padding: 10px;
  background-color: cyan;
  color: white;
}
```

This can be leveraged in an HTML page as follows:

```
<link rel="stylesheet" href="cssdoc.css">

<h1>

  Hello World

</h1>


<div class="outeroption">

<div class="boxoption">Test Your CSS</div>

</div>
```

The code can be in line to an HTML page as well. In this case, the code snippet included in cssdoc.css will be included in the main HTML page inlieu of the `<link rel="stylesheet" href="cssdoc.css">` command. When executed, this program produces the output as shown in *Figure 5.2* for the preceding code snippet:

Figure 5.2: *CSS Output*

Now, let's see some examples of CSS selectors that we are likely to interpret using Selenium commands.

CSS Selectors

There are many types of CSS Selectors but three of them are majorly used, namely, a Type Selector, a Class Selector, and an ID Selector. Type Selector typically refers to an HTML tag type such as a header text (`<h1>` – `<h6>`) or a paragraph (`<p>`). These CSS style sheet markups are applied throughout the selectors in the HTML page. The second type of selector is a Class selector. This can be defined in such a way that whenever a defined class is called, the HTML browser interprets the class selector and applies the styling applicable to the class. The third type of selector is an ID selector. This permits the users to define IDs in an HTML page and applies the styling as defined in the ID. The other types of selectors include the Universal selector, attribute selector, Pseudo class selector, and combinators.

Let us see the selectors used in examples in the following *Table 5.3:*

• h2 { }	Type Selector
• .tip { }	Class Selector
• #selenium book { }	ID Selector
• * { }	Universal Selector
• a[title]{ } • a[href="URL"] { }	Attribute Selectors
• p::last-line { } • p:first-child { }	Pseudo Class Selectors
• article p • article > p • h2 + p • h2 ~ p	Combinators

Table 5.3: *Key CSS Selectors Example*

Now that we know about HTML and CSS, let us get into the specifics of how a Document Object Model is formed. To understand this, let us understand the flow of how an HTML page is rendered in a browser. The flow is as follows:

- Browser Loads the HTML File ◆ Parses the HTML File ◆ Creates a DOM Tree ◆ Renders the page in the Display Unit (PC, laptop, mobile, etc.)

When a CSS or JavaScript file is used, the flow changes a bit. It is shown as follows:

- Browser Loads the HTML File ◆ Parses the HTML File ◆ Creates a DOM Tree ◆ Loads CSS/JS Files ◆ Parse CSS/JS Files ◆ Attach Style/Objects to DOM Trees ◆ Renders the page in the Display Unit (PC, laptop, mobile, etc.)

As you can see, in order to do good automation of web sites using selenium, it is important to understand the basics of HTML, CSS and see how DOM works. This will help us in developing a good Page Object Model to allow us to automate websites efficiently.

Document Object Model

The **Document Object Model (DOM)** is an object-oriented representation of a web page and is a programming interface for XML and HTML documents used for web page rendering. It is also a representation of a page that includes the structure, content, and style used in a page. With the use of a DOM, it is possible to use a program to manipulate how the content is rendered as it is a tree structure and content can be dynamically managed with a scripting language like JavaScript. In simple terms, the DOM is a logical tree of the document with each branch ending as a node. Each node contains an object. These objects can be managed programmatically. These DOM objects have an event handler as well that can be managed programmatically. With the use of a DOM, automation tools such as Selenium can perform various user-centric actions.

Taking inputs from the HTML and CSS section, a simple DOM model can be constructed as shown inthe following *Figure 5.3*:

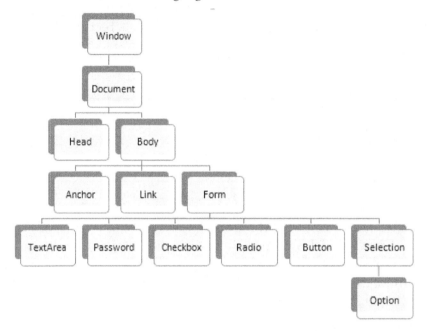

Figure 5.3: *A representation of a Document Object Model*

The elements represented by a DOM tree can be referenced by DOM API functions such as `getElementById()`, `getElemenstByName()`, `getElementsByTagName()`, and `getElementsByClassName()` to fetch details from the DOM tree constructed by the browser.

XPATH can be used to traverse the DOM Tree. XPATH is a path traversing language used specifically for this purpose. It leverages the DOM tree for any page and uses absolute or a relative path to traverse and identify any element in the DOM tree. We willbe using XPATH identifiers extensively in our programs to identify the elements that need to be parsed or acted upon.

Now, let's put some of these concepts into a fruitful action.

Element Locators

One of the key aspects to understand in Selenium is the location of elements. There are multiple ways in which an element can be located in Selenium. Some of the key methods to locate elements are as follows:

- Locators using ID
- Locators using Name
- Locators using LinkText
    - o LinkText
    - o Partial LinkText
- Locators using Tag Names
- Locators using Class Names
- Locators using CSS
- Locators using XPATH

Locators using ID and Name

Let's take a look at thefollowing HTML example and see aJava-based example of identifying the elements using various types of locators:

```
<html>

<body>

<form id="Details">

<input name="Name" type="text"/>

<input name="EmailID" type="text"/>

<input name="Submit" type="submit" value="Submit Details!"/>

</form>

</body>

</html>
```

There are four identifiers that can be used from this form. They are as follows:

- Identifier (By ID) = Details
- Identifers (By Name)
    - o Name
    - o EmailID
    - o Submit

The corresponding code snippets for element extraction will be as follows:

Example of Locator by Identifier

```
WebElementDetailsEle = driver.findElement(By.id("Details"));
```

Example of Locator by Name

The following commands are examples of identifying locators using Names:

```
WebElementNameEle= driver.findElement(By.name("Name"));

WebElementEmailEle= driver.findElement(By.name("EmailID"));

WebElementSubmitEle= driver.findElement(By.name("Submit"));
```

Example of Locator by Links

Let us take an example of Locator by Links by taking the Yahoo URL **https://in.yahoo.com/?p=us**:

- We can extract the link for Cricket using the following command:

  ```
  WebElementLinkEle= driver.findElement(By.linkText("Cricket"));
  ```

- If we want to extract link info for words starting with Cri, it can be done using the following command:

  o If there is a single link starting with "Cri", then the following command will suffice:

  ```
  WebElementPartLinkEle= driver.findElement(By.
  partialLinkText("Cri"));
  ```

  o If there are more than one link starting with "Cri", then use the following command:

  ```
  List <WebElement>PartLinkEleList= driver.findElements(By.
          partialLinkText("Cri"));
  ```

Example of Locator by Tag Names

Let us take an example of Locator by Tag names by taking the Yahoo URL **https://in.yahoo.com/?p=us**:

```
WebDriver driver = new FirefoxDriver();

driver.get("https://in.yahoo.com/?p=us");

List <WebElement>ATaglist = driver.findElements(By.tagName("a"));
```

After the execution of the script, the List element *ATaglist* will have all the elements having the anchor tag <a>.

Example of Locators by Class Names

Let us take an example of Locator by Tag names by taking the LinkedIn Signup URL **https://www.linkedin.com/start/join**:

```
WebDriver driver = new ChromeDriver();

driver.get("https://www.linkedin.com/start/join");

WebElementClassNameEle = driver.findElement(By.className("os-win gr__
linkedin_com"));
```

Locators using CSS

A CSS locator in an HTML Page can be referenced via the following syntax:

- Using a # Notation:
  - o   `CSS = <HTML TAG><#><Attribute Value>`
  - o   `css = TAG_name[<attribute_name>='<value>']`
- Using a "." Notation:
  - o   `CSS = <HTML TAG><.><Attribute Value>`

Take the following example for a form:

```
<input type="text" id="Name" name="Name" class="FormInputs">
<input type="text" id="Email" name="Email" class="FormInputs">
```

In this example, CSS selectors can be chosen as follows:

- `css=input[name='Name']`
- `css=input[name='Email']`

To select the input class, we can use the following command:

- `css=input.FormInputs or css =.FormInputs`

To select name or Email elements, we canuse following as the identifier:

- `css=input#Name or css =#Name`
- `css=input#Email or css =#Email`

Now, let's take a real example and use a Selenium code to understand the concept. Let's take an example of the google.com landing page. This minimalistic landing page has a lot of CSS elements to handle. Some of the CSS elements include the following:

- `Search Text Box = [maxlength]`
- `Microphone Icon = .hb2Smf`
- `Google Search Button = .FPdoLc [value='Google Search']`
- `I'm Feeling Lucky Button = .FPdoLc [value='I\'m Feeling Lucky']`
- `How Search Works Link = #fsl .Fx4vi:nth-of-type(4)`
- `Google Apps Icon =  [title='Google apps']`
- `Google Images Link = [href='https\:\/\/www\.google\.co\.in\/ imghp\?hl\=en\&tab\=wi\&authuser\=0\&ogbl']`

- Gmail Link = [href='https\:\/\/mail\.google\.com\/
  mail\/\?tab\=wm\&authuser\=0\&ogbl']

If we want to use CSS Selectors on the Google.com home page, the following code snippet is a sample code we could use:

```
WebDriver driver = new ChromeDriver();

driver.get("https://www.google.com");

// Fill Text in Search box

driver.findElement(By.cssSelector("[maxlength]")).sendKeys("Testing
Selenium CSS Selectors");

//Click Google Search Button

driver.findElement(By.cssSelector(".FPdoLc  [value='Google  Search']")).
click();

//Or we can click I'm Feeling Lucky Button

driver.findElement(By.cssSelector(".FPdoLc     [value='I\'m     Feeling
Lucky']")).click();

//Or we can click on How Search Works Link

driver.findElement(By.cssSelector("#fsl .Fx4vi:nth-of-type(4)")).click();

//Or we can click on Google Apps Icon

driver.findElement(By.cssSelector("[title='Google apps']")).click();
```

The cssSelector function can be used along with a regular expression provision to select more than one element or to handle dynamically changing websites. The sub string matching regular expressions include starts with (^) and ends with ($), contains (*)

Suppose if we have an input element as the following in an HTML page:

```
<input  id="emailid"  class="inputtext"  type="emailid"  "  value="email@
domain.com" name="emailid">
```

We could use any of the following three commands to choose the emailid selector in our Selenium automation program:

```
//Starts with ^ operator

driver.findElement(By.cssSelector("input[id^='ema']")).
sendKeys("startswith.emailid@domain.com");

//Ends with $ operator

driver.findElement(By.cssSelector("input[id$='lid']")).
```

```
sendKeys("endswith.emailid@domain.com");

//Contains * operator

driver.findElement(By.cssSelector("input[id*='email']")).
sendKeys("contains.emailid@domain.com");
```

Example of Locators by XPATH

XPATH or XML Path for simplicity is a syntax used for identification of any element in an HTML or a web page. It is a simple XML path language. It uses the HTML DOM structure for simplified navigation. So far we understood the following:

- **locator by ID** is used to identify an element by the ID of the element.
- **locator by Classname** is used to identify an element by the class name of the element.
- **locator by name** is used to identify an element by the name of the element.
- **locator by Link Text** is used to identify an element by the text of the link attributed to the element.
- **locator by CSS path** is used to locate elements by a CSS path, including elements having no name, class name, link, or ID associated with it.

The syntax of an XPath is as follows:

```
XPATH = //TAGNAME[@ATTRIBUTE='VALUE']
```

The syntax can be explained in the sequence as follows:

- `//` is typically the path of the element. It could be a relative or an absolute path for selection of the element.
- `TAGNAME` is the tag/element being searched for in the node. This could be an HTML element like `<a>`, `<ul>`, `<div>`, `<img>`, or `<input>` to name a few.
- `@` is the selected attribute.
- `ATTRIBUTE` is the name of the element or node.
- `VALUE` is the value of the `ATTRIBUTE` selected.

Additional relative locator tags include `following-sibling`, `preceding-sibling`, `parent`, `ends-with()`, `starts-with()` and `last()`. These tags are used very extensively in XPath. Relative XPath tags can be referred to using a single / and a * in the XPath.

Let's take the example given for CSS (Google.com) in the previous section and replace four elements with XPath references. We willgenerate code for two of the elements/identifiers using an XPath-based approach. We will use both absolute and relative XPath parameters for this code snippet:

- **Search Text Box:**
  - o **Absolute XPath:** `/html//form[@id='tsf']//div[@ class='a4bIc']/input[@role='combobox']`
  - o **Relative XPath:** `//div[1]/input[@role='combobox']`

- **Microphone Icon:**
  - o **Absolute XPath:** `/html//form[@id='tsf']//div[@ class='A8SBwf']//div[@role='button']/span[@ class='hb2Smf']`
  - o **Relative XPath:** `//div[@role='button']/span`

- **Google Search Button:**
  - o **Absolute XPath:** `/html//form[@id='tsf']//div[@ class='A8SBwf']/div[@class='FPdoLc VlcLAe']/center/ input[@name='btnK']`
  - o **Relative XPath:** `//form[#'tsf']/div[2]/div/?/?/center/ input[@name='btnK']`

- **I'm Feeling Lucky Button:**
  - o **Absolute XPath:** `/html//form[@id='tsf']//div[@ class='A8SBwf']/div[@class='FPdoLc VlcLAe']/center/ input[@name='btnI']`
  - o **Relative XPath:** `//form[#'tsf']/div[2]/div/?/?/center/ input[@name='btnI']`

If we want to use CSS Selectors on the Google.com home page, we can use the following sample code:

```
WebDriver driver = new ChromeDriver();

driver.get("https://www.google.com");

// Select Search button using absolute XPath

WebElement element = driver.findElement(By.xpath("/html//form[@
id='tsf']//div[@class='a4bIc']/input[@role='combobox']")).
sendKeys("Testing Selenium XPath Selectors");


//or using relative XPath

WebElement element = driver.findElement(By.xpath("//div[1]/input[@
role='combobox']")).sendKeys("Testing Selenium XPath Selectors");
```

The key to the usage of XPath as an element identifier is to understand the DOM tree model and how various IDs, Classes, Names and Tags are interlinked in an HTML page. There are quite a few tools available for generation of the CSS and XPath tags that could be used for programming. Some of these tools include Ranorex, Katalon, and Open Source extensions.

We can use tools such as FirePath and ChroPath for generating the Web Element Locators from a webpage to do the Selenium Locator programming. Similarly, there are tools such as the Page Object Generator that allows youto generate base code for Selenium automation that can be customized and beautified to suit the needs of your test automation needs.

Other Locators Available

In addition to the standard locators mentioned above, we have a set of locator identification options in Selenium that permits us to search based on a combination, if we are unsure about the tags. These methods are particularly helpful when dealing with very dynamic web applications that obfuscate the code (by making it cryptic and difficult to read) to generate dynamic pages.

Some of the locators that help us achieve this feature is given below.

- The **ByIdOrName** locator helps to locate an element based on either the id or name match. This is particularly helpful in automating web pages that typically havea standard name or id tag when it comes to forms or common elements.
- The **ByChained** locator helps tolocate an element based on the element hierarchy by running through the hierarchy. It typically accepts multiple (unlimited) locators to act.
- The **ByAll** locator accepts any type of locator to find an element based on the inputs given. The locator can be any of the standard locator (name, id, class name, link text, partial link text, CSS, or XPath).

Custom Locators

To write good Selenium programs, we need to understand some of the advanced concepts of the web application architecture such as CSS, DOM, XPATH, etc. If we handcraft the code with complex logic, it would become a nightmare to maintain a working automation script that delivers all the benefits we forecast for test automation. What about some flexibility in writing custom locators to address flexibility, dynamism, reuse, and efficient use of codes?

We can also write custom locators for simplicity and object reuse, if we find that the XPath elements are very complex to understand. For example, if the CSS or XPath tag identifier for an object is very long such as `By.xpath("/html//form[@ id='tsf']//div[@class='a4bIc']/input[@role='combobox']")`, we can consider writing a custom locator class.

Some ways by which we can achieve the objective of a custom locator are as follows.

- To extend a custom locator, we need to create a custom class for the locator. In this case, it could be **aByComboBox**.

- **ByComboBox** needs to be of a return type of **By**. This is because WebElement expects all method types to be of the type of **By**.

- Return type of **By** is achieved using a creator.

- Finally. the**findElements()** method is overridden to use the search parameters passed.

- Using In find Elements(), we create the XPath element fully based on the context we pass (the parameter could be **id**, **class** and type (i.e.) ComboBox).

- A very simple and quick implementation of a ComboBox custom locator for Google Search can be seen* in the following code snippet:

```java
import java.util.List;

import org.openqa.selenium.By;

import org.openqa.selenium.SearchContext;

import org.openqa.selenium.WebElement;


public class ByComboBox extends By
{
    private final String cbByString;

    public ByComboBox(String cbByString)

    {
this.cbByString = cbByString;

    }

    @Override

    public List<WebElement>findElements(SearchContext context)

    {
            List<WebElement>cbElements = context.findElements(By.
xpath("/html//form[@id='tsf']//div[@class='a4bIc']/input[@role='"
+ cbByString + "']"));

        return cbElements;

    }

}

.
```

We could then use the defined function for a call during our program. This simplifies the programming requirements for automation. Now, let's move on to an important topic of event handling and see how it helps us in developing solid automation capabilities to handle asynchronous and dynamic web applications.

Selenium Event Handling

What are the options a selenium automation engineer has for maintaining logs for report creation whiledealing with dynamic pages with asynchronous events and multiple actions existing on the same page? How does one take care of automation and complex resolution of XPATHs and CSS selectors to be parsed for automation using the logs and reports for debugging? Can the Events be automated simply to help fast track test automation code debugging? The answer is yes and it can be done with efficient use of Event Listener Handlers in Selenium.

`WebDriverEventListener` typically listens to different automation-related events coded in a selenium program. With the method implemented for each of the events, the programmer can act such as writea log, updatea database or write in a report. All of these come handy while checking the resulting outcome or when used for debugging. Similarly, `TestNG` provides an event listener handler as well. `TestNGlisteners` are `ITestListener` and `ITestResult` which are used for logging and reporting, respectively. `TestNG` Listeners typically listens to every test-related event.

Let us take an example of an automation-related event to see how this is done. For example, we will leverage the `WebDriverEventListener` class that comes along with the events package:

Following is the sequence of tasks we need to perform.

- First, we need to create an event listening class.
- We will nameit as `Ch5_EventCaptureExample` under the `CrackingSeleniumInterviewExamplespackage`.
- In the code, we will extend the implementation of `WebDriverEventListener`.
- As a part of the code, for various actions, including before and after an event, we can include boiler-plate code for use. If you are certain about the implementation logic, you can extend these methods as much as you can.
- For the example, let us implement a simple logging statement via `System.`

```
out.println().
```

The code for event capturing class will look as follows:

Event Capturing Class

Ch5_EventCaptureExample.java

```
1    package CrackSeleniumInterviewExamples.Ch5_EventHandler;

2

3    import org.openqa.selenium.By;

4    import org.openqa.selenium.OutputType;

5    import org.openqa.selenium.WebDriver;

6    import org.openqa.selenium.WebElement;

7    import org.openqa.selenium.support.events.WebDriverEventListener;

8

9    public class Ch5_EventCaptureExample implements WebDriverEventListener {

10       @Override

11   public void beforeAlertAccept(WebDriverwebDriver) {

12   System.out.println("Before accepting an alert");

13       }

14

15       @Override

16   public void afterAlertAccept(WebDriverwebDriver) {

17   System.out.println("After accepting an alert");

18       }

19

20       @Override

21   public void afterAlertDismiss(WebDriverwebDriver) {

22   System.out.println("After dismissing an alert");

23       }

24

25       @Override

26   public void beforeAlertDismiss(WebDriverwebDriver) {

27   System.out.println("Before dismissing an alert");

28       }
```

```
29

30      @Override
31   public void beforeNavigateTo(String s, WebDriverwebDriver) {
32   System.out.println("Before Navigating to " + s );
33      }

34

35      @Override
36   public void afterNavigateTo(String s, WebDriverwebDriver) {
37   System.out.println("After Navigating to " + s );
38      }

39

40      @Override
41   public void beforeNavigateBack(WebDriverwebDriver) {
42   System.out.println("Before Navigating back" );
43      }

44

45      @Override
46   public void afterNavigateBack(WebDriverwebDriver) {
47   System.out.println("After Navigating back" );
48      }

49

50      @Override
51   public void beforeNavigateForward(WebDriverwebDriver) {
52   System.out.println("Before Navigating Forward" );
53      }

54

55      @Override
56   public void afterNavigateForward(WebDriverwebDriver) {
57   System.out.println("After Navigating Forward" );
58      }

59

60      @Override
61   public void beforeNavigateRefresh(WebDriverwebDriver) {
```

```
62  System.out.println("Before Navigating Refresh" );
63      }
64
65      @Override
66  public void afterNavigateRefresh(WebDriverwebDriver) {
67  System.out.println("After Navigating Refresh" );
68      }
69
70      @Override
71  public void beforeFindBy(By by, WebElementwebElement,
    WebDriverwebDriver) {
72  System.out.println("Before Find By"+ webElement.getText() );
73      }
74
75      @Override
76  public void afterFindBy(By by, WebElementwebElement, WebDriverwebDriver)
    {
77  System.out.println("After Find By"+ webElement.getText() );
78      }
79
80      @Override
81  public void beforeClickOn(WebElementwebElement, WebDriverwebDriver) {
82  System.out.println("Before Click on "+ webElement.getText() );
83      }
84
85      @Override
86  public void afterClickOn(WebElementwebElement, WebDriverwebDriver) {
87  System.out.println("After Click on "+ webElement.getText() );
88      }
89
90      @Override
91  public void beforeChangeValueOf(WebElementwebElement,
    WebDriverwebDriver, CharSequence[] charSequences) {
92  System.out.println("Before Change Value of "+ webElement.getText() );
```

```
93          }
94
95          @Override
96     public void afterChangeValueOf(WebElementwebElement, WebDriverwebDriver,
       CharSequence[] charSequences) {
97     System.out.println("After Change Value of "+ webElement.getText() );
98          }
99
100         @Override
101    public void beforeScript(String s, WebDriverwebDriver) {
102    System.out.println("Before Script "+ s );
103         }
104
105         @Override
106    public void afterScript(String s, WebDriverwebDriver) {
107    System.out.println("After Script "+ s );
108         }
109
110         @Override
111    public void beforeSwitchToWindow(String s, WebDriverwebDriver) {
112    System.out.println("Before Switch Window "+ s );
113         }
114
115         @Override
116    public void afterSwitchToWindow(String s, WebDriverwebDriver) {
117    System.out.println("After Switch Window "+ s );
118         }
119
120         @Override
121    public void onException(Throwablethrowable, WebDriverwebDriver) {
122    System.out.println("Exception Thrown "+ throwable.getMessage() );
123         }
124
```

```
125      @Override
126   public <X>void beforeGetScreenshotAs(OutputType<X>outputType) {
127
128      }
129
130      @Override
131   public <X>void afterGetScreenshotAs(OutputType<X>outputType, X x) {
132
133      }
134
135      @Override
136   public void beforeGetText(WebElementwebElement, WebDriverwebDriver) {
137
138      }
139
140      @Override
141   public void afterGetText(WebElementwebElement, WebDriverwebDriver,
      String s) {
142   System.out.println("After Get Text \n"+ s  + "\n Web Element is \n"
      + webElement.getText());
143      }
144   }
```

After this, we need to implement the program.

- Create an instance of `EventFiringWebDriver`.
- Create an instance of `Ch5_EventCaptureExample`.
- In the instance of the class `EventFiringWebDriverregisterCh5_ EventCaptureExample`. perform various events/actions:
    a. For example, we willnavigate various sites.
- The event listener keeps track of the actions and performs the logging/ debugging/reporting-related tasks as defined in various functions/methods defined in `Ch5_EventCaptureExample`.
- You can use the logs generated to see how the program performs and make necessary changes.

Let us see how the code we implemented the Ch5_EventCaptureExample class in the actual Listener in the preceding code snippet.Example – Ch5_prog_1_ ListenerExample_Main.java:

Ch5_Prog_1_ListenerExample_Main.java

```java
1   package CrackSeleniumInterviewExamples.Ch5_EventHandler;

2

3   import org.openqa.selenium.*;

4   import org.openqa.selenium.chrome.ChromeDriver;

5   import org.openqa.selenium.support.events.EventFiringWebDriver;

6

7   public class Ch5_Prog_1_ListenerExample_Main {

8   public static void main(String[] args) throws InterruptedException {

9       // Create a new instance of the Chrome driver - Set the Properties
        for the Chrome Driver locations

10      System.setProperty("webdriver.chrome.driver",

11      "C:\\Selenium\\chromedriver.exe");

12

13      WebDriver driver = new ChromeDriver();

14      //Initiate the Event Capturing Class Initiated

15      EventFiringWebDrivereventFiringWebDriver = new
        EventFiringWebDriver(driver);

16          Ch5_EventCaptureExample ch5EventCaptureExample = new Ch5_
            EventCaptureExample();

17      // Let us Register the Capture with EventFiringWebDriver to register

18      // the implementation of WebDriverEventListener

19      // to ensure it listens to the WebDriver events

20      eventFiringWebDriver.register(ch5EventCaptureExample);

21      // And now use this to visit BPB Publication's website

22      eventFiringWebDriver.navigate().to("https://WWW.GOOGLE.COM/");

23      // Check the title of the page

24      System.out.println("Page title is: " + eventFiringWebDriver.
        getTitle());

25      // Let's pick the Check Bing

26          eventFiringWebDriver.navigate().to("https://www.bing.com/
        search?q=selenium");
```

```
27    System.out.println("Page title is: " + eventFiringWebDriver.
      getTitle());
28    System.out.println("The current" + eventFiringWebDriver.
getCurrentUrl() );
29    //Now Let us move to the home page of Selenium HQ
30            eventFiringWebDriver.navigate().to("https://www.seleniumhq.
      org/");
31    System.out.println("Page title is: " + eventFiringWebDriver.
      getTitle());
32    System.out.println("The current" + eventFiringWebDriver.
       getCurrentUrl() );
33    // Let's try some events to cover the Locater concept
34    eventFiringWebDriver.manage().window().setSize(new Dimension(1050,
      708));
35    System.out.println("The current" + eventFiringWebDriver.
       getCurrentUrl() );
36            eventFiringWebDriver.navigate().to("https://www.google.com/
      search?q=selenium");
37    System.out.println("Page title is: " + eventFiringWebDriver.
      getTitle());
38 System.out.println("The current" + eventFiringWebDriver.getCurrentUrl()
   + "Capabilites are \n" + eventFiringWebDriver.getCapabilities());
39    // And now use this to visit BPB Publication's website
40    eventFiringWebDriver.navigate().to("https://bpbonline.com/");
41    System.out.println("Page title is: " + eventFiringWebDriver.
      getTitle());
42    System.out.println("The current" + eventFiringWebDriver.
      getCurrentUrl() );
43    // Let's quit this driver
44    eventFiringWebDriver.quit();
45    //Now to Unregister the listener
46    eventFiringWebDriver.unregister(ch5EventCaptureExample);
47    System.out.print("End of the Code");
48        }
49 }
```

This simple program uses only one of the actions: navigation. All the user actions can be listened to and logged for various automation tasks. A tool like TestNG is very useful while doing automation for the first time on a complex application landscape.

Output:

This simple program produces the following outcome:

Figure 5.4: *Event Handler Program Output*

Asynchronous Interactions in Selenium

Almost all the web applications/sites use Dynamic HTML aided by JavaScript. When a website uses JavaScript, it is always asynchronous. This is because JavaScript is always asynchronous and the input and output is asynchronous most of the time. The popularity of Asynchronous websites such as GMAIL was largely possible due to the usefulness and success of AJAX whileimplementing these applications.

There are two major types of wait functions that allow us to handle the asynchronous nature of the JavaScript programs. They are as follows:

- **Implicit Wait:**
  - o An implicit wait is used for polling the DOM Tree for a certain amount of time while finding an element by the WebDriver. By default, it is set for 0 seconds. The implicit wait is like a global wait. Once it is set, it will wait for each element in the script. An example statement will be as shown in the following code:

- ▪ driver.manage().timeouts().implicitlyWait(30, TimeUnit. SECONDS);

- **Explicit Wait:**

  o This wait is used to instruct code to wait for a particular state to be reached in a web page before progressing. The time limit specified instructs the program to wait for a particular time for an action to occur. If the event happens beforehand, the code progresses.

  o For a timebound wait, a function such as thread.sleep() can be used but this is not recommended. It pauses the program for a certain period before it progresses to check for the website updates. Thread. sleep needs to be handled for an interruption related exception. The code snippet will be as follows:

    - ▪ try { Thread.sleep(1000);} catch (InterruptedExceptionintEx){}

  o The explicit wait keeps checking the element every 500 milli seconds. If the element is found, then it resumes the execution. That is why this should be preferred over Thread.sleep(). This is implemented using a combination of WebDriverWait and ExpectedConditions. This is particularly useful to check for updates before acting as an AJAX-enabled web page.

    - ▪ Let us see this with two examples as follows

      - ▪ **Example 1:**

        - ▪ WebElementwebElement = wait.
          until(ExpectedConditions.
          elementToBeClickable(By.id(>someid>)));

          //Above Example waits for a clickable element (link, button etc.) to appear

      - ▪ **Example 2:**

        - ▪ WebDriverWaitwdWait = new
          WebDriverWait(driver, 20);

          Alert checkForAlert = wdWait.
          until(ExpectedConditions.alertIsPresent());

          //Above Example waits for an alert to appear within 20 seconds

Some of the expected conditions that can be used along with WebDriverWait() for an explicit wait is given in the following table. The expected conditions are that WebDriverWait will keep waiting for the time mentioned until the expected conditions become true.

`alertIsPresent()`	`elementSelectionState ToBe(By locator, boolean selected)`
`elementSelectionStateToBe (WebElement element, boolean selected)`	`elementToBeClickable (By locator)`
`elementToBeClickable (WebElement element)`	`elementToBeSelected (By locator)`
`elementToBeSelected (WebElement element)`	`frameToBeAvailable AndSwitchToIt(By locator)`
`frameToBeAvailableAnd SwitchToIt(String frameLocator)`	`invisibilityOfElement Located(By locator)`
`invisibilityOfElement WithText(By locator, String text)`	`not(ExpectedCondition <?> condition)`
`presenceOfAllElements LocatedBy(By locator)`	`presenceOfElement Located(By locator)`
`refreshed(Expected Condition<T> condition)`	`stalenessOf(Web Element element)`
`textToBePresentIn Element(WebElement element, String text)`	`textToBePresentIn ElementLocated(By locator, String text)`
`textToBePresentInElement Value(By locator, String text)`	`textToBePresentIn ElementValue(WebElement element, String text)`
`titleContains(String title)`	`titleIs(String title)`
`visibilityOf(WebElement element)`	`visibilityOfAllElements (List<WebElement> elements)`
`visibilityOfAllElements LocatedBy(By locator)`	`visibilityOfElementLocated(By locator)`

Table 5.4: Table of the WebDriverWait function checks

While the implicit and explicit waits are used extensively by the programmers, there are some other types of waits used by WebDriver. They include the following:

- **Fluent Wait - **`FluentWait()`
  - o Sometimes, an element appears at certain intervals or after a while and may repeat the action. Things such as stock ticker data appearing on some financial websites is an example. If we want to capture these elements, we may want to use a Fluent Wait.
  - o A Fluent Wait polls regularly for a web element at the interval specified or until the interval specified for the timeout by ignoring exceptions for the element not being present during the polling.

o A Fluent Wait uses a polling frequency and a timeout limit:

- **Example**:

- ```
  Wait fluentWait = new FluentWait(driver).
  withTimeout(60, SECONDS).pollingEvery(3, SECONDS).
  ignoring(NoSuchElementException.class);
  ```

- The preceding example sets a timeout limit of 60 seconds by polling every threeseconds while ignoring an exception for `NoSuchElement`.

- **SetScriptTimeout** –`setScriptTimeout()`

  o This is used for setting the timeout for script-related execution.

  - **Example**:

    - ```
      driver.manage().timeouts().setScriptTimeout (20,SECONDS);
      ```

- **PageLoadTimeout** – `pageLoadTimeout()`

  o This is used for setting the timeout for a web page load.

  - **Example:**

    - ```
      driver.manage().timeouts().pageLoadTimeout(50, SECONDS);
      ```

Screen Size Management

In Selenium, the screen sizes of the browser windows can be resized or modified through various functions available inthe active window. This can be useful while doing cross-browser testing across various configurations and to simulate responsive web design characteristics of the website. Some of the WebDriver-based browser window sizing options in Selenium are as follows:

- Using the browser options by adding window size arguments, we can set the size of the browser window.
- Using the `driver.manage().window().setSize()` functionality, we can set the size of the browser window.
- Using `driver.manage().window().fullscreen()`, we can set the size of the browser to full screen.
- Using `driver.manage().window().maximize()`, we can set the size of the browser to maximum size.
- `driver.manage().window().getPosition()` returns the current point in the window. This could be used to reset or resize the browser.
- `driver.manage().window().setPosition()` can be used to set the browser at a particular location in the window.

Let us see an example for resizing the browser window. The following example uses a simple browser sizing of `800x480` pixels:
      ```

Ch5_Prog_2_WindowResize_Example.java

```
1    package CrackSeleniumInterviewExamples;

2

3    import org.openqa.selenium.*;

4    import org.openqa.selenium.chrome.ChromeDriver;

5    import org.openqa.selenium.chrome.ChromeOptions;

6    import org.openqa.selenium.remote.DesiredCapabilities;

7

8    public class Ch5_Prog_2_WindowResize_Example {

9    public static void main(String[] args) throws InterruptedException {

10   WebElement element;

11   System.setProperty("webdriver.chrome.driver",

12   "C:\\Selenium\\chromedriver.exe");

13   ChromeOptionschromeOptions = new ChromeOptions();

14   chromeOptions.addArguments("window-size=800,480");

15    DesiredCapabilitiesdesiredCapabilities = DesiredCapabilities.chrome();

16   desiredCapabilities.setCapability(ChromeOptions.CAPABILITY, chromeOptions);

17   //this will open chrome with set size

18   WebDriver driver = new ChromeDriver(desiredCapabilities);

19   driver.get("https://www.google.com");

20          Dimension d = new Dimension(1200,1200);

21   //Resize current window to the set dimension

22   driver.manage().window().setSize(d);

23          d = new Dimension(600,980);

24   //Resize current window to the set dimension

25   driver.manage().window().setSize(d);

26   driver.manage().window().fullscreen();

27   driver.manage().window().maximize();

28   driver.close();

29       }

30   }
```

Web UI Automation with Browsers (Firefox, Chrome, Internet Explorer and Safari)

We got introduced to various browsers and saw how to initiate WebDrivers in Selenium in the preceding chapters. From a WebDriver standpoint, all we need to focus will be primarily based on the browser driver and the browser-centric options and configurations. Rest of the programming logic is the same for all browsers, thus making Selenium a tool of choice for cross-browser and cross-platform testing.

Let us take a look at the following JAVA example for initializing the browsers. We will leverage different browsers across different programming languages from *Chapter 6* (Web UI Automation with Selenium) onwards. Let us see the examples of instantiation across various browsers using the JAVA programming language. For the Opera browser, the followingPython example is included as well:

Java:

```
/* Examples to initiate various Drivers */
```

<u>FireFox Browser:</u>

Package Import

```
import org.openqa.selenium.firefox.FirefoxDriver;
```

Code for setup and initiating the script

```
// Configuration of Browser Properties is highly recommended for proper
functioning of the code

System.setProperty("webdriver.firefox.marionette","<<PATH/FOLDER
CONTAINING THE DRIVER>>\\geckodriver.exe");

WebDriver driver=new FirefoxDriver();

// In the example above, we are creating an instance of WebDriver by
creating a // new FirefoxDriver Object and by passing firefox parameters
such as version // and the location of the driver executable
```

Chrome Browser:

Package Import

```
import org.openqa.selenium.chrome.ChromeDriver;
```

Code for setup and initiating the script

```
// Configuration of Browser Properties is highly recommended for proper
functioning of the code
```

```
System.setProperty("webdriver.chrome.driver","<<PATH/FOLDER CONTAINING
THE DRIVER>>\\chromedriver.exe");

WebDriver driver=new ChromeDriver();

// In the example above, we are creating an instance of WebDriver by
creating a // new ChromeDriver Object and by passing Chrome parameters
such as version
// and the location of the driver executable
```

Edge Browser:

Package Import

```
import org.openqa.selenium.edge.EdgeDriver;
```

Code for setup and initiating the script

```
// Configuration of Browser Properties is highly recommended for proper
functioning of the code
System.setProperty("webdriver.edge.driver","<<PATH/FOLDER CONTAINING THE
DRIVER>>\\MicrosoftWebDriver.exe");

WebDriver driver=new EdgeDriver ();

// In the example above, we are creating an instance of WebDriver
by creating a // new EdgeDriver Object and by passing Edge Driver
parameters such as version
// and the location of the driver executable
```

Internet Explorer Browser:

Package Import

```
import org.openqa.selenium.ie.InternetExplorerDriver;
```

Code for setup and initiating the script

```
// Configuration of Browser Properties is highly recommended for proper
functioning of the code

System.setProperty("webdriver.ie.driver","<<PATH/FOLDER  CONTAINING  THE
DRIVER>>\\IEDriverServer.exe");

WebDriver driver=new InternetExplorerDriver();

// In the example above, we are creating an instance of WebDriver by
creating a // new InternetExplorerDriver Object and by passing
```

```
// Internet Explorer Driver parameters such as version
// and the location of the driver executable
```

Safari Browser

Package Import

```
import org.openqa.selenium.safari.SafariDriver;
```

Code for setup and initiating the script

```
// Configuration of Browser Properties is highly recommended for proper
functioning of the code

WebDriver driver=new SafariDriver();

// In the example above, we are creating an instance of WebDriver by
creating a // new SafariDriver Object
// Safari Driver leverages the existing WebDriver object
```

Opera Browser:

For Opera, there is no dedicated driver and it is better to use OperaChromiumDriver extended using ChromeDriver. This technically uses ChromeDriver to do the automation.

Let's take a python example

```
from selenium import webdriver
from selenium.webdriver.chrome import service

#Instantiate the webdriver service for Opera
OperaWebdriver_service = service.Service('<<INCLUDE THE PATH WHERE
OPERADRIVER IS LOCATED')
OperaWebdriver_service.start()

#Set WebDriver capabilities for Opera
operadriver = webdriver.Remote(OperaWebdriver_service.service_url,
webdriver.DesiredCapabilities.OPERA)

#Set Perform a search on Bing Web site
operadriver.get('https://www.bing.com/')
input_txt = operadriver.find_element_by_xpath('/html//input[@id='sb_
form_q']')
input_txt.send_keys('Selenium Opera Driver\n')
```

```
#Close
operadriver.quit()
```

```
# In the example above, we are creating an instance of WebDriver by
creating a # new RemoteDriver Object and by passing
# Opera Driver parameters such as version
# and the location of the driver executable
```

Headless Browser Instantiation

We willcover Headless Browser testing in detail in the next section. For simplicity, the instantiation of the web drivers will be as follows:

PhantomJS Driver:

Package Import

```
import org.openqa.selenium.phantomjs.PhantomJSDriver;
```

Code for setup and initiating the script

```
// Configuration of Browser Properties is highly recommended for proper
functioning of the code
```

```
WebDriver driver=new PhantomJSDriver();
```

```
// In the example above, we are creating an instance of WebDriver by
creating a // new PhantomJSDriver Object and by passing
// Phantom JS Headless Browser Driver parameters such as version
// and the location of the driver executable
```

HtmlUnit Driver:

Package Import

```
import org.openqa.selenium.htmlunit.HtmlUnitDriver;
```

Code for setup and initiating the script

```
// Configuration of Browser Properties is highly recommended for proper
functioning of the code
```

```
WebDriver driver=new HtmlUnitDriver();
```

```
// In the example above, we are creating an instance of WebDriver by
creating a // new HtmlUnitDriver Object and by passing
// Html Unit Headless Browser Driver parameters such as version
// and the location of the driver executable
```

Once instantiated, the code for the remaining actions will be exactly similar. This is the beauty of the library-based application automation approach using Selenium.

Headless Browser Testing

Headless browser testing offers a lot of benefits to the automation programmer. The concept is like this. A webdriver instance is created and run in the background. This is very useful for validating programs that don't mandate many variants of user behavior. Headless browser testing permits the automation suite to be executed any time of the day like a batch program as a browser invocation is not needed in the system. The developer can work on other tasks in parallel while the background execution is going on, and thus a productivity enhancement is a direct benefit. Human intervention-related test failure avoidance, increased the memory consumption avoidance are two additional benefits we can derive.

In general, headless browsers consume fewer resources and thus are faster than typical browser-based test automation. A headless browser script is good where static content needs to be captured like a web scraping or web applications which needs minimal user interactions. We can also run a good application monitoring programs using a headless browser especially, if we want to capture the performance of the browser, background processes, etc. Common features like capturing a screenshot are all feasible with the headless browser just like in a regular webdriver-based application.

A few disadvantages are as follows. Firstly, we are not emulating the real end-user behavior, and hence it is better to avoid it for testing web apps with multiple types of user experience and behavior. Secondly, as the testing is backend, some of the user experience elements and cosmetic issues are difficult to find, unless a human checks the screenshots captured through a headless browser test outcome. Finally, most of the headless browser drivers are open-sourced and do not have similar support or backing like the Selenium tool itself so there is a chance for lack of support in the long run. In spite of all these aspects, headless browser testing is a widely used and a successful phenomenon.

Now, let us see an example of Headless Browser Testing with PhantomJS Driver. To run this program, you need to download the PhantomJS driver and the jar files and configure them in your IDE under the library path of the project. Once configured, we can create a simple path by setting the Driver file (Phantomjs.exe) path and creating a new instance of `PhantomJSWebDriver`. *Please note that PhantomJS is deprecated in 2017 and is planned to be taken out when Selenium 4.0 is launched.* The rest of the code is similar to any other webdriver-based test execution. For example, we are running a simple search on the Bing Search engine. Let us see the code:

Ch5_Prog_3_Headless_Browser_PhantomJS_Example.java

```java
1   package CrackSeleniumInterviewExamples;
2
3   import org.openqa.selenium.By;
4   import org.openqa.selenium.WebDriver;
5   import org.openqa.selenium.WebElement;
6   import org.openqa.selenium.phantomjs.PhantomJSDriver;
7
8   import java.io.File;
9
10  public class Ch5_Prog_3_Headless_Browser_PhantomJS_Example {
11  public static void main(String[] args) throws InterruptedException {
12  //Set the path of the PhantomJS Driver file location
13          File headlessDriverFile = new File("C:\\ Selenium\\phantomjs.exe");
14  System.setProperty("phantomjs.binary.path", headlessDriverFile.
      getAbsolutePath());
15  //Create a new instance
16  WebDriver driver = new PhantomJSDriver();
17  //Let's start a search at Bing.com
18  driver.get("http://www.bing.com");
19  //Let's start a search
20  //Use the XPATH element for Search text /html//input[@id='sb_form_q']
21  WebElement element = driver.findElement(By.xpath("/html//input[@
      id='sb_form_q']"));
22  element.sendKeys("Selenium");
23  element.submit();
24  //Let's check the Title Page and the length of the file
25  System.out.println("Page title is: " + driver.getTitle());
26  System.out.println("Page output length of HTML page is: " +driver.
      getPageSource().length());
27  //Close the driver
28  driver.quit();
29      }
30  }
```

Now, let's see the outcome of this program. As you can see, only twolines of output are relevant for the program. All the actions were done without the invocation of a browser and the user interactions:

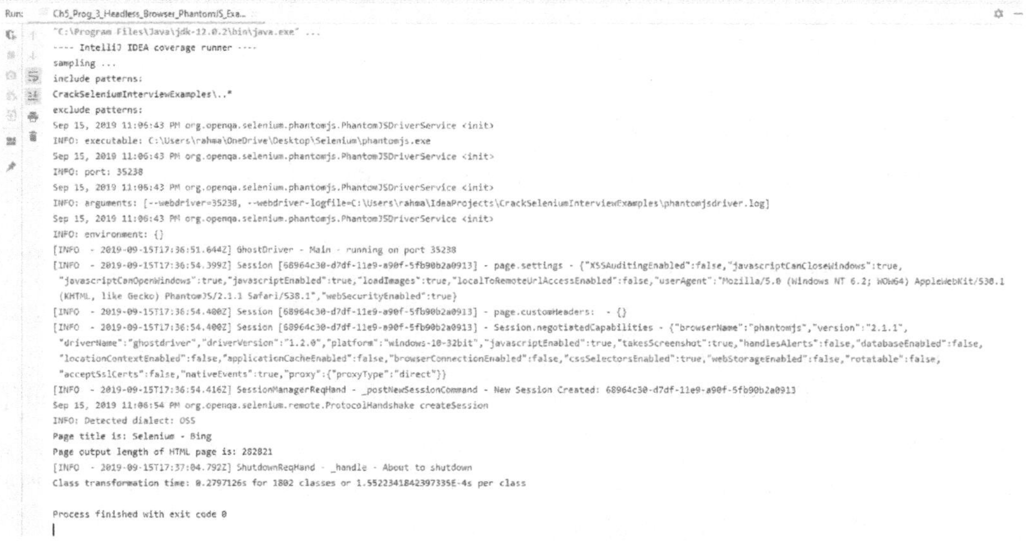

```
Run: Ch5_Prog_3_Headless_Browser_PhantomJS_Exa...
"C:\Program Files\Java\jdk-12.0.2\bin\java.exe" ...
---- IntelliJ IDEA coverage runner ----
sampling ...
include patterns:
CrackSeleniumInterviewExamples\..*
exclude patterns:
Sep 15, 2019 11:06:43 PM org.openqa.selenium.phantomjs.PhantomJSDriverService <init>
INFO: executable: C:\Users\rahma\OneDrive\Desktop\Selenium\phantomjs.exe
Sep 15, 2019 11:06:43 PM org.openqa.selenium.phantomjs.PhantomJSDriverService <init>
INFO: port: 35238
Sep 15, 2019 11:06:43 PM org.openqa.selenium.phantomjs.PhantomJSDriverService <init>
INFO: arguments: [--webdriver=35238, --webdriver-logfile=C:\Users\rahma\IdeaProjects\CrackSeleniumInterviewExamples\phantomjsdriver.log]
Sep 15, 2019 11:06:43 PM org.openqa.selenium.phantomjs.PhantomJSDriverService <init>
INFO: environment: {}
[INFO  - 2019-09-15T17:36:51.644Z] GhostDriver - Main - running on port 35238
[INFO  - 2019-09-15T17:36:54.399Z] Session [68964c30-d7df-11e9-a90f-5fb90b2a0913] - page.settings - {"XSSAuditingEnabled":false,"javascriptCanCloseWindows":true,
 "javascriptCanOpenWindows":true,"javascriptEnabled":true,"loadImages":true,"localToRemoteUrlAccessEnabled":false,"userAgent":"Mozilla/5.0 (Windows NT 6.2; WOW64) AppleWebKit/538.1
 (KHTML, like Gecko) PhantomJS/2.1.1 Safari/538.1","webSecurityEnabled":true}
[INFO  - 2019-09-15T17:36:54.400Z] Session [68964c30-d7df-11e9-a90f-5fb90b2a0913] - page.customHeaders:  - {}
[INFO  - 2019-09-15T17:36:54.400Z] Session [68964c30-d7df-11e9-a90f-5fb90b2a0913] - Session.negotiatedCapabilities - {"browserName":"phantomjs","version":"2.1.1",
 "driverName":"ghostdriver","driverVersion":"1.2.0","platform":"windows-10-32bit","javascriptEnabled":true,"takesScreenshot":true,"handlesAlerts":false,"databaseEnabled":false,
 "locationContextEnabled":false,"applicationCacheEnabled":false,"browserConnectionEnabled":false,"cssSelectorsEnabled":true,"webStorageEnabled":false,"rotatable":false,
 "acceptSslCerts":false,"nativeEvents":true,"proxy":{"proxyType":"direct"}}
[INFO  - 2019-09-15T17:36:54.416Z] SessionManagerReqHand - _postNewSessionCommand - New Session Created: 68964c30-d7df-11e9-a90f-5fb90b2a0913
Sep 15, 2019 11:06:54 PM org.openqa.selenium.remote.ProtocolHandshake createSession
INFO: Detected dialect: OSS
Page title is: Selenium - Bing
Page output length of HTML page is: 282821
[INFO  - 2019-09-15T17:37:04.792Z] ShutdownReqHand - _handle - About to shutdown
Class transformation time: 0.2797126s for 1802 classes or 1.552234184239733SE-4s per class

Process finished with exit code 0
```

Figure 5.5: Headless Browser Testing Output

Conclusion

In this chapter, we focused on the fundamentals of the web application. We understood what makes up a web application and a web page. We looked at the core elements an automation engineer needs to understand while using Selenium for automation. We got introduced to HTML, CSS, DOM, and the important elements and aspects that make up the concept. We discussed some of the core concepts of the web browser automation such as screen size management. We got introduced to the concepts such as headless browser testing which is very important for test automation especially, in web applications having limited user interactions or for testing the infrastructure and continuous build-related needs using automation. We also saw the various types of browsers and how to instantiate the web driver session across browsers. In the upcoming chapters, we will delve into details about the Selenium features, including programming on the top languages used for Selenium automation.

Questions

1. What are the key architectural components of a Web UI?
2. What are the different locators and syntax of XPATH locators?
3. What are the different locators and syntax of CSS locators?

4. How will you handle asynchronous event handlers while using locators?

5. How is an HTML web page structure mapped? What are itskey constituents?

6. How will you build a **Document Object Model (DOM)** tree?

7. What is CSS? What are the benefits of CSS?

8. What is an element locator?

9. What are the ways available to locate an element using Selenium?

10. How will you resize the window using Selenium? What are itsbenefits?

11. What is Headless Browser Testing? What are the benefits and drawbacks of using a Headless Browser?

12. What is a `PhantomJS` driver? How will you use it?

13. What is a `FluentWait()`? Where will you use it?

14. What are the differences between implicit and explicit waits in Selenium? When will you use them?

15. What is the difference between an absolute and relative XPath?

16. How will you implement a custom locator function in Selenium?

17. What is the difference between a DOM and a **Page Object Model (POM)**?

CHAPTER 6
Web UI Automation with Selenium

"Good programmers write code for humans first and computers next."

– Anonymous

In *Chapter 6* we shall leverage the concepts learned so far and try to run some programsusing Python to evaluate some of the core features of Selenium. While not all concepts in Selenium can be covered in a single chapter, we will focus on Python coding with reference to a few examples in this chapteras against Java coding used in Chapter5 to give a distinctive flavour of Selenium ecosystem.

Structure

In this chapter, we will covert he following concepts using the Selenium-centric Python coding:

- Python programs to understand the components of Web UI
- Simulation of screen sizes
- Correlation between various locators using DOM, CSS in an HTML Page
- Python event handling for Selenium
- Use of Python to handle cookies in a web site
- Use of Python code to invoke various browsers

- Use of `WebDriver.Firefox,WebDriver.FireFoxProfile`, `WebDriver.Chrome` and `WebDriver.ChromeOptions()`, `DesiredCapabilities` classes
- Initiating browsers for Internet Explorer, Opera, Safari and PhantomJS
- Use of PhantomJS for Headless Browser Testing to test Web UI
- Use of advanced Webdriver functions in Python

Objective

In this chapter, we will cover the core aspects of WebUI automation to a certain degree, including what is a **HypertextMarkup Language (HTML)**, usage of **Cascading Style Sheets (CSS)** and **Document Object Model (DOM)**, that largely makeup how content is rendered and interacted within a web application, in addition to actions performed by the user. We shall also look at various approaches to locate various web elements, choose the selectors in the Web UI, customize various IDs and elements in a page, have a mechanism to handle events and take care of asynchronous interactions. The objective of this chapter is to address all these points. We shall also look at some nice features of Selenium such as asynchronous interactions, setting up of a proxy configuration, accessing web application through headless browsers, and handling cookies.

Python example to understand the components of Web UI

Let us take a simple example first, which would invoke a web browser using a Python program. Mentioned in *Figure 6.1*, *Ch_6_Prog_1_Inaugurate_Browsers* is a simple program, which can be used to open a browser, open a search site and run a search on "Selenium" as a search string. This program is made modular using "testBrowser" as a function to be called. We can instantiate any type of browser (chrome, firefox etc.) through invoking WebDriver interface and pass it as a handle to the calling function. Depending on the instantiation of the browser through the WebDriver, the program will execute the action in the specified browser and share the results. For example, we are using **the Chrome** browser. However, this can be either Firefox, Safari, Opera, Internet Explorer bowsers or an Edge browser.

```python
from selenium import webdriver

def testBrowser(browserDriver):
    SearchURL = 'https://www.bing.com'
    SearchPhrase = 'Selenium'
    browserDriver.get(SearchURL)
    browserDriver.find_element_by_xpath("/html//input[@id='sb_form_q']").send_keys(SearchPhrase)
    browserDriver.find_element_by_xpath("//html//input[@id='sb_form_go']").click()
    print(browserDriver.current_url)
    print(browserDriver.page_source)
    browserDriver.close()
    browserDriver.quit()


print("Let us try a simple XPATH based search in a website")
driver= webdriver.Chrome()
driver.set_window_size(1120, 550)
testBrowser(driver)
print("Exiting the program successfully")
```

Figure 6.1: Ch_6_Prog_1_Inaugurate_Browsers.py

Correlation between various locators using DOM, CSS in an HTML Page

Now, let us try a simple locator program by invoking the Internet Sample app available at *Heroku App*. The site **http://the-internet.herokuapp.com** has some brilliant examples for a web automation project to test the capabilities. For the example, we will take the simple login example provided on the site. The code mentioned in *Figure 6.3*, as Ch_6_Prog_2_Heroku_Katz_Login_SIDE.py, uses simple locators, such as find_element_by_name, find_element_by_id and find_element_by_xpath, as a means to navigate the web application. This program is modularized and the code is built to run against a unit test framework for Python likeunittest or pytest. A couple of functions have been added to it to check if apop-up alert is present on the page. In addition, to deal with the program, another function is also added to check the availability of a web element. Such a level of modularization and use of a POM (we willcover POMin a future chapter) are good programming practices to follow.

```python
# -*- coding: utf-8 -*-
from selenium import webdriver
from selenium.webdriver.common.by import By
from selenium.webdriver.common.keys import Keys
from selenium.webdriver.support.ui import Select
from selenium.common.exceptions import NoSuchElementException
from selenium.common.exceptions import NoAlertPresentException
import unittest, time, re

class InternetHeroku(unittest.TestCase):
    def setUp(self):
        self.driver = webdriver.Chrome()
        self.driver.implicitly_wait(30)
        self.base_url = "https://www.google.com/"
        self.verificationErrors = []
        self.accept_next_alert = True

    def test_internet_heroku(self):
        driver = self.driver
        driver.get("https://the-internet.herokuapp.com/")
        driver.find_element_by_xpath("(.//*[normalize-space(text()) and normalize-space(.)='Available Examples'])[1]/following::li[1]").click()
        driver.find_element_by_link_text("Form Authentication").click()
        driver.find_element_by_id("username").click()
        print("Entered User Name")
        driver.find_element_by_id("username").clear()
        driver.find_element_by_id("username").send_keys("tomsmith")
        driver.find_element_by_id("password").clear()
        driver.find_element_by_id("password").send_keys("SuperSecretPassword!")
        print("Entered Password")
        driver.find_element_by_xpath("(.//*[normalize-space(text()) and normalize-space(.)='Password'])[1]/following::i[1]").click()
        driver.find_element_by_id("flash").click()
        driver.find_element_by_xpath("(.//*[normalize-space(text()) and normalize-space(.)='Welcome to the Secure Area. When you are done click logou below.'])[1]/following::i[1]").click()
        driver.find_element_by_id("flash").click()
        print("Entered Empty Click")
        driver.find_element_by_xpath("(.//*[normalize-space(text()) and normalize-space(.)='Password'])[1]/following::i[1]").click()
        driver.find_element_by_id("flash").click()
        driver.find_element_by_xpath("(.//*[normalize-space(text()) and normalize-space(.)='SuperSecretPassword!'])[1]/following::div[1]").click()
        print("Let's click the exit button")
        driver.close()
        print("End of the program")

    def is_element_present(self, how, what):
        try: self.driver.find_element(by=how, value=what)
        except NoSuchElementException as e: return False
        return True

    def is_alert_present(self):
        try: self.driver.switch_to_alert()
        except NoAlertPresentException as e: return False
        return True

    def close_alert_and_get_its_text(self):
        try:
            alert = self.driver.switch_to_alert()
            alert_text = alert.text
            if self.accept_next_alert:
                alert.accept()
            else:
                alert.dismiss()
            return alert_text
        finally: self.accept_next_alert = True

    def tearDown(self):
        self.driver.quit()
        self.assertEqual([], self.verificationErrors)

if __name__ == "__main__":
    unittest.main()
```

Figure 6.2: Ch_6_Prog_2_Heroku_Katz_Login_SIDE.py

Let us take another example where we will use the CSS selectors and explore how to navigate the deep-DOM web pages. In the example, we have taken the-internet. herokuapp as a sample.We will navigate the application using the CSS selectors. Mentioned in *Figure 6.3*, the `Ch_6_Prog_3_HerokuApp_Navigation.py` uses the features that we discussed in *Chapter 5* and utilizes find_element_by_css_selector and find_element_by_link_text functions.

```
Ch_6_Prog_3_HerokuApp_Navigation.py
1   # -*- coding: utf-8 -*-
2   from selenium import webdriver
3   from selenium.webdriver.common.by import By
4   from selenium.webdriver.common.keys import Keys
5   from selenium.webdriver.support.ui import Select
6   from selenium.common.exceptions import NoSuchElementException
7   from selenium.common.exceptions import NoAlertPresentException
8   import unittest, time, re
9
10  class InternetHerokuCSS(unittest.TestCase):
11      def setUp(self):
12          self.driver = webdriver.Chrome()
13          self.driver.implicitly_wait(30)
14          self.base_url = "https://www.google.com/"
15          self.verificationErrors = []
16          self.accept_next_alert = True
17
18      def test_internet_heroku_c_s_s(self):
19          driver = self.driver
20          driver.get("https://the-internet.herokuapp.com/")
21          print("Testing Deep DOM example")
22          driver.find_element_by_xpath("(.//*[normalize-space(text()) and normalize-space(.)='Basic Auth'])[1]/following::li[1]").click()
23          driver.find_element_by_link_text("Large & Deep DOM").click()
24          driver.find_element_by_id("sibling-49.1").click()
25          driver.find_element_by_css_selector("tr.row-4 > td.column-17").click()
26          driver.back()
27          print("Done Testing Deep DOM example")
28          print("Test Status Codes using Only CSS locators")
29          driver.find_element_by_link_text("Status Codes").click()
30          driver.find_element_by_css_selector("li > a").click()
31          driver.find_element_by_css_selector("p > a").click()
32          driver.find_element_by_link_text("301").click()
33          print("Test Status Code 301")
34          driver.find_element_by_css_selector("p > a").click()
35          driver.find_element_by_link_text("404").click()
36          print("Test Status Code 404")
37          driver.find_element_by_css_selector("p > a").click()
38          driver.find_element_by_link_text("500").click()
39          print("Test Status Code 500")
40          driver.find_element_by_css_selector("p > a").click()
41          print("Click External Link")
42          driver.find_element_by_css_selector("p > a").click()
43          driver.close()
44          print("Close the Program")
45
46      def is_element_present(self, how, what):
47          try: self.driver.find_element(by=how, value=what)
48          except NoSuchElementException as e: return False
49          return True
50
51      def is_alert_present(self):
52          try: self.driver.switch_to_alert()
53          except NoAlertPresentException as e: return False
54          return True
55
56      def close_alert_and_get_its_text(self):
57          try:
58              alert = self.driver.switch_to_alert()
59              alert_text = alert.text
60              if self.accept_next_alert:
61                  alert.accept()
62              else:
63                  alert.dismiss()
64              return alert_text
65          finally: self.accept_next_alert = True
66
67      def tearDown(self):
68          self.driver.quit()
69          self.assertEqual([], self.verificationErrors)
70
```

Figure 6.3: *Ch_6_Prog_3_HerokuApp_Navigation.py*

Python event handling for Selenium

Now, let us take an example of how to handle events in Python for a Selenium automation program. We had an example in Java while we were discussing this topic in *Chapter 5*. Let us see how it wouldlook like in a Python program. For example, we shall be performing a search in the Bing search engine.The program mentioned in *Figure 6.4* as `Ch_6_Prog_5_Python_Event_Listener.py` gives a modular view of how the `CustomPythonListener` class can be implemented. To implement a custom listener, we would extend the Abstract Event Listener and Event Firing WebDriver classes and execute the interface functions with our custom implementations. In the example, we have used a simple print statement to check the log of events and function calls based on the action performed by themain web driver.

```python
Ch_6_Prog_5_Python_Event_Listener.py
1   import unittest
2   from selenium import webdriver
3   from selenium.webdriver import Chrome
4   from selenium.webdriver.support.events import EventFiringWebDriver, AbstractEventListener
5
6   class CustomPythonListener(AbstractEventListener):
7       def before_navigate_to(self, url, driver):
8           print("Event Handler Function for actions before navigating to ", url)
9       def after_navigate_to(self, url, driver):
10          print("Event Handler Function for actions after navigating to ", url)
11      def before_navigate_back(self, driver):
12          print("Event Handler Function for actions before navigating back ", driver.current_url)
13      def after_navigate_back(self, driver):
14          print("Event Handler Function for actions after navigating back ", driver.current_url)
15      def before_navigate_forward(self, driver):
16          print("Event Handler Function for actions before navigating forward ", driver.current_url)
17      def after_navigate_forward(self, driver):
18          print("Event Handler Function for actions after navigating forward ", driver.current_url)
19      def before_find(self, by, value, driver):
20          print("Event Handler Function for before find")
21      def after_find(self, by, value, driver):
22          print("Event Handler Function for after_find")
23      def before_click(self, element, driver):
24          print("Event Handler Function for before_click")
25      def after_click(self, element, driver):
26          print("Event Handler Function for after_click")
27      def before_change_value_of(self, element, driver):
28          print("Event Handler Function for before_change_value_of")
29      def after_change_value_of(self, element, driver):
30          print("Event Handler Function for after_change_value_of")
31      def before_execute_script(self, script, driver):
32          print("Event Handler Function for before_execute_script")
33      def after_execute_script(self, script, driver):
34          print("Event Handler Function for after_execute_script")
35      def before_close(self, driver):
36          print("Event Handler Function before closing the browser driver")
37      def after_close(self, driver):
38          print("Event Handler Function after closing the browser driver")
39      def before_quit(self, driver):
40          print("Event Handler Function for before_quit")
41      def after_quit(self, driver):
42          print("Event Handler Function for after_quit")
43      def on_exception(self, exception, driver):
44          print("Event Handler Function for on_exception")
45
46  class Test(unittest.TestCase):
47      def test_logging_file(self):
48          myWebDriver = webdriver.Chrome()
49          eventListenerDriver = EventFiringWebDriver(myWebDriver, CustomPythonListener())
50          eventListenerDriver.get("https://www.bing.com")
51          eventListenerDriver.find_element_by_xpath(".//html//input[@id='sb_form_q']").send_keys("Testing Event in Selenium Using Python")
52          eventListenerDriver.find_element_by_xpath("//html//input[@id='sb_form_go']").click()
53          eventListenerDriver.close()
54
55  if __name__ == "__main__":
56      unittest.main()
```

Figure 6.4: Ch_6_Prog_5_Python_Event_Listener.py

This program would produce the following output:

```
In [8]: runfile('C:/Users/rahma/Ch_6_Prog_5_Python_Event_Listener.PY', wdir='C:/Users/rahma')
Event Handler Function for actions before navigating to  https://www.bing.com
Event Handler Function for actions after navigating to  https://www.bing.com
Event Handler Function for before find
Event Handler Function for after_find
Event Handler Function for before_change_value_of
Event Handler Function for after_change_value_of
Event Handler Function for before find
Event Handler Function for after_find
Event Handler Function for before_click
Event Handler Function for after_click
Event Handler Function before closing the browser driver
.Event Handler Function after closing the browser driver

----------------------------------------------------------------------
Ran 1 test in 14.902s

OK
```

Figure 6.5: Output of Python Event Listener Class Implementation Program

Simulation of screen sizes

Continuing on the Java examples used in *Chapter 5*, let us see how to emulate screen sizes and browser settings in Python.

1. We can set a browser position using the `set_window_position()` function available in WebDriver using the following command:

   a. `driver.set_window_position(x=150, y=250)`

2. We can set the window size by specifying the X, Y start coordinates, width and height using the following `Set_Window_rect()` function:

   a. `driver.set_window_rect(x=150, y=250, width=400, height=400)`

3. We can maximize the browser window using the following `maximize_window()` function:

   a. `driver.maximize_window()`

4. We can use full desktop size using the following `fullscreen_window()` function as well:

   a. `driver.fullscreen_window()`

5. For setting a window size, we can use `set_window_size()` function:

   a. `driver.set_window_size(300, 750)`

6. To get the current window position, we can use the following `get_window_position()` function:

   a. `driver.get_window_position()`

The use of varying window sizes will be very useful and relevant in performing cross-browser testing.

Asynchronous interaction

There are two ways to handle the asynchronous interaction. First, by leveragingthe asynchronous JavaScript inline function.Second, byleveraging the various types of waits such as implicit wait, explicit wait and fluent wait.

Let us take the first option of executing the JavaScript inline. See *Figure 6.6.*

```
Ch_6_Async_example.py
1   //Async Script execution of a JavaScript Code in Python
2   execute_async_script(script, *arguments)
3
4   driver.execute_async_script("return Math.PI")
5   //Above code prints value of mathematical constant PI (22/7)
6
7   driver.execute_async_script("function myFunction(a, b) { return a*b;}", 5,125)
8   //Above code prints 625
9
```

Figure 6.6: Asynchronous Example

Let us now take an example of printing all the DOM objects on a page using the asynchronous JavaScript function. See *Figure 6.7.*

```
Ch_6_Async_example_JS.py
1   p = browserDriver.find_elements_by_tag_name("p")
2   inputs = browserDriver.execute_script(
3       "var p = arguments[0], inputs = []; for (var i=0; i < p.length; i++){" +
4       "inputs.push(document.getElementById(p[i].getAttribute('for'))); } return inputs;", p)
5   print(inputs)
6
```

Figure 6.7: Asynchronous Example Using JavaScript

If we will execute the script mentioned in *Figure 6.7* in a search engine, such as Bing, the output would look like:

[None, None]

In a web page with labels and classes, we can use thisJavaScript to modify and extract the DOM tree. The content available in the Python program can also be utilized usedfor Selenium.

The second way to introduce asynchronous wait in Selenium is to use the available language-specific Async-Await features such as asyncio function available in Python. This can be seen in the code snippet mentioned in *Figure 6.8.* Async-wait function along with the use of creating the task and other mechanisms allows the programmers to create parallelism in programming. This feature is available in the latest versions of the languages including Python 3.7.4 and may not be available in earlier versions of Python or JavaScript. The code snippet for use of asynchronous wait in Python can be clubbed with a web page specific asynchronous wait to handle dynamic behaviour of the programs.

```python
# Ch_6_AsyncIO_JS.py
1   import asyncio
2   import time
3
4   async def say_something_async(delay, messagepassed):
5       await asyncio.sleep(delay)
6       print(messagepassed)
7
8   async def main():
9       print(" This function started at {time.strftime('%X')}")
10      await say_something_async (1, 'Hello World')
11      await say_something_async (2, 'Happy Coding')
12      print("This function finished at {time.strftime('%X')}")
13
14  asyncio.run(main())
15
```

Figure 6.8: AsyncIO Example

Let us get to the available simple asynchronistic options that we covered in detail in *Chapter 5*. *Figure 6.9* shows a program that we have taken as an example. This will be used to evaluate the outcomes.

```python
# Ch_6_Prog_7_Browser_Invocations_New.py
1   from selenium import webdriver
2   from selenium.webdriver.common.keys import Keys
3   import time
4   from selenium.webdriver.support import expected_conditions as EC
5   from selenium.webdriver.support.ui import WebDriverWait
6   from selenium.webdriver.common.by import By
7
8   time.sleep(3)
9   driver = webdriver.Chrome(executable_path ="C:\\ Selenium\\chromedriver.exe")
10  driver.get("http://www.duckduckgo.com")
11  time.sleep(2)
12  assert "DuckDuckGo" in driver.title
13  elem = driver.find_element_by_id("search_form_input_homepage")
14  elem.send_keys("Google")
15  elem.send_keys(Keys.RETURN)
16  time.sleep(7)
17  driver.save_screenshot("screenshot_DDG.png")
18  print("Success 1")
19
```

Figure 6.9: Ch_6_Prog_7_Browser_Invocations_New.py

As you can see in *Figure 6.9*, the program has been able to capture the essential implicit wait and explicit wait options with the following code snippets:

```
time.sleep(3)
```

```
driver.implicitly_wait(5)
```

```
elem=WebDriverWait(driver, 10).until(EC.presence_of_element_located((By.ID,"email")))
```

As you can see, the above program covers the example of the implicit wait and explicit wait options. The screen output will look like:

Success 1

The actual search screenshot will be like the following:

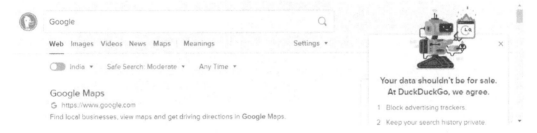

Figure 6.10: Browser Invocation Output

Use of Python to handle cookies in a web site

Almost all the web sites use cookies for tracking user behaviour, preferences and state of various transactions performed. This gives an advantage to the websites to offer better user experience by remembering the preferences, actions, breadcrumb of activities performed, personalization, order statuses etc., for a seamless personalized experience. However, all this comes at a cost of privacy and tracking of personal information, which is done by multiple parties including ad agencies that keep a tab on the info for advertisements. Hence, cookies play a major role in website content and it is important to test this aspect well both fromthe functional stability standpoint and the privacy standpoint.

Let us take a simple example of printing the cookies on a website. We are modifying the first program of this chapter a bit to do the same. See *Figure 6.11*.

```
◆ Ch_6_Prog_8_Cookies_Check.py
1    from selenium import webdriver
2
3    def testBrowser(browserDriver):
4      SearchURL = 'https://www.bing.com'
5      SearchPhrase = 'Selenium'
6      browserDriver.get(SearchURL)
7      print("Let us try a simple XPATH based search in a website")
8      browserDriver.find_element_by_xpath("/html//input[@id='sb_form_q']").send_keys(SearchPhrase)
9      browserDriver.find_element_by_xpath("//html//input[@id='sb_form_go']").click()
10     print(browserDriver.current_url)
11     for cookie in browserDriver.get_cookies():
12       print("%s -> %s" % (cookie['name'], cookie['value']))
13     browserDriver.close()
14     browserDriver.quit()
15
16   print("Let Us try XPATH search and Cookie Check")
17   driver= webdriver.Chrome()
18   driver.set_window_size(1120, 550)
19   testBrowser(driver)
20   print("Exiting the program successfully")
```

Figure 6.11: Cookies Management Program

In the program, the following code snippet would do the work for us:

```
for cookie in browserDriver.get_cookies():

    print("%s -> %s" % (cookie['name'], cookie['value']))
```

For adding the cookie, we can use the add_cookie function with the following syntax:

```
driver.add_cookie({'name':'key', 'value':'value', 'path':'/'})
```

For deleting the cookie, we can use the delete_cookie or delete_all_cookies functions with the following syntax:

```
# Deleting Cookies By name

driver.delete_cookie("CookieName")

# Or all of them

driver.delete_all_cookies()
```

For the program given in *Figure 6.11*, the output would be as follows:

```
Let us try a simple XPATH based search in a website
https://www.bing.com/search?q=Selenium&qs=n&form=QBLH&sp=-1&pq=selenium&sc=8-8&sk=&cvid=29D97B48D96C4787A7165CB0CD5A5334
_SS -> SID=2A6BAA7F9A4A67401EA0A7A79B76662B&HV=1568529813&bIm=781
SRCHHPGUSR -> CW=1087&CH=401&DPR=1&UTC=330&WTS=63704126606
_EDGE_S -> mkt=en-in&F=1&SID=2A6BAA7F9A4A67401EA0A7A79B76662B
MUIDB -> 2B3DE5D19F74682C0B1FE8099E486906
_EDGE_V -> 1
ipv6 -> hit=1568533413509&t=4
SRCHUSR -> DOB=20190915
SRCHUID -> V=2&GUID=534A2DAC0EAF41179ABD53C7130BF368&dmnchg=1
MUID -> 2B3DE5D19F74682C0B1FE8099E486906
SRCHD -> AF=NOFORM
Exiting the program successfully
```

Figure 6.12: Cookies Program Output

Use of Python code to invoke various browsers

In Python, the ways to invoke various browsers are almost similar to the examples we saw in *Chapter 2* and *Chapter 5*. In this section, we shall touch upon some additional classes that configure the browser profiles, options and capabilities.

Let us see the following aspects in detail:

Webdrivers

```
WebDriver.Firefox
```

```
WebDriver.Chrome
```

```
WebDriver.Ie
```

```
WebDriver.Opera
```

```
WebDriver.PhantomJS
```

```
WebDriver.Remote
```

Key functions of WebDriver

WebDriver.DesiredCapabilities

WebDriver.FirefoxProfile

WebDriver.ChromeOptions

WebDriver.ActionChains

WebDriver.TouchActions

WebDriver.Proxy

WebDriver.Firefox and WebDriver. FireFoxProfile classes

For initiating the Firefox, we can use multiple modes. The simplest one would be a simple `driver= webdriver.Firefox()`. Other options to initiate the Firefox browser includes the use of the configuration of Firefox capabilities and options. The two code snippets that show one way to initiate the Firefox browser are given below. We can also use `FirefoxProfile` class to set the profile configuration. We will refer to the `FireFoxProfile` class later.

```python
options = Options()
options.add_argument("-profile")
options.add_argument("GECKO DRIVER LOCATION")
firefox_capabilities = DesiredCapabilities.FIREFOX
firefox_capabilities['marionette'] = True
print("Capability Set")
driver = webdriver.Firefox(capabilities=firefox_capabilities,
                           firefox_options=options,
                           GECKO DRIVER LOCATION)
driver= webdriver.Firefox(firefox_profile=None,
firefox_binary=None, timeout=30, capabilities=None,
 proxy=None, executable_path='GECKO DRIVER LOCATION',firefox_
options=None)
```

For setting up a Firefoxbrowser profile,we can use `FirefoxProfile` class. By using `set_preference()` function, we can set all the browser preferences. This is similar to opening up the browser settings and updating each of the hundreds of options we have at our disposal to configure. If the profile setting is handy in terms of corporate application profiles, it needs to be tested for certain types of configurations. For example, a firm may restrict the saving of files or download of plugins via a web browser as a security measure. If we want to validate an application in a controlled environment, these features would come very handy.

```python
firefox_profile = webdriver.FirefoxProfile()

firefox_profile.set_preference("browser.cache.disk.enable",False)
firefox_profile.set_preference("browser.cache.memory.enable",False)
firefox_profile.set_preference("browser.cache.offline.enable",False)
firefox_profile.set_preference("browser.download.dir",tempDir)
firefox_profile.set_preference("javascript.enabled",False)
firefox_profile.set_preference("media.autoplay.enabled",False)
firefox_profile.set_preference("network.cookie.lifetimePolicy",2)
firefox_profile.set_preference("network.dns.disablePrefetch",True)
firefox_profile.set_preference("plugin.state.java",0)
firefox_profile.set_preference("signon.rememberSignons",False)
firefox_profile.set_preference("webdriver.load.strategy","unstable")
firefox_profile.set_preference('app.update.auto',False)
firefox_profile.set_preference('app.update.enabled',False)
firefox_profile.set_preference('browser.download.dir',destination)
```

```
firefox_profile.set_preference('enable.native.events',True)
firefox_profile.set_preference('html5.offmainthread',False)
firefox_profile.set_preference('network.http.pipelining',True)
firefox_profile.set_preference('network.http.pipelining.maxrequests',8)
firefox_profile.set_preference('network.http.pipelining.ssl',True)
firefox_profile.set_preference('network.http.spdy.enabled',False)
firefox_profile.set_preference('webdriver.enable.native.events',True)
```

After the profile setting is complete, we can update the browser settings using update_preferences() function. Post this setup; we can invoke the Firefox WebDriver class for our automation.

WebDriver.Chrome and WebDriver.ChromeOptions()

For initiating Chrome, we can use multiple modes. The simplest is a `driver= webdriver.Chrome()`. However, we can also use `ChromeOptions()` class to set various parameters with the help of the **add_argument** function for various choices.

```
def set_chrome_options():
        chrome_options = webdriver.ChromeOptions()
        chrome_options.accept_untrusted_certs = True
        chrome_options.assume_untrusted_cert_issuer = True
        chrome_options.add_argument("--no-sandbox")
        chrome_options.add_argument("--disable-impl-side-painting")
        chrome_options.add_argument("--disable-breakpad")
        chrome_options.add_argument("user-data-dir=" + profilePath)
        chrome_options.add_argument('window-size=1920x1080')

        #For running Browser in a Headless Manner
        chrome_options.add_argument("--headless")
        chrome_options.add_argument("--disable-gpu")
        chrome_options.add_argument("--start-fullscreen")

        return chrome_options


driver = webdriver.Chrome(chrome_options = set_chrome_options)
```

DesiredCapabilities

Let us see how we can set the DesiredCapabilities.To do this, we are referring to the code snippet for a Selenium Grid that we configured in an earlier *Chapter 4*. In addition, to perform a test on a particular configuration of a browser, we can use the DesiredCapabilities to configure the parameters such as the platform, browser version, JavaScript features etc. However, one point to note is that DesiredCapabilities class can only be used for running in grid for browser capability test with different browser configuration.

Let us see an example through a code snippet for the usage of DesiredCapabilities.

```python
from selenium import webdriver

selenium_grid_url = "http://198.0.0.8:4444/wd/hub"

# Create a desired capabilities object as a starting point.
capabilities = DesiredCapabilities.CHROME.copy()
capabilities['platform'] = "LINUX"

# Instantiate an instance of Remote WebDriver with the desired capabilities.
driver = webdriver.Remote(desired_capabilities=capabilities,
                          command_executor=selenium_grid_url)
```

The default capabilities for various types of browsers are mentioned below. The detailed summary is available on the Python documentation website for Selenium accessible at **https://selenium-python.readthedocs.io/api.html**.

ANDROID	{'browserName': 'android', 'platform': 'ANDROID', 'version': ''}
CHROME	{'browserName': 'chrome', 'platform': 'ANY', 'version': ''}
EDGE	{'browserName': 'MicrosoftEdge', 'platform': 'WINDOWS', 'version': ''}
FIRE FOX	{'acceptInsecureCerts': True, 'browserName': 'firefox', 'marionette': True}
HTML UNIT	{'browserName': 'htmlunit', 'platform': 'ANY', 'version': ''}
HTMLUNIT WITHJS	{'browserName': 'htmlunit', 'javascriptEnabled': True, 'platform': 'ANY', 'version': 'firefox'}
INTERNET EXPLORER	{'browserName': 'internet explorer', 'platform': 'WINDOWS', 'version': ''}
IPAD	{'browserName': 'iPad', 'platform': 'MAC', 'version': ''}
IPHONE	{'browserName': 'iPhone', 'platform': 'MAC', 'version': ''}

OPERA	`{'browserName': 'opera', 'platform': 'ANY', 'version': ''}`
PHANTOMJS	`{'browserName': 'phantomjs', 'javascriptEnabled': True, 'platform': 'ANY', 'version': ''}`
SAFARI	`{'browserName': 'safari', 'platform': 'MAC', 'version': ''}`
WEBKITGTK	`{'browserName': 'MiniBrowser', 'platform': 'ANY', 'version': ''}`

Table 6.1: Default Capabilities for WebDrivers

Initiating browsers for Internet Explorer, Opera, Safari and PhantomJS

Invocation of browsers for a newer set of browsers is simple with the webdriver classes outlined for each of the browsers.

1. **Internet Explorer**
   - `driver = webdriver.Ie`
2. **OPERA Browser**
   - `driver = webdriver.Opera`
3. **PhantomJS**
   - `Driver = webdriver.PhantomJS`

We will cover the use of a headless browser in the next section.

Use of PhantomJS for Headless Browser Testing

NOTE

PhantomJS has been deprecated since 2017 and may not be relevant in future releases of Selenium. This is more of reference

Let us see an example for the Headless Browser using PhantomJS. Following program is a simple search on two search engines – DuckDuckGo and Bing.

```
Ch_6_Prog_5_Headless_Py.py
1    from selenium import webdriver
2    driver = webdriver.PhantomJS()
3    driver.set_window_size(1120, 550)
4    driver.get("https://duckduckgo.com/")
5    driver.find_element_by_id('search_form_input_homepage').send_keys("Selenium")
6    driver.find_element_by_id("search_button_homepage").click()
7    print(driver.current_url)
8    driver.save_screenshot("screenshot_DuckDuckGo_SeleniumSearch.png")
9    driver.get("https://www.bing.com")
10   driver.find_element_by_xpath("/html//input[@id='sb_form_q']").send_keys("Selenium")
11   driver.find_element_by_xpath("/html//input[@id='sb_form_go']").click()
12   print(driver.current_url)
13   driver.save_screenshot("screenshot_Bing_SeleniumSearch.png")
14   driver.quit()
```

Figure 6.13: Ch_6_Prog_5_Headless_PY.py Program

The screen output for the print statements would look something like the following:

https://duckduckgo.com/?q=Selenium&t=h_

https://www.bing.com/search?q=Selenium&go=Submit&qs=ds&form=QBLH

The screenshots taken from the program would look like:

Figure 6.14: *Headless Browser Program Screenshot using Headless PhantomJS Browser*

When you execute this program, we will get a failed execution for the DuckDuckGo search. These are some of the challenges to address. The search failed as the locator search was not successful. We may need to add exception handling functions by using assert and validate title functions to exit gracefully.

WebDriver.ActionChains

Actions Chains class gives a way to handle a sequence of actions in a chain style to be executed simply. For example, a drag-and-drop action or a file-upload action or choosingan item in a multi-level menu can all be performed using an action chain. A simple way to highlightthis is as follows:

```
ActionChains(webDriver).key_down(Keys.CONTROL).send_keys('C').key_
up(Keys.CONTROL).perform()
```

The *ActionChains* statement can be split into multiple atomic level statements as given below. To explain in a simpler manner, the sequence specifiedin the *ActionChains* statement is a combination of a group of individual statements executed in the order specified below.

```
chainActions = ActionChains(webDriver)
```

```
chainActions.key_down(Keys.CONTROL)
```

```
chainActions.send_keys('C')
```

```
chainActions.key_up(Keys.CONTROL)
```

```
chainActions.perform()
```

WebDriver.TouchActions

Selenium also provides touch actions to touch-enabled devices and native or responsive web applications. `TouchActions` class has some functions that can be performed in a touch interface such as scroll, tap, select, move, double-click, drag-and-drop etc.

Some of the actions with syntax are as follows:

```
TouchActions(driver).double_tap(web_element)
//Web element is the element you want to tap – such as a button or a link

TouchActions(driver).flick(50, 60)
//XSpeed & YSpeed are pixel flicks per second

TouchActions(driver).flick_element(web_element, 50, 60)
//Flicking on a web element at a speed

TouchActions(driver).long_press(web_element)
//Perform a long press on a particular web element
```

```
TouchActions(driver).move(100,100)
//Move to a particular location in screen

TouchActions(driver).perform()
//Perform all stored actions at a go

TouchActions(driver).release(100,100)
// Release a previous hold at a coordinate

TouchActions(driver).scroll(200,200)
// Touch and Scroll to a particular coordinate

TouchActions(driver).scroll_from_element(web_element, 400, 600)
// Touch and Scroll from a particular web element to a particular coordinate

TouchActions(driver).tap(web_element)
// Tap on a particular web element

TouchActions(driver).tap_and_hold(200,200)
// Tap and hold on to a particular coordinate
```

All the touch actions will be very useful in the current context for the state the devices is in as all the devices (desktops, laptops, tablets and mobile phones) have a touch interface and most of the actions performed in a responsive web application will be touch-centric. Hence, it is better to understand the `TouchActions` class and leverage the features for efficient automation.

WebDriver.Proxy

Most of the corporate applications are behind a firewall or a demilitarized zone, and to communicate with applications or servers in a different zone or on the Internet, a proxy server may be required to protect the infrastructure. Hence,a use of proxy to make applications talk to each other becomes important. `WebDriver.Proxy` class gives a way to the programmers to establish the necessary connections to perform the actions.

Let us see the program to set a Webdriver proxy for a Chrome browser.

The first method is to use `DesiredCapabilities` option to set the proxy setting.

```
from selenium import webdriver

PROXY_SERVER_IP = "YOUR IP ADDRESS of the PROXY" //http://AA.BB.CC.DD:XXXXX
where XXXXX is port and AA.BB.CC.DD is the Proxy server IP
```

```
webdriver.DesiredCapabilities.CHROME['proxy']={

    "httpProxy": PROXY_SERVER_IP,

    "ftpProxy": PROXY_SERVER_IP,

    "sslProxy": PROXY_SERVER_IP,

    "noProxy":None,

    "proxyType":"MANUAL",

    "autodetect":False

}
```

```
driver = webdriver.Chrome() // or webdriver.Firefox()
```

```
driver.get('http://www.whatsmyip.net/') // Use a website to check your
public IP through the proxy
```

A second method is to use the Proxy() class and add the same to the DesiredCapabilities of the browser. Thus, the program above would be modified as:

```
from selenium.webdriver.common.proxy import Proxy, ProxyType

# Configure Proxy Option
Proxy_class = Proxy()
Proxy_class.proxy_type = ProxyType.MANUAL

# Proxy IP & Port
Proxy_class.http_proxy = "AA.BB.CC.DD:XXXXX"
Proxy_class.socks_proxy = "AA.BB.CC.DD:XXXXX"
Proxy_class.ssl_proxy = "AA.BB.CC.DD:XXXXX"

# Configure capabilities
desiredcapabilities = webdriver.DesiredCapabilities.CHROME
Proxy_class.add_to_capabilities(desiredcapabilities)
driver = webdriver.Chrome()
// or webdriver.Firefox()
driver.get('http://www.whatsmyip.net/')
// Use a website to check your public IP through the proxy
```

Both the code snippets perform more or less the same work.

Conclusion

In this chapter, we explored the Web UI automation in detail and used Python for programming examples to explain the WebUI automation concept., So far, we have been able to explore how to perform Selenium automation, how to leverage various features available in Selenium, how to set up a Selenium Grid, how to leverage WebDriver to perform various automation scripts. We also looked at some of the advanced concepts of Selenium. In the upcoming chapters, to expand our horizon of understanding, we'll check out moreadvanced concepts such as how to create a Page Object Model, how to modularize the scripts better, how to perform smooth exception handling etc.

Questions

1. How do you set up a proxy in Selenium using Python for a Firefox browser?

2. How do you set up a `FirefoxProfile` in Selenium? What are the benefits of it?

3. What are the benefits of headless testing in Selenium? How will you setup headless testing using `Chrome()`?

4. What is the use of `DesiredCapabilities` class? How is it useful?

5. What are the functions available in `TouchActions` class? Where will you use `TouchActions` class?

6. How does `ActionChains` class work in Selenium? How can ActionChains class be used? When will you use it?

7. How will you go about handling cookies in Selenium? What is the role of function add and delete cookies in Selenium?

8. How do you manage event handling in Python for a Selenium program? What are the different event handling functions available?

9. What are the asynchronous operations handling mechanisms in Python for usage in a Selenium script?

10. What is Async-Await functionality? How will you use it?

11. How will you set screen sizes in Selenium using Python?

CHAPTER 7

Selenium Coding with Other Languages (JavaScript, Ruby)

"The first rule of any technology used in a business is that automation applied to an efficient operation will magnify the efficiency. The second is that automation applied to an inefficient operation will magnify the inefficiency.

– Bill Gates"

Until now, we have looked at Selenium automation using the two most popular languages of choice, that is, Java and Python. In this chapter, we willlook at some of the concepts using other programming languages such as JavaScript and Ruby. We will also try to cover some programming examples in other languages (PHP, C#, etc.) that Selenium supports. Most of the concepts covered in this chapter will be a replication of the concepts covered earlier.

Structure

This chapter will cover programming examples in JavaScript, Ruby and other languages so that you can understand and explore the following concepts:

- Launch and closure of browsers
- Browser level automation tasks, including –
  - o URL/Web page navigation and URL information gathering

o Page-level automation like page info gathering, element identification and data capturing

o CSS and XPathelement locators, selectors and locator ID customization

o Management of **Document Object Model (DOM)**

o Simulation of screen sizes

o UI element level automation, covering the following points –

- State inquiry, event handling, asynchronous interactions

- UI element styling, moving between frames and windows, handling pop-ups and windows

- History and locations, handling cookies, dragging and dropping

- Changing user agents

- Fetching data from forms

- Filling and submitting forms

Objective

The objective of this chapter is to cover the concepts of Selenium in other programming languages such as Ruby, JavaScript and PHP etc.

Launch and closure of browsers

In this section, we will refer to the code snippets related to the opening and closing of browsers in different languages. The approach would be very straightforward as discussed orpointed out in the earlier chapters. This would cover the following points:

1. Importing/including the classes you intend to use
2. Defining the parameters of a WebDriver
3. Opening the browser
4. Opening a URL
5. Performing an action
6. Closing the browser

Setting up Node.JS/JavaScript environment for Selenium testing

---

TIPS

You can download the Node.js installers for your development from the following sites:

- **https://nodejs.org/en/** – The site would give you the ideal version for your operating system.

- **https://nodejs.org/en/download/** –The site would give you a choice to pick the installer or downloadable version suitable for your platform including add-ons, available in the downloader site.

You may download the latest version of your choice for installation. The installation process is very straightforward and self-explanatory. Since at the time of writing this book, the Selenium Alpha-5 version was the most apt choice, we have picked this up.

After the installation of Node.JS, you need to install Selenium-WebDriver to run your tests. This can be carried out by opening the Node.js command prompt and running the following command:

npm install selenium-webdriver

As a next step, you need to ensure you have a good JavaScript-friendly integrated development environment. There are plenty of choices. Some of the top ones to consider are as follows:

IntelliJ IDEA, MS Visual Studio Code, Komodo IDE, Koding, Eclipse with Node.JS Plug-in - nodeclipse, Atom and Brackets

The programs used in this book were created using MS Visual Studio Code and Atom IDEs.

Example of JavaScript

Let us take an example of a JavaScript Program and understand the program in detail:

To understand a Java Script program in detail, let us look at the example:

```javascript
var webdriver = require('selenium-webdriver'),
    By = webdriver.By,
    until = webdriver.until;
var driver = new webdriver.Builder().forBrowser('chrome').build();
driver.get('https://sites.google.com/view/crackingseleniuminterview/home');
console.log('Opening Web site');
// Take a Screenshot
var fs = require('fs')
var err = ''
console.log('Taking Screenshot of the results');
driver.sleep(5000).then(function() {
    driver.getTitle().then(function(title) {
        console.log("The Title is ::: " + title);
        driver.takeScreenshot().then(function(ScreenShotImage, err) {
            fs.writeFile('simple_screen_shot_1.png', ScreenShotImage, 'base64', fu
nction(error) {
                if (error != null) {
                    console.log("Error occured during screenshot" + error);
                    err = error;
                }
            });
        });
        if (err != null) {
            console.log('Test passed');
        } else {
            console.log('Test failed');
        }
        driver.quit();
    });
});
```

After running the program, the console log would look like as follows:

```
[Running] node "c:\Users\rahma\node_modules\selenium-webdriver\testing\Ch_7_Prog_1_Simple_site_Open_Close.js"
Opening Web site
Taking Screenshot of the results
Test passed

[Done] exited with code=0 in 29.191 seconds
```

Figure 7.1: *Example of Simple JavaScript Program —=*

Since one of the actions from the code is to take a screenshot of the page loaded, the output would be as follows:

Figure 7.2: *Screenshot of Selenium Automation Website*

Let us dissect the code in detail:

1. We defined the WebDriver with the following lines of code:

```
var webdriver = require('selenium-webdriver'),
        By = webdriver.By,
        until = webdriver.until;
```

2. We defined the browser driver in the following code using `Builder()`:

```
var driver = new webdriver.Builder().forBrowser('chrome').build();
```

3. We opened a URL using the following code:

```
driver.get('https://sites.google.com/view/crackingseleniuminterview/home');
```

4. We performed a WebDriver action with the following lines of code:

```
driver.sleep(5000).then(function() {
driver.getTitle().then(function(title) {
```

5. We closed the WebDriver with the following code:

```
    driver.quit();
```

6. We also took a screenshot with the following piece of code:

```
driver.takeScreenshot().then( function (ScreenShotImage, err) {
fs.writeFile('simple_screen_shot_1.png', ScreenShotImage,
'base64', function (error) { if (error != null) {
        console.log("Error occured during screenshot" + error);
        err = error;
```

```
      }
    });
  }
```

As you can see, the JavaScript code is almost similar to the Python or a Java code with changes only in the syntax of programming language and the functions used to run the program.

Setting up Ruby environment for Selenium testing

TIPS

You can download the Ruby installers for your development from the following sites:

- **https://rubyinstaller.org/** – The sitewould give you a choice to pick the installer or downloadable version suitable for your platform including add-ons, available in the downloader site.

You may download the latest version of your choice for installation. The installation process is very straightforward and self-explanatory. Since at the time of writing this book, the Selenium Alpha-5 version was the most apt choice, we have picked this up.

If you want to install any other gems (or libraries), you can use the *gem install* command.

If you want to use the available developer kits or any other Ruby Gems (libraries for simple references), install them as well.

ruby dk.rbinit and ruby dk.rb install

After the installation of Ruby, you need to install Selenium-WebDriver to run your tests. This could be carried out by opening the Ruby command prompt and running the following command:

gem install selenium-webdriver

As a next step, you can choose to install any of the following libraries, if you want to test Selenium Grid, headless browser or perform Behaviour Driven Design (BDD) based testing using Cucumber etc.

gem install rspec/gem install selenium-cucumber/gem install selenium-phantomjs/gem install selenium-grid

As a next step, you need to ensure you have a good Ruby-friendly Integrated development environment. There are plenty of choices.

MS Visual Studio Code, Eclipse with Ruby-dltk, Atom, VIM, EMACS and JetBrainsRubyMine

The programs used in this book were created using MS Visual Studio Code and RubyMine IDEs.

Example of Ruby

Now, let us take an example in Ruby to do the same task we performed in the JavaScript. To do this, we willopen a browser using WebDriver, print the page title and take a screenshot after a wait of a few seconds.

```ruby
require 'rubygems'
require 'selenium-webdriver'

def setup
    @driver = Selenium::WebDriver.for :firefox
end

def teardown
  @driver.quit
end

def run
    setup
    yield
    teardown
end

run do
    @driver.get "https://sites.google.com/view/crackingseleniuminterview/home"
    puts("Page title is #{@driver.title}")
    wait = Selenium::WebDriver::Wait.new(:timeout => 10)
    puts("Successful Selenium Wait")
    @driver.save_screenshot("..\\..\\Cracking Your Selenium Interview Book\\Images\\CrackingSelenium.png")
    puts("Successful Screenshot")
    puts("End of Program")
end
```

After running the above program, the Console output of the program would be like as follows:

```
C:\Users\rahma\OneDrive\Desktop\Selenium\Programs\Ruby>ruby Ch_7_Prog_2_Ruby_Example.rb
Page title is Selenium Automation
Successful Selenium Wait
Successful Screenshot
End of Program
```

Figure 7.3: Example of Ruby Program Output / Screenshot

In this case, the output of the screenshot would exactly appear the way it was produced while running the JavaScript program.

Page navigation

Let us take an example of Ruby for navigating a web page using a WebDriver.

Example of Ruby

The example given below gives a view of how we can use the Selenium WebDriver to navigate web pages, leverage the form to enter data using web elements By clicking on links and buttons.

```ruby
require "json"

require "selenium-webdriver"

require "rspec"

include RSpec::Expectations


def setup

    @driver = Selenium::WebDriver.for :chrome

    @accept_next_alert = true

    @driver.manage.timeouts.implicit_wait = 120

    @verification_errors = []

end

def teardown

    @driver.quit

end


def run

    setup

    yield

    teardown

end


run do

    puts("get @driver.get https://rahmankalilur.wixsite.com/
crackingselenium")

    @driver.get "https://rahmankalilur.wixsite.com/crackingselenium"

    puts("Filling the form")
```

```ruby
@driver.find_element(:id, "comp-jxad7hnvinput").clear
@driver.find_element(:id, "comp-jxad7hnvinput").send_keys "Test"
@driver.find_element(:id, "comp-jxad7ho5input").clear
@driver.find_element(:id, "comp-jxad7ho5input").send_keys "Test@Test.Test"
@driver.find_element(:id, "comp-jxad7hoeinput").clear
@driver.find_element(:id, "comp-jxad7hoeinput").send_keys "Test"
@driver.find_element(:id, "comp-jxad7hoptextarea").clear
@driver.find_element(:id, "comp-jxad7hoptextarea").send_keys "Test"
@driver.find_element(:id, "comp-jxad7hoylink").click
puts("Filled the form")
@driver.save_screenshot("wixite_cracking_selenium_forms.png")
puts("Waiting for the menus to appear")
puts("Clicking First Link")
wait = Selenium::WebDriver::Wait.new(:timeout => 120)
wait.until{@driver.find_element(:id, 'DrpDwnMn01label')}
@driver.find_element(:id, "DrpDwnMn01label").click
@driver.save_screenshot("wixite_cracking_first_link.png")
puts("Clicking Second Link")
wait = Selenium::WebDriver::Wait.new(:timeout => 120)
wait.until{@driver.find_element(:id, 'DrpDwnMn02label')}
@driver.find_element(:id, "DrpDwnMn02label").click
@driver.save_screenshot("wixite_cracking_second_link.png")
puts("Clicking Third Link")
wait = Selenium::WebDriver::Wait.new(:timeout => 120)
wait.until{@driver.find_element(:id, 'DrpDwnMn03label')}
@driver.find_element(:id, "DrpDwnMn03label").click
@driver.save_screenshot("wixite_cracking_third_link.png")
puts("Clicking Fourth Link")
wait = Selenium::WebDriver::Wait.new(:timeout => 120)
wait.until{@driver.find_element(:id, 'DrpDwnMn04label')}
@driver.find_element(:id, "DrpDwnMn04label").click
@driver.save_screenshot("wixite_cracking_fourth_link.png")
puts("Clicking Fifth Link")
```

```
        wait = Selenium::WebDriver::Wait.new(:timeout => 120)
        wait.until{@driver.find_element(:id, 'DrpDwnMn05label')}
        @driver.find_element(:id, "DrpDwnMn05label").click
        @driver.find_element(:id, "DrpDwnMn0moreContainer0label").click
        @driver.save_screenshot("wixite_cracking_fifth_link.png")
        puts("Clicking Sixth Link")
        wait = Selenium::WebDriver::Wait.new(:timeout => 120)
        wait.until{@driver.find_element(:id, 'DrpDwnMn06label')}
        @driver.find_element(:id, "DrpDwnMn06label").click
        @driver.save_screenshot("wixite_cracking_sixth_link.png")
        @driver.close
        puts("Quit the Browser")
end

def verify(&blk)
  yield
  rescue ExpectationNotMetError => ex
    @verification_errors << ex
end
```

Let us see how this program would work in Ruby.

1. The first set of code is included with the Ruby gems or modules/libraries for usage:

```
require "json"
require "selenium-webdriver"
require "rspec"
include RSpec::Expectations
```

2. Next, we defined the setup for WebDriver, timeouts, alerts etc:

```
def setup
@driver = Selenium::WebDriver.for :chrome
@accept_next_alert = true
        @driver.manage.timeouts.implicit_wait = 120
        @verification_errors = []
    end
```

Moreover, defined the closure of the WebDriver:

```
def teardown
    @driver.quit
end
```

3. Next, we defined the execution sequence for the execution:

```
def run
    setup
    yield
    teardown
end
```

4. Then, we defined the core logic of sequential activities in the "run" setup of the program, which would do the following four things:

    a. Open the URL for automation

    b. Find web elements

    c. Fill out a form

    d. Take screenshots

    e. Click on all the key links of a dynamic menu in the website appearing across pages

```
run do
    puts("get @driver.get https://rahmankalilur.wixsite.com/
crackingselenium")
    @driver.get "https://rahmankalilur.wixsite.com/crackingselenium"
    puts("Filling the form")
    @driver.find_element(:id, "comp-jxad7hnvinput").clear
    @driver.find_element(:id, "comp-jxad7hnvinput").send_keys "Test"
    @driver.find_element(:id, "comp-jxad7ho5input").clear
    @driver.find_element(:id, "comp-jxad7ho5input").send_keys "Test@Test.Test"
    @driver.find_element(:id, "comp-jxad7hoeinput").clear
    @driver.find_element(:id, "comp-jxad7hoeinput").send_keys "Test"
    @driver.find_element(:id, "comp-jxad7hoptextarea").clear
    @driver.find_element(:id, "comp-jxad7hoptextarea").send_keys "Test"
    @driver.find_element(:id, "comp-jxad7hoylink").click
    puts("Filled the form")
```

```ruby
@driver.save_screenshot("wixite_cracking_selenium_forms.png")
puts("Waiting for the menus to appear")
puts("Clicking First Link")
wait = Selenium::WebDriver::Wait.new(:timeout => 120)
wait.until{@driver.find_element(:id, 'DrpDwnMn01label')}
@driver.find_element(:id, "DrpDwnMn01label").click
@driver.save_screenshot("wixite_cracking_first_link.png")
puts("Clicking Second Link")
wait = Selenium::WebDriver::Wait.new(:timeout => 120)
wait.until{@driver.find_element(:id, 'DrpDwnMn02label')}
@driver.find_element(:id, "DrpDwnMn02label").click
@driver.save_screenshot("wixite_cracking_second_link.png")
puts("Clicking Third Link")
wait = Selenium::WebDriver::Wait.new(:timeout => 120)
wait.until{@driver.find_element(:id, 'DrpDwnMn03label')}
@driver.find_element(:id, "DrpDwnMn03label").click
@driver.save_screenshot("wixite_cracking_third_link.png")
puts("Clicking Fourth Link")
wait = Selenium::WebDriver::Wait.new(:timeout => 120)
wait.until{@driver.find_element(:id, 'DrpDwnMn04label')}
@driver.find_element(:id, "DrpDwnMn04label").click
@driver.save_screenshot("wixite_cracking_fourth_link.png")
puts("Clicking Fifth Link")
wait = Selenium::WebDriver::Wait.new(:timeout => 120)
wait.until{@driver.find_element(:id, 'DrpDwnMn05label')}
@driver.find_element(:id, "DrpDwnMn05label").click
@driver.find_element(:id, "DrpDwnMn0moreContainer0label").click
@driver.save_screenshot("wixite_cracking_fifth_link.png")
puts("Clicking Sixth Link")
wait = Selenium::WebDriver::Wait.new(:timeout => 120)
wait.until{@driver.find_element(:id, 'DrpDwnMn06label')}
@driver.find_element(:id, "DrpDwnMn06label").click
@driver.save_screenshot("wixite_cracking_sixth_link.png")
```

```
    @driver.close
    puts("Quit the Browser")
end
```

As a result, the output would appear as follows:

```
C:\Users\rahma\OneDrive\Desktop\Selenium\Programs\Ruby>ruby Ch_7_Prog_3_WixSites_Navigation.rb

DevTools listening on ws://127.0.0.1:64527/devtools/browser/17d8c6bf-199b-45ca-9786-6ad76d00c274
get @driver.get https://rahmankalilur.wixsite.com/crackingselenium
Filling the form
Filled the form
Waiting for the menus to appear
Clicking First Link
Clicking Second Link
Clicking Third Link
Clicking Fourth Link
Clicking Fifth Link
Clicking Sixth Link
Quit the Browser
```

***Figure 7.4:** Output of Test Execution*

In addition, the screenshots of the program flow would appear as follows:

***Figure 7.5:** Screenshots of Navigation*

Hence, once we log into the page, we would see a site login screen after clicking on the login link mentioned on the site. When we click on the same, we willget some sample data to be filled in. This is shown in in the figure below (*Figure 7.6*).

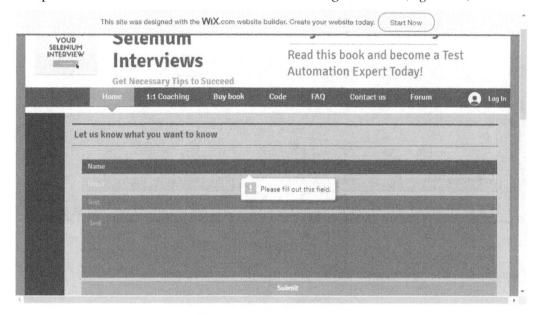

Figure 7.6: *Test Execution Screenshots*

In addition, to navigate in the above example, the types of identifiers that we can use are as follows:

```
@driver.find_element(:id, "comp-jxad7hnvinput").send_keys "Test"
```

The link identifier (not included in the example), which we can use to click on the FAQ link given in *Figure 7.6* would be as follows:

```
@driver.find_element(:link, "FAQ").click
```

We can also use CSS Locator, XPath and other locators with a known identifier in the web page to locate. To demonstrate this, an example is mentioned in the next section.

JavaScript example on asynchronous execution

Before we look into the program, let us see how asynchronous execution works in a JavaScript.

Many of the interpreter-oriented languages use a synchronous model of programming. What this means is that, whenever an action or event happens, you need to wait for the activity to complete before you can move to the next statement.

Thiswouldbe linear and the overall time to execute a program may exceed the sum of all the individual actions taken together. In a synchronous model, the program is stopped until the task is done and in other words, the program is dormant.

In the case of asynchronous programming, using threads or similar aspects, the program can continue to do tasks in parallel while waiting for the tasks to complete. When the action completes, the program gets information about the completion of the task and it can consolidate and continue.

When it comes to the JavaScript, as it is an interpreted language, it is typically a synchronous and single-threaded model. However, JavaScript can be performed in an asynchronous mode using threads and **Asynchronous JavaScript and XML (AJAX)** API and JavaScript functions such as setTimeOut() etc.

As one of the ways, Selenium can leverage the asynchronous JavaScript by using a Promise Object that actually represents the completion of an asynchronous JavaScript operation. It could be a completion, rejection or a failure of the task specified. More details about the JavaScript's Promise class function is given in *Chapter 10*.

The example mentioned below provides a view of how we can use Selenium WebDriver to navigate web pages, use the form to enter data using web elementsby clicking on links and buttons.

```javascript
const { Builder, By, Key, until } = require('selenium-webdriver')
const assert = require('assert')

describe('Untitled', function() {
  this.timeout(600000)
  let driver
  let vars
  beforeEach(async function() {
    driver = await new Builder().forBrowser('chrome').build()
    vars = {}
  })
  afterEach(async function() {
    await driver.quit();
  })
  it('Untitled', async function() {
    // Test name: Untitled
    // Step # | name | target | value | comment
    // 1 | open | / |  |
```

```
await driver.get("https://www.dogpile.com/")

var fs = require('fs')

// 2 | Take a Screenshot

await driver.takeScreenshot().then(

    function (ScreenShotImage, err) {

        fs.writeFile('dogpile_screen_shot_1.png', ScreenShotImage,
'base64', function (error) {

            if (error != null)

                console.log("Error occured during screenshot" +
error);

        });

    }

);

// 3 | click | id=q |  |

await driver.findElement(By.id("q")).click()

// 4 | type | id=q | selenium |

await driver.findElement(By.id("q")).sendKeys("selenium")

// 5 | sendKeys | id=q | ${KEY_ENTER} |

await driver.findElement(By.id("q")).sendKeys(Key.ENTER)

// 6 | Take a Screenshot

await driver.takeScreenshot().then(

    function (ScreenShotImage, err) {

        fs.writeFile('dogpile_screen_shot_2.png', ScreenShotImage,
'base64', function (error) {

            if (error != null)

                console.log("Error occured during screenshot" + error);

        });

    }

);

// 7 | click | css=.aylf-bing-sidebar__result:nth-child(9) > .aylf-
bing-sidebar__title |  |

await driver.findElement(By.css(".aylf-bing-sidebar__result:nth-
child(9) > .aylf-bing-sidebar__title")).click()
```

```
// 8 | close |  |  |
await driver.close()
})
})
```

The output would look like as follows:

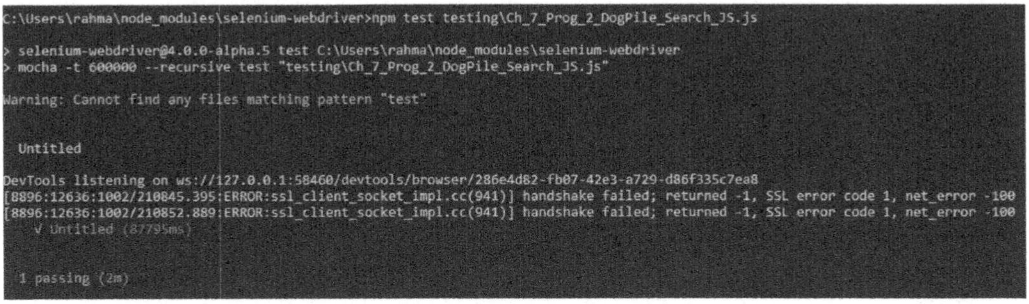

Figure 7.7: *Test Execution Output*

The screenshots taken would appear as follows:

Figure 7.8: *Output of the Screenshot*

Similar to the Ruby program earlier, the JavaScript program above has two locator code snippets, that is, locater by ID and locator by CSS. Additionally, this program runs asynchronously using the await function, which allows the program to wait for asynchronous actions to complete the execution.

1. Locator by ID:

```
await driver.findElement(By.id("q")).click()
```

2. Locator by CSS Selector:

```
await driver.findElement(By.css(".aylf-bing-sidebar__result:nth-
child(9) > .aylf-bing-sidebar__title")).click()
// 8 | close |  |  |
```

Filling out a web form – A JavaScript example

Now, let us take an example of how we can leverage WebDriver to auto-populate a form and submit content. Since the code in the example is generated using an IDE, it can be modularized and used in a Page Object Model (POM) mode. An example of this is provided in *Chapter 8* for your reference. In the example given below, we are following a simple linear model of programming.

```javascript
// Generated by Selenium IDE
const { Builder, By, Key, until } = require('selenium-webdriver')
const assert = require('assert')

describe('CrackingSeleniumInterviewGoogleSites', function() {
  this.timeout(300000)
  let driver
  let vars
  beforeEach(async function() {
    driver = await new Builder().forBrowser('firefox').build()
    vars = {}
    console.log("Starting the Program");
  })
  afterEach(async function() {
//    await driver.quit();
    console.log("Closing the Program");
  })
  it('CrackingSeleniumInterviewGoogleSites', async function() {
    // Test name: CrackingSeleniumInterviewGoogleSites
    // Step # | name | target | value | comment
    // 1 | open | /view/crackingseleniuminterview/login |  |
    await driver.get("https://sites.google.com/view/
crackingseleniuminterview/login")
    var fs = require('fs')
    // 2 | Take a Screenshot
    await driver.takeScreenshot().then(
        function (ScreenShotImage, err) {
```

```
              fs.writeFile('crackingselenium_googlesites_screen_shot_1.
png', ScreenShotImage, 'base64', function (error) {
                  if (error != null)

                      console.log("Error occured during screenshot" +
error);

              });

        }

   );

   // 3 | selectFrame | index=0 |  |

   await driver.switchTo().frame(0)

   // 4 | click | css=.quantumWizTextinputSimpleinputInput |  |

   await driver.findElement(By.css(".
quantumWizTextinputSimpleinputInput")).click()

   // 5 | type | css=.quantumWizTextinputSimpleinputInput | Selenium |

   await driver.findElement(By.css(".
quantumWizTextinputSimpleinputInput")).sendKeys("Selenium")

   // 6 | click | css=.freebirdFormviewerViewItemsTextShortText >
.quantumWizTextinputPaperinputMainContent |  |

   await driver.findElement(By.css(".
freebirdFormviewerViewItemsTextShortText >
.quantumWizTextinputPaperinputMainContent")).click()

   // 7 | click | name=entry.1621524406 |  |

   await driver.findElement(By.name("entry.1621524406")).click()

   // 8 | type | name=entry.1621524406 | Is Selenium Good |

   await driver.findElement(By.name("entry.1621524406")).sendKeys("Is
Selenium Good")

   // 9 | type | name=entry.420674755 | Ofcourse it is brilliant tool. |

   await driver.findElement(By.name("entry.420674755")).
sendKeys("Ofcourse it is brilliant tool.")

   // 10 | Take a Screenshot

   await driver.takeScreenshot().then(

       function (ScreenShotImage, err) {

              fs.writeFile('crackingselenium_googlesites_screen_shot_2.
png', ScreenShotImage, 'base64', function (error) {

                  if (error != null)

                      console.log("Error occured during screenshot" + error);
```

```
        });

    }

);
    // 11 | click | css=.freebirdFormviewerViewItemsGridRowGroup:nth-
child(4) > .freebirdFormviewerViewItemsGridCell:nth-child(3) |   |

    await driver.findElement(By.css(".freebirdFormviewerViewItemsGri
dRowGroup:nth-child(4) > .freebirdFormviewerViewItemsGridCell:nth-
child(3)")).click()

    // 12 | click | css=.freebirdFormviewerViewItemsDateDateSelectionInp
ut:nth-child(1) .quantumWizTextinputPaperinputInput |   |

    await driver.findElement(By.css(".freebirdFormviewerViewItemsDateDa
teSelectionInput:nth-child(1) .quantumWizTextinputPaperinputInput")).
click()

    // 13 | type | css=.freebirdFormviewerViewItemsDateDateSelectionInpu
t:nth-child(1) .quantumWizTextinputPaperinputInput | 11 |

    await driver.findElement(By.css(".freebirdFormviewerViewItemsDateDa
teSelectionInput:nth-child(1) .quantumWizTextinputPaperinputInput")).
sendKeys("11")

    // 14 | type | css=.freebirdFormviewerViewItemsDateDateSelectionInpu
t:nth-child(3) .quantumWizTextinputPaperinputInput | 11 |

    await driver.findElement(By.css(".freebirdFormviewerViewItemsDateDa
teSelectionInput:nth-child(3) .quantumWizTextinputPaperinputInput")).
sendKeys("11")

    // 15 | type | css=.freebirdFormviewerViewItemsTimeTimeInputs
> .freebirdFormviewerViewItemsTimeNumberEdit:nth-child(1)
.quantumWizTextinputPaperinputInput | 12 |

    await driver.findElement(By.css(".
freebirdFormviewerViewItemsTimeTimeInputs > .freebirdFormviewerViewIte
msTimeNumberEdit:nth-child(1) .quantumWizTextinputPaperinputInput")).
sendKeys("12")

    // 16 | type | css=.freebirdFormviewerViewItemsTimeNumberEdit:nth-
child(3) .quantumWizTextinputPaperinputInput | 34 |

    await driver.findElement(By.css(".freebirdFormviewerViewItemsTi
meNumberEdit:nth-child(3) .quantumWizTextinputPaperinputInput")).
sendKeys("34")

    // 17  | Take another Screenshot

  await driver.takeScreenshot().then(

        function (ScreenShotImage, err) {

            fs.writeFile('crackingselenium_googlesites_screen_shot_3.
png', ScreenShotImage, 'base64', function (error) {
```

```
            if (error != null)
                console.log("Error occured during screenshot" + error);
        });
    }
);
// 18 | verifyTitle | Simple Form Data Collection |  |
console.log(await driver.getTitle())
// 19  | Take another Screenshot
await driver.takeScreenshot().then(
    function (ScreenShotImage, err) {
        fs.writeFile('crackingselenium_googlesites_screen_shot_5.
png', ScreenShotImage, 'base64', function (error) {
            if (error != null)
                console.log("Error occured during screenshot" + error);
        });
    }
);
// 20  | Close the Driver
await driver.close()
  })
})
```

This program works using web element's by locators, sending the values to be filled by using SendKeys() method for text input and click() method for choosing a radio button, checkbox or a pulldown menu items, in addition to the submit button clicking. This is similar to the examples we covered in the programs in the preceding sections.

One more additional concept we covered in this program is the ability to switch between windows and frames. The driver.switchTo() command in JavaScript allows us to switch between windows and frames.

```
await driver.switchTo().frame(0)
```

Filling out a web form – A Ruby example

Now, let us see a similar example for filling out a web form by using Ruby.

```
require "json"
```

```ruby
require "selenium-webdriver"
require "rspec"
include RSpec::Expectations

def setup
    @driver = Selenium::WebDriver.for :chrome
    @accept_next_alert = true
    @driver.manage.timeouts.implicit_wait = 30
    @verification_errors = []
end

def teardown
    @driver.quit
end

def run
    setup
    yield
    teardown
end

run do
    puts("Open Site")
    @driver.get "http://crackingseleniuminterviews.simplesite.com/"
    @driver.find_element(:link, "CONTACT").click
    puts("Click Contacts")
    puts("Fill Contact form")
    @driver.find_element(:name, "Name").click
    @driver.find_element(:name, "Name").clear
    @driver.find_element(:name, "Name").send_keys "Selenium User"
    @driver.find_element(:name, "Email").clear
    @driver.find_element(:name, "Email").send_keys "seleniumuser@
exactsiteemailaddress.is.not.needed.com"
    @driver.find_element(:name, "Message").clear
    @driver.find_element(:name, "Message").send_keys "testing selenium is
very cool"
        @driver.find_element(:xpath,  "(.//*[normalize-space(text())  and
```

```
normalize-space(.)='Message*'])[1]/following::span[1]").click
    puts("end of submission")

end
def verify(&blk)
  yield
  rescue ExpectationNotMetError => ex
    @verification_errors << ex
end
```

The above example is a simple program that uses Ruby and Selenium WebDriver. This program will open a website, help you to navigate to a contact form and submit the contact content in the form. The locators by name, XPATH and link are used for the program.

Headless browser testing – JavaScript

Let us see a code snippet of how we can run headless testing using JavaScript. Similar to the Python and Java examples that we covered in the earlier chapters, it is a simple case of setting the parameters, configuring the WebDriver settings for the browsers and passing the headless parameters as arguments using the headless() command as an option while setting up. The rest of the code would exactly remain the same as the normal WebDriver program.

```
const chrome = require('../chrome');
const firefox = require('../firefox');
const {Builder, By, Key, until} = require('..');
const width = 1280;
const height = 800;

let driver = new Builder()
    .forBrowser('chrome')
    .setChromeOptions(
        new chrome.Options().headless().windowSize({width, height}))
    .setFirefoxOptions(
        new firefox.Options().headless().windowSize({width, height}))
    .build();

let fs = require('fs');

driver.get('https://sites.google.com/view/crackingseleniuminterview/
```

```
home')
driver.takeScreenshot().then(
    function(image, err) {
        require('fs').writeFile('Ch_7_Prog_7_JS_Headless.png', image,
'base64', function(err) {
            console.log(err);
        });
    }
);
driver.quit()
```

Headless browser testing – Ruby

Similar to the JavaScript code in the preceding section, the code for Ruby is almost similar toa headless program. As a second method, we will use a class headless by instantiating the object using the `Headless.new` and destroying it before the program is closed using the `Headless.destroy` functions. The rest of the code would exactly remain the same as the WebDriver program. In the program below, the use of the headless class commented using # tag, which covers both the type of headless program outputs.

```
require 'selenium-webdriver'
require 'rspec/expectations'
#require 'headless'

def setup
  #@headless = Headless.new
  #@headless.start
  options = Selenium::WebDriver::Chrome::Options.new
  options.add_argument('--headless')
  options.add_argument('--disable-gpu')
  @driver = Selenium::WebDriver.for :chrome, options: options
end

def teardown
  @driver.quit
#  @headless.destroy
end
```

```ruby
def run
  setup
  yield
  teardown
end

run do
  @driver.get "https://sites.google.com/view/crackingseleniuminterview/home"
  puts(@driver.title)
  @driver.save_screenshot('Ch_7_Prog_7_Ruby_Headless.png')
end
```

Let us now see the screenshots produced by the program:

Figure 7.9: Selenium Headless Program Output from Ruby

Ruby Cookies Management example

Now, let us see an example for managing cookies using the WebDriver.

```ruby
require "json"
require "selenium-webdriver"
require "rspec"
include RSpec::Expectations
```

```ruby
def setup
    @driver = Selenium::WebDriver.for :firefox
    @accept_next_alert = true
    @driver.manage.timeouts.implicit_wait = 30
    @verification_errors = []
end

def teardown
    @driver.quit
end

def run
    setup
    yield
    teardown
end

def print_cookies
  @driver.manage.all_cookies.each { |cookie|
      puts "#{cookie[:name]} => #{cookie[:value]}"
  }
end

run do
  @driver.get "http://www.google.com"
  puts("before cookies")
  print_cookies
  puts("Adding cookies")
  @driver.manage.add_cookie(:name => 'key-1', :value => 'value-1')
  @driver.manage.add_cookie(:name => 'key-2', :value => 'value-2')
  puts("After Adding cookies")
  print_cookies
  puts("deleting cookies")
  @driver.manage.delete_cookie "key-2"
  @driver.manage.delete_all_cookies
  puts("After Deleting cookies")
  print_cookies
```

```ruby
  puts("End of Program")
end
```

As you can see in the above program, we have added a cookie using the add_cookie command and deleted the cookies using the `delete_cookie` or `delete_all_ cookies` commands. This is similar to the examples that we covered earlier using the Python and Java programs in *Chapter 6*.

The custom function `print_cookies` would prints all the cookies stored against the browser by the website we are navigating through the WebDriver. The output of this program would appear as follows:

```
[Running] ruby "c:\Users\rahma\OneDrive\Desktop\Selenium\Programs\Ruby\Ch_7_Prog_8_Ruby_Cookies.rb"
before cookies
NID => 188=upjYOtcBdAkpWCovDcJJqskofqAwm4FkCfZlTz1boUht-o_npfk0Ra13EZVUhI5VZ-kssaHHu0t6FSFe4DhIeq1H78vMedX3jxjHr12CjyTnAbrL0wWJKPyTGtxq
1P_JAR => 2019-10-5-8
Adding cookies
After Adding cookies
NID => 188=upjYOtcBdAkpWCovDcJJqskofqAwm4FkCfZlTz1boUht-o_npfk0Ra13EZVUhI5VZ-kssaHHu0t6FSFe4DhIeq1H78vMedX3jxjHr12CjyTnAbrL0wWJKPyTGtxq
1P_JAR => 2019-10-5-8
key-1 => value-1
key-2 => value-2
deleting cookies
After Deleting cookies
End of Program

[Done] exited with code=0 in 22.888 seconds
```

Figure 7.10: *Test Execution Output - Cookies*

As you can see, initially we had one cookie with the id NID and we added two more cookies namely key-1 and key-2. After the deletion of the cookies, when the program ended, there were only zero cookies left for us. Likewise, this exercise can be run against multiple sites to see the number of cookies the websites store for tracking and marketing purposes.

Ruby-screen size emulations

Let us now see how we can perform screen size emulations with the help of a Ruby program. To do this, we can use various instance methods defined in the Ruby Class:Selenium::WebDriver::Window available to us such as full_screen, maximize, minimize, move_to, position, rect, resize_to, size etc. Some of the methods such as rect, move_to have been deprecated in the new Selenium 4.0 version. Some of the functions in Selenium that are usable and future centric are given in the following example.

```ruby
require "json"
require "selenium-webdriver"
require "rspec"
include RSpec::Expectations

def setup
```

```ruby
    @driver = Selenium::WebDriver.for :firefox
    @driver.manage.timeouts.implicit_wait = 30
end

def teardown
    @driver.quit
end

def run
    setup
    yield
    teardown
end

run do
  puts "Start of Program"
  @driver.get "http://www.google.com"
  # get initial window size
  puts @driver.manage.window.size
  # set window size using Dimension struct
  target_size = Selenium::WebDriver::Dimension.new(1024, 768)
  @driver.manage.window.size = target_size
  puts @driver.manage.window.size
  # resize window
  @driver.manage.window.resize_to(800, 320)
  puts @driver.manage.window.size
  # maximize window
  @driver.manage.window.maximize
  puts @driver.manage.window.size
  # set to permissible maximum sized window
  max_width, max_height = @driver.execute_script("return [window.screen.
availWidth, window.screen.availHeight];")
  @driver.manage.window.resize_to(max_width, max_height)
  puts @driver.manage.window.size
  # Move window
  @driver.manage.window.move_to(300, 400)
```

```ruby
  puts @driver.manage.window.size
  # Go Full Screen
  @driver.manage.window.full_screen
  puts @driver.manage.window.size
  # mInimize window
  @driver.manage.window.minimize
  puts @driver.manage.window.size
  puts("End of Program")
end
```

When executed, the program would produce the following output:

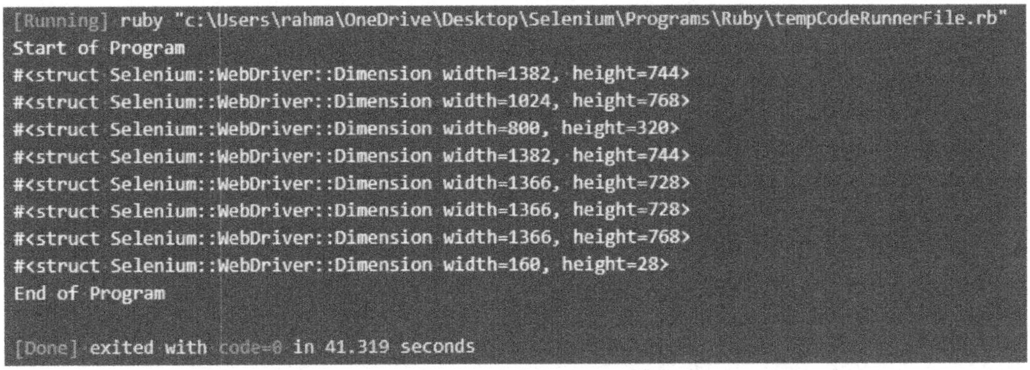

```
[Running] ruby "c:\Users\rahma\OneDrive\Desktop\Selenium\Programs\Ruby\tempCodeRunnerFile.rb"
Start of Program
#<struct Selenium::WebDriver::Dimension width=1382, height=744>
#<struct Selenium::WebDriver::Dimension width=1024, height=768>
#<struct Selenium::WebDriver::Dimension width=800, height=320>
#<struct Selenium::WebDriver::Dimension width=1382, height=744>
#<struct Selenium::WebDriver::Dimension width=1366, height=728>
#<struct Selenium::WebDriver::Dimension width=1366, height=728>
#<struct Selenium::WebDriver::Dimension width=1366, height=768>
#<struct Selenium::WebDriver::Dimension width=160, height=28>
End of Program

[Done] exited with code=0 in 41.319 seconds
```

Figure 7.11: Test Execution Output – Window Resizing

In the image above, you can see the variance in the browser screen sizes (tracked by the dimension class) as per the operation performed.

Ruby example for moving between frames and windows

Let us see the examples on how to switch between various windows and frames using Selenium WebDriver and Ruby programming language.

```ruby
#Selenium WebDriver Commands in Ruby for Switching Windows
driver.switch_to.window("windowName")


#Selenium WebDriver Commands in Ruby for Navigating all window handles
driver.window_handles.each do |windowhandle|
    driver.switch_to.window windowhandle
end

#Selenium WebDriver Commands in Ruby for Switching Frames
driver .switch_to.frame "BrowserFrameName"
```

As you can see in the code snippet above, it is important to understand the window or frame you are on to act for your automation program. The commands are almost similar in all the programming languages.

With reference to the above-mentioned code snippet, the first command navigates to a window named `windowName`; the second snippet navigates through all the open windows available to the browser one-by-one. The final code snippet navigates to a frame named "`BrowserFrameName`". This is useful for automating actions in iFrame-based navigational features of a web application.

Ruby example handling pop-ups and alerts

The Ruby class named Class: `Selenium::WebDriver::Alert` has features that will be useful for handling various pop-ups and alerts. Some of the key methods available for navigation include the following:

- **`accept:`** to accept the alert
- **`dismiss:`** to dismiss and ignore the alert
- **`send_keys:`** to type a text in the alert if it has a data entry field or it could be an *Enter* key using `Key.ENTER` or a similar control key
- **`text:`** gives the alert text getting displayed

Alert handling in Ruby using `accept, dismiss` and `send_keys` can be showcased in the following code snippet:

```
alert = driver.switch_to.alert

alert.accept

alert.dismiss

alert.send_keys "Key.ENTER"

puts(alert.text)
```

The code snippet above covers all the key alert methods available in Selenium WebDriver using Ruby.

Ruby example handling drag and drops

Sometimes a large volume of data or contentmay need to be dragged from one web element to another. This can be done simply and effectively through the functions available in Selenium. The code snippet given below covers all the key alert methods available in Selenium WebDriver using Ruby.

```
#identify the source and destination web elements

sourcwebelement = @driver.find_element(:name => 'source_web_element')

targetwebelement = @driver.find_element(:name => 'target_web_element')
```

```
#Drag the Source element to Target
@driver.action.drag_and_drop(sourcwebelement, targetwebelement).perform
```

This Drag and Drop action can be performed by using an action sequence.

The same action can be performed with the help of an action sequence through the `Class: Selenium::WebDriver::ActionBuilder` class. This will be performed in the following manner.

```
#Drag the Source element to Target in action - We can use more than one
web element
@driver.action.key_down(:shift).
                click(firstwebelement).
                click(secondwebelement).
                key_up(:shift).
                drag_and_drop(targetwebelement, thirdwebelement).
                perform
```

Other functions one can use using `ActionBuilder` class includes the following methods:

- **click:** for clicking on a web element
- **click_and_hold:** for clicking on a web element and holding it
- **context_click:** for right-clicking the mouse on the web element
- **double_click:** for double-clicking a web element such as a link or a button
- **drag_and_drop:** As seen in the example above
- **drag_and_drop_by:** for another drag and drop example
- **initialize:** for initializing the ActionBuilder class
- **key_down:** tomove down the element by emulating the down key
- **key_up:** to move up the element by emulating the up key
- **move_by:** to move the pointer by a specified set of pixels
- **move_to:** to move to a specific element
- **perform:** to perform the actions specified
- **release:** torelease the keys
- **send_keys:** for sending keys to the elements included in the action builder

Ruby example for locators

Now let us see how we can leverage WebElement locators in Ruby

```
#Selenium Locators
# We can search based on the following Parameters
  class: 'class name',
  class_name: 'class name',
  css: 'css selector',
  id: 'id',
  link: 'link text',
  link_text: 'link text',
  name: 'name',
  partial_link_text: 'partial link text',
  tag_name: 'tag name',
  xpath: 'xpath'


#Getting values through various locators
find_element - Get the first matching element based on Parameters passed
find_elements - Get the list of elements matching the parameters passed


#Locator by ID
# <input id="crackseleniuminterview">...</input>
weblocatorelement = driver.find_element(:id, "crackseleniuminterview")


#Locator By Class Name
# <div class="selenium-ruby" style="display: none; ">...</div>
weblocatorelement = driver.find_element(:class, 'selenium-ruby')
weblocatorelement driver.find_element(:class_name, 'selenium-ruby')
#locator by Tag Name
# <div class="selenium-ruby" style="display: none; ">...</div>
weblocatorelement = driver.find_element(:tag_name, 'div')


#locator by Name
# <input id="reviewer" name='reviewer' type='text'>…</input>
weblocatorelement = driver.find_element(:name, 'reviewer')


#locator by Link Text
# <a href="https://bpbonline.com/search?q=C">C</a>
weblocatorelement = driver.find_element(:link, 'C')
```

```
weblocatorelement = driver.find_element(:link_text, 'C')
```

```
#locator by Partial Link Text
```
#Example from the site above - BPBOnline.com <a href="/products/web-applications-using-jsp?_pos=1&_sid=d16c8f49a&_ss=r" style="font-family: "SF Pro Display","SF Pro Icons","Helvetica Neue","Helvetica","Arial",sans-serif;

font-size:14px;text-align:center;color:#555;">Web Applications Using JSP</a>
```
weblocatorelement = driver.find_element(:partial_link_text, 'JSP')
```

```
#locator by XPATH
```
```
#Example from the site above BPBONLINE.COM <span>Home</span>
```
```
#XPATH = //*[@id="page-body"]/header/div[3]/div/div/div/div/nav/div/ul/li[1]/a/span
```
```
weblocatorelement = driver.find_element(:xpath, '//*[@id="page-body"]/header/div[3]/div/div/div/div/nav/div/ul/li[1]/a/span')
```

```
#locator by CSS
```
```
#Example From The Site => https://www.w3.org/Style/CSS/
```
```
#CSS Selector = "a[href*='TR/CSS/'] > cite"
```
```
weblocatorelement = driver.find_element(:css, a[href*='TR/CSS/'] > cite)
```

Ruby Example for submission of forms data

In the program given below, we have used the Ruby programming language to fill a form automatically. While the program is a linear one, the same can be modularized using the POM, which we will cover in the next chapter. For this program, we are using the locators available in the Selenium classes for Ruby. For the comparison purposes, we will explore the outputs as well.

```
require "json"

require "selenium-webdriver"

require "rspec"

include RSpec::Expectations


def setup

    @driver = Selenium::WebDriver.for :chrome
```

```ruby
    @accept_next_alert = true

    @driver.manage.timeouts.implicit_wait = 30

    @verification_errors = []

end

def teardown

    @driver.quit

end

def run

  setup

  yield

  teardown

end

run do

    @driver.get "https://docs.google.com/forms/d/e/1FAIpQLSdPjNwlIuToBeV
nTPIIRhg2_8t5HX-o0PwaSIvSeUmFr1KasA/viewform"

    #windowhandleslist

    @driver.save_screenshot 'Ch_7_Prog_11_Ruby_Form_Prefill.png'

      @driver.find_element(:xpath,  "(.//*[normalize-space(text())  and
normalize-space(.)='Selenium  Test  User  -  Form  Data  Collection'])[1]/
following::div[4]").click

    @driver.find_element(:xpath, "(.//*[normalize-space(text()) and
normalize-space(.)='Choice 1'])[1]/following::div[7]").click

    @driver.find_element(:xpath, "(.//*[normalize-space(text()) and
normalize-space(.)='Option 1'])[1]/following::div[6]").click

    @driver.find_element(:name, "entry.1621524406").click

    @driver.find_element(:name, "entry.1621524406").clear

    @driver.find_element(:name, "entry.1621524406").send_keys "Test"

    @driver.find_element(:name, "entry.420674755").click

    @driver.find_element(:name, "entry.420674755").clear

    @driver.find_element(:name, "entry.420674755").send_keys "Tested Again
```

and Again... and Again... and Again... How many times does a test gets Tested Again and Again... and Again... and Again... How many times does a test gets Tested Again and Again... and Again... and Again... How many times does a test gets Tested Again and Again... and Again... and Again... How many times does a test gets Tested Again and Again... and Again... and Again... How many times does a test"

```
@driver.find_element(:xpath, "(.//*[normalize-space(text()) and
normalize-space(.)='Choose A Drop Down'])[1]/following::div[4]").click

@driver.find_element(:xpath, "(.//*[normalize-space(text()) and
normalize-space(.)='Option 1'])[3]/following::span[1]").click

@driver.find_element(:xpath, "(.//*[normalize-space(text()) and
normalize-space(.)='Choose a Scale'])[1]/following::div[54]").click

@driver.find_element(:xpath, "(.//*[normalize-space(text()) and
normalize-space(.)='Row 1'])[1]/following::div[6]").click

@driver.find_element(:xpath, "(.//*[normalize-space(text()) and
normalize-space(.)='Row 2'])[1]/following::div[13]").click

@driver.find_element(:xpath, "(.//*[normalize-space(text()) and
normalize-space(.)='Row 3'])[1]/following::div[20]").click

@driver.find_element(:xpath, "(.//*[normalize-space(text()) and
normalize-space(.)='Row 4'])[1]/following::div[27]").click

@driver.find_element(:xpath, "(.//*[normalize-space(text()) and
normalize-space(.)='Row 1'])[3]/following::div[4]").click

@driver.find_element(:xpath, "(.//*[normalize-space(text()) and
normalize-space(.)='Row 1'])[3]/following::div[20]").click

@driver.find_element(:xpath, "(.//*[normalize-space(text()) and
normalize-space(.)='Row 2'])[3]/following::div[12]").click

@driver.find_element(:xpath, "(.//*[normalize-space(text()) and
normalize-space(.)='Row 2'])[3]/following::div[28]").click

@driver.find_element(:xpath, "(.//*[normalize-space(text()) and
normalize-space(.)='Row 3'])[3]/following::div[4]").click

@driver.find_element(:xpath, "(.//*[normalize-space(text()) and
normalize-space(.)='Row 3'])[3]/following::div[28]").click

@driver.find_element(:xpath, "(.//*[normalize-space(text()) and
normalize-space(.)='Row 4'])[3]/following::div[12]").click

@driver.find_element(:xpath, "(.//*[normalize-space(text()) and
normalize-space(.)='Row 4'])[3]/following::div[20]").click

@driver.find_element(:xpath, "(.//*[normalize-space(text()) and
```

```
normalize-space(.)='Date'])[1]/following::input[1]").click

    @driver.find_element(:xpath, "(.//*[normalize-space(text()) and
normalize-space(.)='Date'])[1]/following::input[1]").click

    @driver.find_element(:xpath, "(.//*[normalize-space(text()) and
normalize-space(.)='Date'])[1]/following::input[1]").clear

    @driver.find_element(:xpath, "(.//*[normalize-space(text()) and
normalize-space(.)='Date'])[1]/following::input[1]").send_keys "10-10-
2019"

    @driver.find_element(:xpath, "(.//*[normalize-space(text()) and
normalize-space(.)='Time'])[1]/following::input[1]").click

    @driver.find_element(:xpath, "(.//*[normalize-space(text()) and
normalize-space(.)='Time'])[1]/following::input[1]").clear

    @driver.find_element(:xpath, "(.//*[normalize-space(text()) and
normalize-space(.)='Time'])[1]/following::input[1]").send_keys "12"

    @driver.find_element(:xpath, "(.//*[normalize-space(text()) and
normalize-space(.)=':'])[1]/following::input[1]").clear

    @driver.find_element(:xpath, "(.//*[normalize-space(text()) and
normalize-space(.)=':'])[1]/following::input[1]").send_keys "34"

    @driver.save_screenshot 'Ch_7_Prog_11_Ruby_Form_Postfill.png'

    @driver.find_element(:xpath, "(.//*[normalize-space(text()) and
normalize-space(.)=':'])[1]/following::span[1]").click

    puts @driver.title

    @driver.save_screenshot 'Ch_7_Prog_11_Ruby_Form_Submit_Confirmation.
png'

    @driver.close

end


def windowhandleslist

    @driver.window_handles.each do |windowhandle|

    puts(windowhandle)

    @driver.switch_to.window windowhandle

end


end
```

Since in the program mentioned above, we have used a variety of web elements, such as a text box, radio button, checkboxes, pull-down menu, date/time element types, after executing the code, the output would be as follows:

```
[Running] ruby "c:\Users\rahma\OneDrive\Desktop\Selenium\Programs\Ruby\
Ch_7_Prog_11_Ruby_Form_Filler.rb"

Simple Form Data Collection


[Done] exited with code=0 in 29.864 seconds
```

In addition, the output of the screenshots will be as follow:

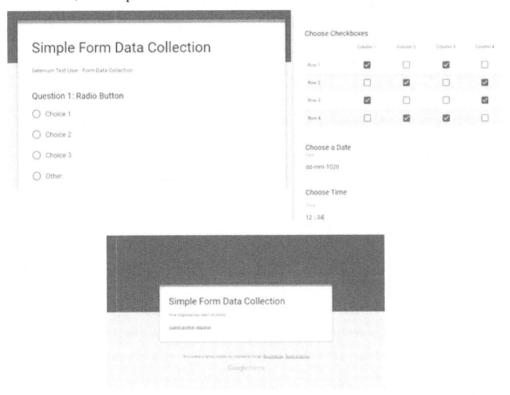

Figure 7.12: Output of the Screenshot

Key Selenium aspects to keep in mind from this program are as follows:

- Filling the element based on the XPATH and NAME locators. This is shown below:

    ```
    @driver.find_element(:xpath, "(.//*[normalize-space(text())
    and normalize-space(.)='Option 1'])[1]/following::div[6]").click

    @driver.find_element(:name, "entry.1621524406").click
    ```

```
@driver.find_element(:name, "entry.1621524406").clear

@driver.find_element(:name, "entry.1621524406").send_keys "Test"
```

- Getting the screenshot using the functionsave_screenshot
- Rest of the information is very straight forward

Ruby example getting form element values

Let us see some web element operations in Ruby for Selenium with reference to the following code snippets:

1. Clicking a button

```
#RUBY WEB ELEMENT OPERATIONS

#Handling a Button CLick

@driver.find_element(:id, web_id_element_for_button).click

#e.g

@driver.find_element(:id, 'SUBMIT').click
```

2. Filling a text box

```
# Filling a Text Box

@driver.find_element(:id, web_id_element_for_a_text_box).send_keys
'Text Inputs'
```

3. Checking checkboxes and performing select/unselect in a check box

```
# Check Box Examples for checking if it is selected, clicking a
check box and clearing the same.

@driver.find_element(:id, web_id_element_for_a_checkbox).selected?

@driver.find_element(:id, web_id_element_for_a_checkbox).click

@driver.find_element(:id, web_id_element_for_a_checkbox).clear
```

4. Selecting an element from a pull-down menu

```
# Selecting an element

elementselect = @driver.find_element(:tag_name, "elementselect")

all_options_in_select = elementselect.find_elements(:tag_name,
"option")

all_options_in_select.each do |options|

  puts "Value is: " + options.attribute("value")

  options.click

end
```

5. Checking whether an element is displayed on the screen

```
#Checking if this is displayed?
driver.find_element(:id,'webelementtocheck').displayed?
```

6. Getting a web element's text

```
#getting element's text

driver.find_element(:id,'webelementtocheck').text
```

7. Getting a web element's attribute (when a class is used as a locator)

```
#getting element's attributes

driver.find_element(:id,'webelementtocheck').
attribute('webelementclass')
```

JavaScript example for WebElementPromise

One of the nice features available in JavaScript programming language when dealing with web elementsis the WebElementPromise feature. WebElementPromise is an actionable promise defined in JavaScript. This JavaScript Promise is acted upon via a WebElement that calls the function. Since it uses a proxy of sorts on a web, we can write a function to do multiple actions because of the action performed. For example, two similar actions using web elementsare mentioned below. The first one is a straight forward action whereas the second one is a web element promise capable of doing more than one action because of the web element action.

```
driver.findElement({link: 'web-element-link'}).click();

driver.findElement({link: 'web-element-link'}).then(function(weproelink)
{
    return weproelink.click();

});
```

Conclusion

In this chapter, we have covered the key essential features of WebDriver automation using the JavaScript and Ruby programming languages. In the next chapter, we shall look at the conceptual approach, which is important for building a test automation framework using Selenium such as POM. In addition, we will also look at how we can bring the entire components of the test automation framework into onepicture. Having a strong grasp of the basic components of test automation, how to interweave them together to build a solid framework, having a strong approach for test automation and being flexible to accommodate the futuristic changes will be a key to successful implementation. In the next chapter, we will discuss some of the advanced concepts such as how to establish a test automation framework and how to go about designing a solid approach for test automation.

Questions

1. How will you open a web browser using JavaScript and Selenium WebDriver?

2. What is the use of WebElementPromise in JavaScript?

3. What is the use of ThenableWebDriver Class?

4. How will you use ActionChains in the Ruby programming language?

5. What is the difference between JavaScript and Ruby when it comes to the automation of Selenium WebDrivers?

6. Where will you use Ruby and Python for web automation? What are the pros and cons of one over another?

7. What are the key differences between Java and JavaScript when it comes to testing automation?

8. How will you automate headless browser testing using Ruby and JavaScript in Selenium?

Building a Test Automation Framework with Selenium

"Why did the Roman Empire collapse? What is Latin for office Automation?"

– Alan J Perlis

One of the most important aspects of any test automation project is the requirement to build a test automation framework. This includes multiple tasks in addition to coding in selenium. Building a good test automation framework requires a meticulous planning mind with the end state and long-term vision of the organization in mind. In this chapter, we will take a look at one type of approach we could follow for establishing a test automation framework with Selenium. This chapter will be a conceptual one in nature and we will have a technical implementation discussion in the next chapter.

Structure

We will look at the following concepts to test the automation knowledge. We shall also look at some reference and tips to the following points.

Test Automation Strategy / Approach:

- Building an Automation Strategy
- Choosing a Programming Language

- Defining the Automation Framework Architecture
- Choosing a Unit Test Framework
- Designing Core Components of a Framework – Modularization
- Designing Test Components of a Framework
- Designing Reporting Mechanism
- How to perform Source Code Control, Build, and Continuous integration if used in DevOps
- How to integrate with Other Tools

Objectives

In this chapter, we will explore the various aspects of test automation to evaluate what are some good tips to follow, what to automate, when to automate, what is the right approach, what are some suggested approaches? What are the different ways in which we can automate efficiently? We will focus more on the theoretical and concept-based understanding of test automation.

Building a Test Automation Strategy

We have tremendous growth in computerization and business processes are automated as a result. The expansion of Industry 3.0 led innovation (i.e. computerized automation), the amount of codegenerated, and the business logic and functionality getting added is increasing phenomenally as well.

With the approaches taken by businesses and a move towards continuous testing, concepts such as DevOps and Continuous integration will cause a major dent in the manual testing of end-to-end processes, applications, etc. Test automation is a key to deliver value the organizations will be looking forward.

However, an extensive dependency on the UI/front-end based automation may not work in the current age and context. Continuous automation need not happen only at the UI level but it can be done much earlier by inverting the testing Pyramid. What it means is that we can automate testing of APIs, microservices, and interfaces at an earlier phase of SDLC.

It is also important for the organization to decide what can be automated, why it should be automated, and how it can be automated before embarking on a journey in test automation. To achieve this, building a test automation strategy is the first step of a test automation project.

One of the sample approaches for building a Test Automation Strategy may look like the *figure 8.1* below There could be more than one way to decide on a test automation approach and a one-size-fits-all approach may not apply to different organizations and units.

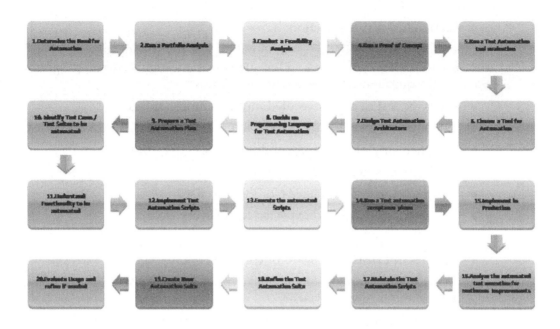

Figure 8.1: *Selecting a Test Strategy – Steps to be followed*

Key actions for building a test automation strategy

For building a good automation strategy, the test automation architect needs to ask some important questions before finalizing the strategy. Some of the questions are as follows:

1. **Determine the need for automation:**

   To determine the need for automation, it is important to analyze and understand if there should be any automation. Automation is not a silver bullet to all the problems unless it is done in a very thorough and well-thought manner. Hence, the first important question is to determinewhen it would be the right time to automate. Is it early in the development in the lifecycle Vs. just before-go-live and in-cycle automation vs. stable phase automation are some of the questions the project team needs to address.

2. **Which test automation tool to choose?**

   Some questions to look for while deciding the test automation tool to use would be what are the features you should be looking at for your test automation framework? Is it functionality or affordability of the tool that you are looking for? Is it the ease of use or the features? Is it the extensibility or compatibility that you are looking for?

3. **Automation test script selection:**

As mentioned earlier, 100% test automation is a myth and purposeful and meaningful automation is key to the success of a test automation program. Some of the questions to be asked are as follows:

- Does the test case get executed multiple times repeatedly?
- Doesthe test case require manual intervention and verification checks?
- Are there any pre and postcondition checks to be done?
- Are the steps to be followed unambiguous?
- What are the test data needs for the test case?
- Are test conditions and expected results very clear?
- Can the script be modularized?
- Is the script straightforward or complex?
- Is there a long term need and goal to use test automation? Is it strategic or use and throw approach?
- Is the automation required for regression testing or a new functionality?
- Is there a need for test script and test data reusability via automation?
- Is there a progressive growth of features in the application/product under test?
  - o Is there an increasing need for regression testing?
- Are the requirements clear and not volatile?

All these questions and the steps outlined in *Figure 8.1* give a method to build a solid test automation strategy.

Choosing a programming language

There are a lot of options available to do test automation using a myriad of programming languages and tools. Some of the tools do not mandate extensive programming knowledge. However, some of the tools/frameworks require a very good programming language in various languages to build a solid test automation framework.

Selenium is such a framework built on a brilliant programming approach followed by a genius tester. As the requirements for test automation vary across applications and products, it is important to choose a programming language that can deliver the requirements for building a solid test automation strategy.

One challenge to remember is that once you decide to go ahead with a programming language for test automation; for example, VB Script for MicroFocus UFT or JavaScript for Protractor, your investment gets locked in a way. However, with a flexible framework such as Selenium, one has an opportunity to automate in multiple languages such as Java, JavaScript, Ruby, C#, Python, PHP, etc. This allows users to use common libraries available in multiple languages.

However, it may take away the efficiency a framework gives in terms of common functions and libraries written in one language to be compatible in another. The key to success is to choose a language that makes your application in a decent state to be migrated to any new automation tool or framework your project/application team decides to use.

Defining the automation framework architecture

One of the most important aspects to choose a test automation strategy is the decision on the automation tool and the type of automation; Be it scripted or script-less automation. If one needs to script in a tool using a programming language, availability of skills, ease of programming, ability to generate modularized scripts and libraries, and ease of maintenance aspects need to be clearly understood and a decision needs to be made accordingly.

Test automation typically starts when the application is in the 'golden window' or when it is stable. However, a good practice will be to start focusing on features and functionalities that are not likely to change and progress with the modular model of testing even before the application is ready. This will be achieved via the use of good library/utility-based test automation by building objects and library functions for use in test automation. This could be at an object or a user action element level.

For the Page Object Model, test automation engineers can use the abstraction-based approach. It is also important to start automaton in earlier phases by inverting the test pyramid as it useful for the application developers to build high-quality build before it is made available for testing.

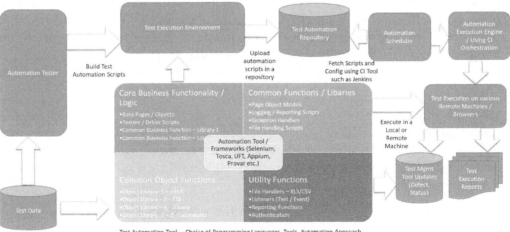

Figure 8.2: Test Automation Framework Example

Once the framework is finalized, the implementation team needs to ensure that the core principles are maintained with a future centric vision in mind. Things such as the ability to port into a new tool, ease of maintenance, and the ability to minimize the maintenance of test automation script are some of these essentials.

Choosing a unit test framework

Once the test automation scripts are developed, it is important to test the scripts, modules, and functions developed. This can be done using a unit test framework. There are many such unit test frameworks and they vary based on choice of the programming language and the platforms used. One can consider TestNG, Junit, NUnit, PyTest, PHPUnit, Test Unit, Groovy, Rest Assured, and Robot Framework for the unit test framework of choice. Each of these tools delivers a unique service depending either on the language used or the type of testing (UI Unit Testing vs. Microservice/API testing, etc.)

The key benefits of a unit test framework include the following:

- Ability to automatically run the tests once the code is committed through a schedule or a continuous integration tool such as Jenkins.
- Remove manual dependency to validate the builds and reduce the time involved in application development.

Designing core components of framework – modularization

As you can see in the preceding *Figure 8.2*, one of the key benefits of modularized test automation framework is the simplicity it brings to the entire approach. We just need to manage the maintenance of a single module or a class or a function. Think about a login/logout function being used in more than 1000 test cases under a test. What will happen if you need to maintain a change in the locators or an identifier changing in either the login or a logout script? With the centrally managed and modularized component, the test automation framework becomes a lot easy to manage.

One more important aspect to consider is the abstraction of the functions and classes. This will help in the extension of a base class. Once the class is extended, we can then implement functions of relevance for the feature getting automated. This layered abstraction is a recognized practice whilebuilding a good test automation framework as well.

In addition to the components specified in the preceding *Figure 8.2*, some of the modular components that can be included are as follows:

- Verification Components (Assertion/Verification, etc.)

- GUI/Web site interaction components
- Language/Technology specific components (Programming Language/Operating System Specific)
- Web Browser Specific components
- Parallel Execution Utility/Components
- Test Data Management Components
- File Handling Components
- Database Utilities
- Error handling Components
- Exception Handlers
- Logging Components
- Reporting Components
- File Parser Components
- Visual Comparison Components
- Mobile App Components
- Cloud-based App Handlers
- File Generators such as XML, HTML, CSV, and Reports
- Report Generators
- Report Formatters
- Rerun Enablers
- File Utilities (Upload, Parsing, and Updaters)
- Email Components
- Date and Timestamp Utilities
- International Localization Utilities
- Test Driver Components
- Automation Controller Components
- Modular Automation Components
- Keywords Library
- Data Handler Components
- Cross Browser Setup Components
- Parallel Execution Components
- Environment Setup Components
- Automation Configuration Components

The benefits of modularization are multifold. To start with, we can do efficient test automation programming as the code is easy to understand and maintain. With a very long linear program, it becomes very difficult to control the logic and validate failures or having a graceful exit or exception handling becomes a challenge. With a modular program, these challenges are addressed thoroughly. We can build a strong library of modular programs.

If you take Selenium as an example, it's a classic case of modularization with purpose. The functions and classes are easy to understand and use. Secondly, there is a major benefit of reuse of a module. You just need to create it once and you can reuse as many times as you want. This results in a lot of benefits to the automation programmer. Ease of maintenance is the next major benefit. As we have the functions in a module, we need to make changes in very few places if the functionality driven by the module changes instead of changing in 100s/1000s or places in a big test automation suite, if followed linearly against a modular fashion.

Designing test components of a framework

Just like how a test automation suite and the libraryare used, it is always a good practice to reuse repeatable test steps into a reusable component and build a library of tests as well. The test components will be very useful to be interwoven into a full test suite. Steps such as Login, Logout, performing a particular action, checking an assertion, and verifying something will be always useful.

Testing frameworks such as TestNG, Unit Test, NUnit, Junit, etc. have a mechanism to provide such a facility. A good test automation framework will account for such a reusable test component use. In a behavior-driven testing suite such as Cucumber that uses Gherkin as a language for specifying test cases in a (Given -> When -> Then) format or a test-driven testing suite using an Arrange->Act->Assert to automate the test cases, it is required to build components that could be used to test the automation script.

Let us take a look at the Gherkin/Cucumber example for checking the weather:

Feature: Is the temperature Hot today?
Everyone wants to know when the temperature is over 35 degrees Celsius
Scenario: Temperature is 32 degrees Celsius
Given temperature is 32 degrees Celsius
When Queried "Is the temperature Hot today?"
Then I should say "No. It is not Hot"
Scenario: Temperature is 40 degrees Celsius
Given temperature is 40 degrees Celsius
When Queried "Is the temperature Hot today?"
Then I should say "Yes. It is Hot today"

> **Scenario:** Temperature is 35 degrees Celsius
> Given temperature is 35 degrees Celsius
> When Queried "Is the temperature Hot today?"
> Then I should say "No. It is not Hot"

Table 8.1: Gherkin BDD example for Test Automation

With the tool such as Cucumber, we can generate code that is suitable for our end-to-end test automation suite.

Coming to testing components, specific components testing tools such as Junit or TestNG have the following capabilities. Other tools have similar or language-specific components that could be used for running tests on the test automation framework. Some of the TestNG specific testing components include the following:

- Test Setup Functions
- Test Teardown functions
- Before Annotations such as:
  - o `@BeforeSuite` executes a method containing a set of actions for tasks before a test suite starts.
  - o `@BeforeTest` executes a method containing a set of actions for tasks before any @test method in the suite.
  - o `@BeforeGroups` executes a method containing a set of actions for tasks before a set of actions get executed in a grouped method.
  - o `@BeforeMethod` executes a method containing a set of actions for tasks before any @test method in the suite gets executed.
  - o `@BeforeClass` executes a method containing a set of actions for tasks before a set of actions get executed in the first method in the class specified.
- After Annotations such as:
  - o `@AfterSuite` executes a method containing a set of actions for tasks after a test suite starts.
  - o `@AfterTest` executes a method containing a set of actions for tasks after a test case starts.
  - o `@AfterGroups` executes a method containing a set of actions for tasks after a set of actions get executed in a grouped method.
  - o `@AfterMethod` executes a method containing a set of actions for tasks after each @test method gets executed.
  - o `@AfterClass` executes a method containing a set of actions for tasks after a set of actions get executed in the first method in the class specified.

- @Listeners defines the listener functions to test the execution and log them for debugging and validation purposes.

- @DataProvider defines a method to provide data to a function.

- @Factory provides a list of test objects used by the testing framework/TestNG and returns Object[] which could be used to check and act.

- @Test defines a class or a method/function as a part of the test. We can define as many methods as a part of a test with this definition.

Different tools and frameworks have different sets of components/functions/methods to enable testing of the test automation scripts. TestNG, Junit, and UnitTest are some good choices to consider and use with Selenium. These methods also help the programmers by providing better control over test execution. It also gives a mechanism to prioritize the test cases and connect to external data, perform better data type validation,error checking, and produce a better-quality reporting feature.

Designing reporting mechanism

One more key aspect of a test automation framework is the ability to report the test execution status and logging the progress with various levels of logging. The ability to produce test execution summary, exception summary, and screenshots as pieces of evidence for test management tools are very useful features. Some of the advanced automation tools have these features like an inbuilt mechanism.

To build such features using Selenium, it is good to use frameworks such as TestNG and extend the features to deliver incremental features needed for the automation framework. To begin with, one could use the Junit TestWatcher option to build a report. The TestWatcher class can be modified by overriding the failed() and succeeded() functions defined for reporting the failure or success of a selenium test execution.

As an alternative to Junit, TestNG, Allure, and Extent Reports provide a much comprehensive summary. The features of Extent Reports and TestNG aremuch more drillable and refined. It is a good idea to leverage detailed analytics and insights provided by these reporting features. For comprehensive end-to-end automation with Continuous integration approach, it is very difficult to analyze the failures and take necessary corrective actions if one is not able to analyze the logs. These reports provide a mechanism to address this issue. We just need to change the MAVEN requirement of the POM.xml file to include the features we want in our testing.

How to perform Source Code Control, Build, and Continuous Integration in DevOps

One of the greatest benefits of the DevOps model is to leverage the automation tools available to build a release pipeline. Automated code built using Selenium can be integrated with other tools to make this happen seamlessly.

One of the biggest challenges faced by developers and automation scriptwriting testers is the ability to version control and manage the code. It becomes critical for the team to ensure the right versioning is done and an automated build is done as soon as the code is committed. To do automated build and for source control, the team can leverage tools such as GitHub, Subversion, Gitlab, Artifactory, and Bitbucket to name a few. Traditional source code control by legacy firms can also be used but the level of integration could be tricky.

When used with Continuous integration tools such as Jenkins, Bamboo, Travis, Circle, Teamcity,+ AWS Code build, Microsoft VSTS, Codeship, etc., we can achieve the objective of doing an end-to-end build of automated test scripts.

For Continuous Build, one can pick from Ant, Maven, JAM, Gulp, and other tools. This purely depends on how you have built the Continuous Integration pipeline for your project and environment.

Tool Type	Tools
Continuous Build Tools	Gradle, Build, Continuum, Cruise Control, Apache Ant, Maven, MS Build, Nant., Ruby on Rails, Urban Code, Gulp, Grunt, Broccolli, JAM, Make, Quickbuild, LuntBuild, Densify, Final Builder
Source Code Management Tools	BitBucket, GitHub, Atlassian Crucible, FishEye, GitLab, Nexus, Gitlab, Nexus, Gerrit, Gogs, Microsoft VSTS, Kallithea, Rational Team Concert, Rational ClearCase, Compuware ISPW, Perforce Helix Core
Testing Tools	Gatling, Selenium, FitNesse, Cucumber, Junit, JMeter, Appium, TestNG, Mocha, Protractor, Jasmine, SpecFlow, Cucumber.JS, Concordion, Watir, CA TDM, Nightwatch.JS, Parasoft SOATEST, Screenster, Squash TA, Gauntlt, Perfecto Mobile, TestComplete-Test, GenRocket, CodeScene, Cyara, Karma, SahiPro, PyTest, Locust, Microfocus UFT, MicroFocus ALM, Parasoft DTP, Katalon Studio, Google Test, SauceLabs, BrowserStack, CrossBrowserTesting, Cypress, QUnit, CA TDM, Ranorex Studio

Continuous Integration Tools	TeamCity, Shippable, Continua CI, Snap, Jenkins, Harness, Concourse, Hudson, ProductionMap, Jenkins X, Travis, Codeship, Gitlab, NeverCode, Drone, MS VSTS, Semaphore, Solano, Hydra, CircleCI, BuildKite, Buddy, AWS Codebuild, Apache Gump, Bamboo

Table 8.4: *List of DevOps/Continuous Integration Tools available for Test Automation*

How to integrate with other tools

One of the key aspects of the end-to-end continuous integration is to build your release pipeline. This could be a unique pipeline with different sets of tools and technologies followed based on the need. Every pipeline is unique by nature and there is no one-size-fits-all template of a build pipeline applicable to all types of enterprises and customers. As a part of the strategy, it is important to decide the need first and understand the capabilities of the tools involved and the amount of programming/coding/ integration needed before deciding on the tools, infrastructure and methods to implement.

Conclusion

In this chapter, we covered the key essentials for building a test automation framework. In the next chapter, we willsee some of the advanced features of selenium test automation such as the Page Object Model and how we can bring the entire test automation framework components into the picture. Having a strong grasp of the basics of test automation components, how to interweave them together to build a solid framework having a strong approach for test automation and being flexible to accommodate the futuristic changes will be a key to successful implementation. In the next chapter, we willcover some of the most important topics in Selenium such as creating a Page Object Model, how to do file and database interactions, how to setup reporting in Selenium, how to integrate with the CI/CD pipeline, and other topics that are crucial for implementation of a good test automation framework.

Questions

1. Why building a test automation framework is important?

2. What are some of the core components to be considered while building a framework?

3. Why is source control management important in a test automation project?

4. What are some of the continuous integration tools that we can use for building a test automation framework?

5. What is meant by a test automation controller? How can you implement a test automation controller using Selenium?

6. What is the benefit of modularization in test automation framework? How will you implement Modularization?

7. What are the benefits of using libraries in a test automation framework? How will you go about implementing one?

8. What are some of the good build tools available?

9. What will be your approach to test automation framework for a product getting built in an agile fashion? When and what will you automate?

10. What are some of the challenges faced while doing test automation maintenance? What would be your ideas to overcome them?

Advanced Features of Selenium Using Java and Python

> *"The bitterness of poor quality remains long after the sweetness of meeting the schedule has been forgotten."*
>
> *- Anonymous*

Some of the core features of Selenium used by most of the automation projects include Page Object Model, File Handling, Reporting, Database interactions and continuous integration using CI/CD pipeline tools. It is very important to know about these concepts. This chapter covers advanced Selenium concepts such as advanced features of Page Object Model (POM), Reading and Writing Files, XLS, CSV, Reporting, Use of Object Repository, Integration with Jenkins, GitHub, Maven, and Database connectivity using examples in Java and Python.

Structure

We will look at the following concepts to test the automation knowledge; and leverage content as a reference and tips to be followed. These include coverage on the following topics.

- Test Automation Approach
- Page Object Model Features

- File Handling
- Reporting
- Database Management and Connectivity
- Integration with Jenkins, GitHub, and Maven

Objectives

Understand the concepts outlined as per the objectives and be in a position to handle POM, file and database handlers and use the packages to produce meaningful reports using Python and Java programming examples in Selenium.

Page Object Model

One of the great features of Selenium web automation is the use of a very solid object-oriented design pattern – the **Page Object Model (POM)**. With the use of the POM, it is very easy to maintain the code and reduce the amount of effort required to do efficient automation. The POM is an object created at each web page level that is utilized like a design of the page pattern. In other words, the Page Object of a page acts as an interface to the web page you are automating with. Typically, a POM is extended to a PageFactory and all the pages of an application can be built, maintained, and managed in a simple and an easy-to-understand manner. A Page Object Model is the easiest way to replicate a complex web application easily. POMs become very handy when a very large application with hundreds of pages needs to be automated. With a traditional way of linear or record-and-playback automation, the overall effort needed to automate is exhaustive. The effort needed to maintain and manage changes will be exorbitant. Using the POM is also a good way to write test cases in a business-relevant language. This is possible using frameworks such as Cucumber and other ATDD frameworks available. It is also easier to segregate the logic between the automated test cases and the actual code that is being automated. This segregation is very important as the scripts can be built into an object repository that can be referred to across the automation suite. This gives a good maintainability capability as well. A Page Factory is an extension of a Page Object and uses implicit @FindBy() instead to define the FindElement or FindElements methods using the By() methods in a Page Object without a Page Factory. It also allows caching of the web elements, it can be very useful in automating applications with an exhaustive set of pages, and hundreds of webelements as the cached search is a lot quicker than a non-cached one that is typically used in a Page Object.

A Page Object Model Design Pattern consists of two key components. First, a page class that covers the page is tested and then, a test case class is used to invoke the POM and test the functionality. The web element locators and the test scripts using the POM and the web elements are stored and run separately. Let us see this in a simple diagram as follows:

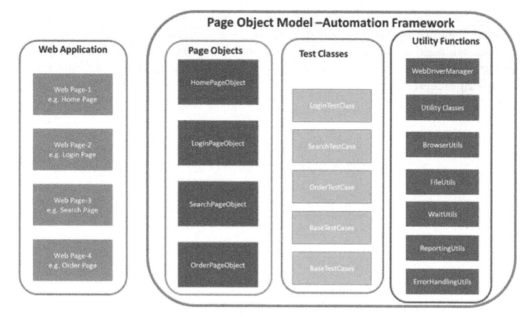

Figure 9.1: *Page Object Model Framework*

As you can see in the preceding diagram, with the use of the design patterns and modular design, we will be able to build a lot simpler application automation design. Let us see some of the examples to understand how we can design a Page Object Model framework using Java and Python, to begin with.

Page Object Model using Java

Let us take an example of a Java Page Object Model. This example takes a custom site built for this book – **http://crackingseleniuminterviews.simplesite.com/**. The landing page looks as shown inthe following screenshot:

Figure 9.2: *Cracking Selenium Interviews POM Example*

For automation, we will create a Page Object Model for the contact form at **http://crackingseleniuminterviews.simplesite.com/443702024**. To create a Page Object Model, we need to identify the Web Element Locators and then use them for our automation purposes. The contact form for the example looks as shown in the following screenshot:

Figure 9.3: Cracking Selenium Interviews POM Example - Form

The first program is the Page Object Model for the Contact Page. The full program is given in the following screenshot. We will dissect this program in detail shortly:

```java
import java.util.List;
import java.util.Map;
import org.openqa.selenium.support.CacheLookup;
import org.openqa.selenium.support.FindBy;
import org.openqa.selenium.support.PageFactory;
import org.openqa.selenium.support.ui.ExpectedCondition;
import org.openqa.selenium.support.ui.Select;
import org.openqa.selenium.support.ui.WebDriverWait;
import org.openqa.selenium.WebDriver;
import org.openqa.selenium.WebElement;

public class CrackingSeleniumSimpleSitePage {
    private Map<String, String> data;
    private WebDriver driver;
    private int timeout = 15;
```

```java
@FindBy(name = "Name")
@CacheLookup
private WebElement contactName;

@FindBy(name = "Email")
@CacheLookup
private WebElement contactEmail;

@FindBy(name = "Message")
@CacheLookup
private WebElement contactMessage;

@FindBy(css = "button.contact-form-button")
@CacheLookup
private WebElement send;

private final String pageLoadedText = "Get Your own FREE website";

private final String pageUrl = "/443702024";

public CrackingSeleniumSimpleSitePage() {

}

public CrackingSeleniumSimpleSitePage(WebDriver driver) {
    this();
    this.driver = driver;

}

    public CrackingSeleniumSimpleSitePage(WebDriver driver, Map<String,
String> data) {
s
        this.data = data;
    }

    public CrackingSeleniumSimpleSitePage(WebDriver driver, Map<String,
String> data, int timeout) {
        this(driver, data);
        this.timeout = timeout;
    }
```

```
/**
 * Click on Contact Link.
 *
 * @return the CrackingSeleniumSimpleSitePage class instance.
 */
public CrackingSeleniumSimpleSitePage clickContactName() {
    contactName.click();
    return this;
}

/**
 * Click on Contact Link.
 *
 * @return the CrackingSeleniumSimpleSitePage class instance.
 */
public CrackingSeleniumSimpleSitePage clickContactEmail() {
    contactEmail.click();
    return this;
}

/**
 * Click on Get Your Own Free Website. Click Here Link.
 *
 * @return the CrackingSeleniumSimpleSitePage class instance.
 */
public CrackingSeleniumSimpleSitePage clickContactMessage() {
    contactMessage.click();
    return this;
}

/**
 * Click on Send Button.
 *
 * @return the CrackingSeleniumSimpleSitePage class instance.
 */
public CrackingSeleniumSimpleSitePage clickSendButton() {
    send.click();
    return this;
}

public CrackingSeleniumSimpleSitePage setContactName(String
contactname){
```

```java
        contactName.sendKeys((contactname));
        return this;
    }

    public CrackingSeleniumSimpleSitePage setContactEmail(String
contactemail){
        contactEmail.sendKeys((contactemail));
        return this;
    }

    public CrackingSeleniumSimpleSitePage setContactMessage(String
contactmsg){
        contactMessage.sendKeys((contactmsg));
        return this;
    }
    public CrackingSeleniumSimpleSitePage setContactName(){
        return this;
    }

    public CrackingSeleniumSimpleSitePage setContactEmail(){
        return this;
    }

    public CrackingSeleniumSimpleSitePage setContactMessage(){
        return this;
    }

    public void SubmitData(String contactname,String contactemail,String
contactmsg)
    {
        contactName.sendKeys((contactname));
        contactEmail.sendKeys((contactemail));
        contactMessage.sendKeys((contactmsg));
        send.click();
    }

    /**
     * Fill every fields in the page.
     *
     * @return the CrackingSeleniumSimpleSitePage class instance.
     */
    public CrackingSeleniumSimpleSitePage fill() {
```

```
        setContactName();
        setContactEmail();
        setContactMessage();
        return this;
    }
    /**
     * Submit the form to target page.
     *
     * @return the CrackingSeleniumSimpleSitePage class instance.
     */
    public CrackingSeleniumSimpleSitePage submit() {
        clickSendButton();
        CrackingSeleniumSimpleSitePage target = new
CrackingSeleniumSimpleSitePage(driver, data, timeout);
        PageFactory.initElements(driver, target);
        return target;
    }


}
```

In the preceding program, the following sections of code are important. In the following section, we define the Page Object Model using Page Factory:

```
import org.openqa.selenium.support.CacheLookup;

import org.openqa.selenium.support.FindBy;

import org.openqa.selenium.support.PageFactory;
```

We define the Web Element Locators using the following code by defining the Web Element types (Name, XPATH, CSS Locator, etc.) using the @FindBy option available in a PageFactoryclass. @CacheLookup allows the caching of the elements for faster identification. Once the Page Objects are instantiated, we can use the functions created along with the Page Objects to finish the automation:

```
    @FindBy(name = "Name")
    @CacheLookup
    private WebElement contactName;

    @FindBy(name = "Email")
    @CacheLookup
    private WebElement contactEmail;

    @FindBy(name = "Message")
```

```
@CacheLookup
private WebElement contactMessage;

@FindBy(css = "button.contact-form-button")
@CacheLookup
private WebElement send;
```

The get/set functions and submit functions help us work on the elements in a simple manner like the SubmitData function mentioned in the preceding code:

```
public void SubmitData(String contactname,String contactemail,String contactmsg)
{
    contactName.sendKeys((contactname));
    contactEmail.sendKeys((contactemail));
    contactMessage.sendKeys((contactmsg));
    send.click();
}
```

The POM tester page – CrackingSeleniumSimpleSitePageTest.java runs the test using the Page Object Model by leveraging the example code as follows:

```
import org.openqa.selenium.WebDriver;
import org.openqa.selenium.chrome.ChromeDriver;
import org.openqa.selenium.WebDriver;
import org.openqa.selenium.support.PageFactory;
import org.testng.annotations.Test;

public class CrackingSeleniumSimpleSitePageTest
{
    @Test
    public void enterDataChrome() {
        System.out.println("=====Browser Session Started - Chrome ");
        // This will launch browser and specific url
        WebDriver webDriver=BrowserHelper.setBrowser("chrome", "http://crackingseleniuminterviews.simplesite.com/443702024");
    //Created Page Object using Page Factory
        CrackingSeleniumSimpleSitePage checksite=PageFactory.initElements(webDriver, CrackingSeleniumSimpleSitePage.class);
        System.out.println("=====Application Started=====");
```

```
        System.out.println("=====Data Entry starts=====");
// Call the method
        checksite.SubmitData("Selenium User", "Selenium.User@
seleniuminterviews.com","selenium is a brilliant tool");
        System.out.println("=====Data Entered");
        webDriver.close();
        System.out.println("=====Application ended=");
    }
    @Test
    public void enterDataFireFox() {
        System.out.println("=====Browser Session Started -Firefox
====");
        // This will launch browser and specific url
        WebDriver webDriver=BrowserHelper.setBrowser("firefox","http://
crackingseleniuminterviews.simplesite.com/443702024");
        //Created Page Object using Page Factory
        CrackingSeleniumSimpleSitePage checksite=PageFactory.
initElements(webDriver, CrackingSeleniumSimpleSitePage.class);
        System.out.println("=====Application Started=====");
        System.out.println("=====Data Entry starts=====");
// Call the method
        checksite.SubmitData("Selenium User", "Selenium.User@
seleniuminterviews.com","selenium is a brilliant tool");
        System.out.println("=====Data Entered");
        webDriver.close();
        System.out.println("=====Application ended=");
    }

}
```

We can also define a centralized browser helper to help us with Web Driver initialization, browser window sizing, and passing the driver object for reference. This utility function will be very handy for automation tasks:

```
import org.openqa.selenium.WebDriver;

import org.openqa.selenium.chrome.ChromeDriver;

import org.openqa.selenium.firefox.FirefoxDriver;

import org.openqa.selenium.ie.InternetExplorerDriver;

import org.openqa.selenium.safari.SafariDriver;
```

```java
public class BrowserHelper {
    static WebDriver driver;
    static String WEBDRIVER_PATH = "C:\\Selenium\\";

    public static WebDriver setBrowser(String browName, String URL){

        if (browName.equalsIgnoreCase("firefox")){
            driver = new FirefoxDriver();
        } else if (browName.equalsIgnoreCase("chrome")){
            String wdp= WEBDRIVER_PATH.concat("chromedriver.exe");
            System.out.println(wdp);
            System.setProperty("webdriver.chrome.driver",wdp);
            driver = new ChromeDriver();
        } else if (browName.equalsIgnoreCase("safari")){
            System.setProperty("webdriver.safari.driver",
                    WEBDRIVER_PATH.concat("safaridriver.exe"));
            driver = new SafariDriver();
        } else if(browName.equalsIgnoreCase("IE")){
            System.setProperty("webdriver.IE.driver",
                    WEBDRIVER_PATH.concat("IEDriverServer.exe"));
            driver = new InternetExplorerDriver();
        }
        driver.manage().window().maximize();
        driver.get(URL);
        return driver;

    }

    public void closeBrowser(WebDriver driver){
        driver.quit();
    }
}
```

In the preceding code, the following two lines of code are the most important ones. The first line of code is the creation of the Page Object using `PageFactory`. `InitElements` of the `CrackingSeleniumSimpleSitePage` Page Object:

```
//Created Page Object using Page Factory
        CrackingSeleniumSimpleSitePage checksite=PageFactory.
initElements(webDriver, CrackingSeleniumSimpleSitePage.class);
```

The second important line of code is the passing of the values through the SubmitData function for submission:

```
// Call the method
        checksite.SubmitData("Selenium User", "Selenium.User@
seleniuminterviews.com","selenium is a brilliant tool");
```

When we execute this program, we get the following outputs:

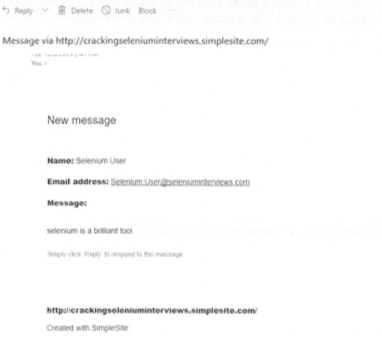

Figure 9.4: Email sent through the POM example

The test program produces the following output by running the same test in both Chrome and Firefox browsers using the functions annotated by the @Test tag in the TestNG-based test program. The methods enterDataChrome() and enter DataFirefox() mentioned in the program is executed:

```
[RemoteTestNG] detected TestNG version 6.13.1

=====Browser Session Started - Chrome

C:\Selenium\chromedriver.exe

Starting ChromeDriver 76.0.3809.68 (420c9498db8ce8fcd190a954d51297672c15
15d5-refs/branch-heads/3809@{#864}) on port 7146

=====Application Started=====

=====Data Entry starts=====
```

```
=====Data Entered

=====Application ended=

=====Browser Session Started -Firefox ====

 [Ch1571163946775   Marionette   INFO   Listening on port 49469

=====Application Started=====

=====Data Entry starts=====

=====Data Entered

1571163979481Marionette   INFO   Stopped listening on port 49469

=====Application ended=

PASSED: enterDataChrome

PASSED: enterDataFireFox


===============================================

    Default test

    Tests run: 2, Failures: 0, Skips: 0

===============================================


===============================================

Default suite

Total tests run: 2, Failures: 0, Skips: 0

===============================================
```

As a recap, the following things were done for the Page Object Models:

Page	Page Object	Test Class/Utility Class
Cracking Selenium Interviews – Contact Page	CrackingSeleniumSimpleSitePage – Contact POM	• CrackingSeleniumSimpleSite PageTest – Test Runner • BrowserHelper – For setting up the Web Driver using various Web Drivers

Table 9.1: Page Object Model and Utility reference

Now, let us see how we can implement a bit complex Page Object Model for an e-commerce style website, using Python in our next example.

Page Object Model using Python

In the second example, we will use a website similar to a B2B/B2C style web application that corresponds to most of the application. We have taken two core

Page Object Models: one for the landing page and the other for a user administration page. We have identified a couple of more pages to be a part of the POM as well. For utility, we have built a few functions that can be helpful for the application. Let us see how the POM works in Python with this example:

Page	Page Object	Test Class/Utility Class
Orange HRM Landing Page **Orange HRM – User Addition / Registration Page**	Orange_HRM HomePage - **HomePage.py** Orange_HRM User Registration page - **RegistrationPage.py** **UserSearchPage.py** – User Search POM for searching users before registering **UserManagementPage. py** – A POM for a user name search on the registration page	● Locators.Py – Locator class that holds all the Web Element Locator definitions ● POMExampleSetup.py – Definition of Utils classes for starting and closing of the POM objects ● ScreenShotUtil.py – Utility class for taking screenshots as evidence ● test_OrangeHRM_HomePage. py – Test class to run the Page Object Model for Home POM created ● test_OrangeHRM_RegistrationPage. py – Test class to run the Page Object Model for user registration POM created

Table 9.2: Reference for Web Pages, Page Objects and Utility Classes used

Let us see the flow of the programs.

Firstly, we need to define the locators for various web elements we will be using in the program. This can be identified by clicking on the web element, right clicking and inspecting it or using Chrome or Firefox extensions to get various types of locators such as CSS, XPATH, and ID to identify the locators. As a recommendation, one can use Firefox developer tools at bare minimum or good extensions such as firepath or Ranorex to get the locators.

The idea of the Locators class is to get all the locators for various pages in the OrangeHRM application and use them in the POMs for various pages. This is used commonly with the Locator identifier. The definition of Find By will be implemented during the locator usage. We can use a naming convention such as _xp or _css or _id to indicate the locator type as well.

Locators.py:

```
class Locators(object):
# https://opensource-demo.orangehrmlive.com/
#home page locator
    logo = '//*[@id="divLogo"]/img'
    user_name = '//*[@id="txtUsername"]'
```

```
    password = '//*[@id="txtPassword"]'

    login = '//*[@id="btnLogin"]'

    forgot_pass = '//*[@id="forgotPasswordLink"]/a'

    forgot_pass_xp = '//*[@id="forgotPasswordLink"]/a'
# https://opensource-demo.orangehrmlive.com/index.php/admin/
viewSystemUsers
#User Management Locators
    user_admin = '//*[@id="menu_admin_viewSystemUsers"]'

    user_admin_menu = '#menu_admin_viewAdminModule > b'

    user_admin_mgmt = 'menu_admin_UserManagement'

    user_add_user = '//*[@id="btnAdd"]'

    user_search_field = '//*[@id="searchSystemUser_userName"]'

    user_search_button = '//*[@id="searchBtn"]'
# https://opensource-demo.orangehrmlive.com/index.php/admin/
saveSystemUser
# Add User page locator
    user_role_role ='//select[@id="systemUser_userType"]'

    employee_name = 'systemUser_employeeName_empName'

    user_name_log = '//*[@id="systemUser_userName"]' #JohnSmith

    user_status = '//select[@id="systemUser_status"]'

    user_password = '//*[@id="systemUser_password"]'

    user_password_conf = '//*[@id="systemUser_confirmPassword"]'

    save_user_button = '//*[@id="btnSave"]'

    cancel_user_button = '//*[@id="btnCancel"]'
```

Once the locator class is defined, we can define the Page Object Utility functions such as setup of the POMs, Web Drivers, and Configurations, etc. In the following example, we are hard wiring the Web Driver as a Chrome. The same can be modified to make it a dynamic function as well, based on the parameters passed. This is an example you can try to make it work by trying your code.

POMExampleSetup.py

```
import unittest

import datetime

from selenium import webdriver
```

```python
class POMExampleSetup(unittest.TestCase):

    def setUp(self):
        self.driver = webdriver.Chrome("c:\\Selenium\\chromedriver.exe")
        # Can be any browser
        # self.driver = webdriver.Firefox(WEB_DRIVER_PATH)
    print("**************************************************************")
        print ("CLASS Initiated at : " + str(datetime.datetime.now()))
    print("**************************************************************")
        self.driver.implicitly_wait(10)
        self.driver.maximize_window()

    def tearDown(self):
      if (self.driver!=None):
        self.driver.close()
        self.driver.quit()
    print("**************************************************************")
        print("PROGRAM ended at : " + str(datetime.datetime.now()))
    print("**************************************************************")
```

Let us see the key **Page Object Model (POM)** for the Orange HRM's landing page also known as the Home Page. This POM uses the Locators defined in Locators.py for setting and getting the values of the Web Element and submits the data using the WebDriver functions.

HomePage.py

```python
from selenium.webdriver.common.by import By
from Locators import Locators

class Home(object):
    def __init__(self, driver):
        self.driver = driver
        self.logo = driver.find_element(By.XPATH, Locators.logo)
        self.user_name = driver.find_element(By.XPATH, Locators.user_name)
        self.password = driver.find_element(By.XPATH, Locators.password)
        self.login = driver.find_element(By.XPATH, Locators.login)
```

```
        self.forgot_pass = driver.find_element(By.XPATH, Locators.forgot_pass)
def getLogo(self):
    return self.logo

def getUserName(self):
    return self.user_name

def getPassword(self):
    return self.password

def getLogin(self):
    return self.login

def getForgotPass(self):
    return self.forgot_pass

def setUserName(self,uName):
    self.user_name.clear()
    self.user_name.send_keys(uName)

def setPassword(self,pwd):
    self.password.clear()
    self.password.send_keys(pwd)

def clickLogin(self):
    self.login.click()

def clickForgotPass(self):
    self.forgot_pass.click()
```

Now, let us see the testing of the second object model built in Python. This is for user registration and the page has a form that needs to be filled. To access this page, we need to login to the website using the HomePage POM and then navigate to the registration page to perform the user registration task.

The register class is a simple instantiation of the Register POM with the locators we defined in Locators.py for the Registration Page.

The POM homepage is invoked first for login and once we are on the registration page, we use the Registration POM to fill in the data in the form to submit the entry.

The testing page for the Page Object Model lookslike the following (test_ OrangeHRMUser_Registration.py).

This program extends the base class (POMExampleSetup), instantiates the Web Driver, invokes the POM for the Home Page using RegisterPageObject = Register(driver), and passes the web element interaction actions. The program also contains some error handling mechanisms and screen capture actions. In the following example, you can see that the program is very simple in nature and very straightforward:

RegistrationPage.py

```python
from selenium.webdriver.common.by import By

from selenium.webdriver.support.select import Select

from HomePage import Home

from Locators import Locators


class Register(object):
    def __init__(self, driver):
        self.driver = driver
# registration page locators defining , you can directly call the WebElement from here
        self.user_admin_menu = driver.find_element(By.CSS_SELECTOR, Locators.user_admin_menu)

        print("self.user_admin_menu")

        self.user_admin_mgmt = driver.find_element(By.ID, Locators.user_admin_mgmt)

        print("self.user_admin_mgmt")

        self.user_admin = driver.find_element(By.XPATH, Locators.user_admin)

        self.user_add_user = driver.find_element(By.XPATH, Locators.user_add_user)

        self.user_search_field = driver.find_element(By.XPATH, Locators.user_search_field)

        self.user_search_button = driver.find_element(By.XPATH, Locators.user_search_button)

        print("user_search_button")

        print("user_role")

        print(self.driver.current_url)
```

```python
        self.employee_name = driver.find_element(By.XPATH, Locators.
employee_name)
        print("employee_name")
        self.user_name_log = driver.find_element(By.XPATH, Locators.user_
name_log)
        self.user_status = driver.find_element(By.XPATH, Locators.user_
status)
        self.user_password = driver.find_element(By.XPATH, Locators.user_
password)
        print("self.user_password")
        self.user_password_conf = driver.find_element(By.XPATH, Locators.
user_password_conf)
        self.save_user_button = driver.find_element(By.XPATH, Locators.
save_user_button)
        self.cancel_user_button  = driver.find_element(By.XPATH,
Locators.cancel_user_button)
        print("all initialization done")
#you can return WebElement from method and call it also, and useful
method with parameter you define here

#    def getUser_role(self):
#         return self.user_role_role

    def setUserSearch(self,userName):
        self.user_search_field.clear()
        self.user_search_field.send_keys(userName)

    def setEmpName(self,eName):
        self.employee_name.clear()
        self.employee_name.send_keys(eName)

    def setUserNameLog(self,uName):
        self.user_name_log.clear()
        self.user_name_log.send_keys(uName)

#    def setUser_role(self):
#         self.user_role_role.select_by_visible_text('ESS')

    def setStatus(self, UserStatus):
```

```python
        self.user_status.clear()
        self.user_status.send_keys(UserStatus)

    def setPassword(self, pwd):
        self.user_password.clear()
        self.user_password.send_keys(pwd)

    def setConfirmPassword(self, pwd):
        self.user_password_conf.clear()
        self.user_password_conf.send_keys(pwd)

    def submitRegistration(self):
        self.save_user_button.click()

    def submitUserSearch(self):
        self.user_search_button.click()

    def clickAddUser(self):
        self.user_add_user.click()

    def clickUserAdminMgmt(self):
        self.user_admin_mgmt.click()

    def clickUserAdminMenu(self):
        self.user_admin_menu.click()

    def clickUserAdmin(self):
        self.user_admin.click()
```

ScreenShotUtil.py

ScreenShotUtil is a function to capture screenshots. We can define multiple utility functions such as these (that are not available in the common libraries) for simplification of the code and the purpose of modularization:

```python
from selenium import webdriver

class ScreenShotUtil(object):

    def __init__(self, driver):
        self.driver = driver
```

```python
    def ScreenShotUtil(self, file_path):
        self.driver.get_screenshot_as_file(file_path)
```

UserSearchPage.py

The UserSearch object is a utility function used for clicking on the drop-down menu on the user search page. This can be used to query users. The same activity can be implemented using an action chain to get the results:

```python
from selenium.webdriver.common.by import By

from Locators import Locators

class UserSearch(object):

    def __init__(self, driver):
        self.driver = driver

# home page locators defining
        self.add_user = driver.find_element(By.XPATH, Locators.add_user)
        self.user_search_field = driver.find_element(By.XPATH, Locators.user_search_field)
        self.user_button = driver.find_element(By.XPATH, Locators.user_button)
```

UserManagementPage.py

The UserManagementPage object is a utility function used for clicking on the user admin link from the drop-down menu on the user search page. This can be used to query users. The same activity can be implemented using an action chain to get the results:

```python
from selenium.webdriver.common.by import By

from Locators import Locators

class UserManagement(object):

    def __init__(self, driver):
        self.driver = driver
```

```
        self.user_admin = driver.find_element(By.XPATH, Locators.user_
admin)
```

test_OrangeHRM_HomePage.py

Now, let us see the testing of this Page Object Model builtin Python:

- The testing page for the Page Object Model lookslike the following test_OrangeHRM_HomePage.py.
- This program extends the base class (POMExampleSetup).
- This instantiates the Web Driver.
- This invokes the POM for the Home Page using homePageObject = Home(driver).
- Passes the web element interaction actions.
- The program also contains some error handling mechanisms and screen capture actions.
- In the example, you can see that the program is very simple in nature and straightforward:

```
from POMExampleSetup import POMExampleSetup
from HomePage import Home
from ScreenShotUtil import ScreenShotUtil
import unittest


class Orange_HomePage(POMExampleSetup):

    def test_Home_Page(self):
        screenshot_path = "\\Test_OrangeHRM"
        driver = self.driver
        self.driver.get("https://opensource-demo.orangehrmlive.com/")
        self.driver.set_page_load_timeout(20)
        screen_shot = ScreenShotUtil(driver)
        expected_title = "OrangeHRM"
        try:
            if driver.title == expected_title:
                print("WebPage loaded successfully")
                self.assertEqual(driver.title,expected_title)
        except Exception as exErr:
```

```python
            print(exErr+"WebPage Failed to load")
        homePageObject = Home(driver)
        if homePageObject.getLogo().is_displayed():
            print(" Logo Successfully Displayed")
        else:
            print("Logo not Displayed")
        try:
            homePageObject.setUserName("Admin")
            homePageObject.setPassword("admin123")
            screen_shot.ScreenShotUtil("beforesubmithome.png")
            homePageObject.clickLogin()
        except Exception as exErr:
            print(exErr)
            print("Missing Web Elements :: Element not present")
        screen_shot.ScreenShotUtil("aftersubmithome.png")
        expected_title = "OrangeHRM"
        try:
            if driver.title == expected_title:
                print("New WebPage loaded successfully")
                self.assertEqual(driver.title,expected_title)
        except Exception as exErr:
            print(exErr)
            print(" New WebPage Failed to load")


if __name__ == '__main__':
    unittest.main()
```

test_OrangeHRMUser_Registration.py

Similarly, for the Registration Page Object Model built in Python, we have a test class named `test_OrangeHRMUser_Registration.py` built for the testing purposes.

- This program extends the base class (`POMExampleSetup`).

- Instantiates the Web Driver.

- Invokes the POM for the Home Page using `homePageObject = Home(driver)`.

- Then, passes the web element interaction actions.

- Once the page gets loaded, this program invokes the registration POM using regPageObject = Register(driver).
- The program also contains some error handling mechanisms and screen capture actions.
- In the example, you can see that the program is very simple in nature and straightforward:

```python
import unittest

from time import sleep

from POMExampleSetup import POMExampleSetup

from HomePage import Home

from RegistrationPage import Register

from ScreenShotUtil import ScreenShotUtil


class OrangeHRM_Registration(POMExampleSetup):

    def test_RegistrationFlow(self):

# Screenshots relative paths
        screenshot_path = "\\Test_OrangeHRM"
        driver = self.driver
        self.driver.get("https://opensource-demo.orangehrmlive.com/")
        self.driver.set_page_load_timeout(10)
        print( self.driver.current_url )
        screen_shot = ScreenShotUtil(driver)
        expected_title = "OrangeHRM"
        homePageObject = Home(driver)
        homePageObject.setUserName("Admin")
        homePageObject.setPassword("admin123")
        screen_shot.ScreenShotUtil("beforesubmithome_reg.png")
        homePageObject.clickLogin()
        screen_shot.ScreenShotUtil("aftersubmithome_reg.png")
        print( self.driver.current_url )

        self.driver.get('https://opensource-demo.orangehrmlive.com/index.
```

```
php/admin/viewSystemUsers')
        print( self.driver.current_url )
        regPageObject = Register(driver)
        regPageObject.clickAddUser()
     self.driver.get('https://opensource-demo.orangehrmlive.com/index.
php/admin/saveSystemUser')
        print( self.driver.current_url )
        self.driver.set_page_load_timeout(10)
        regPageObject = Register(driver)
        regPageObject.clickUserAdminMenu()
        regPageObject.clickUserAdminMgmt()
        regPageObject.clickUserAdmin()
        print(self.driver.current_url)
        self.driver.set_page_load_timeout(10)
# TO BE CONTINUED
#calling registration page object to proceed with registration flow
        if regPageObject.user_admin.is_displayed():
    #           print(regPageObject.user_role.text)
            print(regPageObject.current_url)
            screen_shot.ScreenShotUtil("Registration.png")
        else:
            print("User Registration page not loaded")
        try:
            regPageObject.setEmpName("John Smith")
            regPageObject.setUserNameLog("SelPyPOMUser")
            regPageObject.setPassword("SeleniumUser!")
            regPageObject.setConfirmPassword("SeleniumUser!")
            regPageObject.setStatus("Enabled")
            sleep(2)
            screen_shot.ScreenShotUtil("UserRegistration.png")
            regPageObject.submitRegistration()
            sleep(4)
```

```
        screen_shot.ScreenShotUtil("PostUserRegistration.png")
    except Exception as e:
        print("Exception occurred "+e)

if __name__ == '__main__':
    unittest.main()
```

When we execute the program, we get the following screens.

First, when we invoke the page, we get the landing page for the website. When we fill the data in the forms using web element actions, we get the page as shown in the following screenshot:

Figure 9.5: Orange HRM POM - Landing Page

Once we log in, we will get the dashboard page as a reference. These screens are captured using the `ScreenShotUtil` function written:

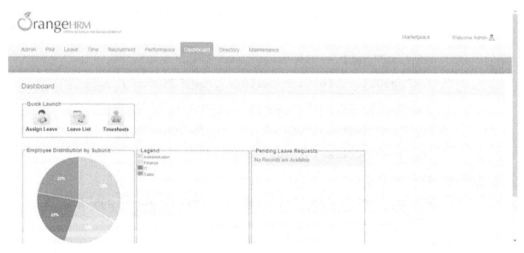

Figure 9.6: Orange CRM - Home Page - Post Login Screen

When we execute the Python script, we get the following console output as well:

```
PS C:\Selenium\PythonPOM>& C:/ProgramData/Anaconda3/python.exe c:/
Selenium/PythonPOM/test_OrangeHRM_HomePage.py

DevTools listening on ws://127.0.0.1:59684/devtools/browser/0a259675-
554b-4dbe-b3ac-a79f61df0a3e
***************************************************************
Starting Execution at :2019-10-12 22:17:48.703683
***************************************************************
WebPage loaded successfully
 Logo Successfully Displayed
New WebPage loaded successfully
***************************************************************
Run Completed at :2019-10-12 22:21:21.013490
***************************************************************

.

-----------------------------------------------------------------

Ran 1 test in 238.211s

OK
```

Table 9.1: Orange HRM - POM - Python Example - Console Output

File and database handling

For performing data-driven testing, we need to be conversant in handling different file types such as a flat file, CSV file, properties file or an XLS in addition to dealing with databases. In this section, we will see some examples for handling various types of files and databases.

Working with Excel files

One of the key requirements for a successful implementation of the data-driven test automation is the need to handle files. It is very important to know how to handle various types of files to handle various automation actions, read and update data, and deliver the expected results through test automation.

We will address these with an example-driven program. Ch_9_Prog_4_Selenium_ POI_Example.java uses the Apache POI library for file handling. The POI has many functions to handle various types of files such as **Dreadful Drawing Format**

(DDF), Horrible Property Set Format (HPSF), Common Spreadsheet Format (SS), Horrible Spreadsheet Format (HSSF), Open Office XML Spreadsheet Format (XSSF), Common Slideshow Format (SL), Horrible Slideshow Format (HSLF), Open Office XML Slideshow Format (XSLF), and other types, including Utilities and User models.

For our example, we will be using the SS and XSSF spreadsheet formats.

This program works as follows:

1. We open input and output file streams using `FileInputStreamand FileOutputStream`.

2. Open an XLS Workbook using the `WorkbookFactory.create()` function.

3. Read the content using the Workbook ⮕ `getSheet()` ⮕ `getRow()` ⮕ `getCell()` functions.

4. Now, we can iterate through the XLS Worksheet using additional functions. For this example, we have hardcoded five rows and five columns.

    a. However, we can use an iterator to navigate through all the rows and columns. The following example throws exceptions if we do not have the specified number of columns and rows.

    b. For example, it will throw an exception if the XLS has content only for two rows and two columns.

    c. Hence, it is important to handle the exceptions well and the use of an iterator is a better idea to handle the situation.

5. Similar to getting cell values, we can set the cell values using the `setCellValue` function.

    a. We can do this by navigating through and setting the value.

        Workbook ⮕`getSheet()`⮕`getRow()`⮕`createCell()`⮕`setCellValue()` (e.g.)

        • `xssfSheet.getRow(0).createCell(5).setCellValue("Test 1");`

6. You can also write custom functions such as handling different types of Excel data without causing exceptions by handling different types of data in a different manner.

    a. This is critical when you are updating an Excel file as Excel has a finicky way to handle data due to its data richness and settings. These functions will be very helpful and can go a long way.

The complete example of the program is as follows:

```
import org.apache.poi.ss.usermodel.*;

import org.apache.poi.xssf.usermodel.XSSFSheet;
```

```java
import org.apache.poi.xssf.usermodel.XSSFWorkbook;

import java.io.*;

public class Ch_9_Prog_4_Selenium_POI_Example {
    static FileInputStream fileInputStream;
    static FileOutputStream fileOutputStream;
    static File fileToHandle;
    public static < exception extends Throwable > void main(String[] args)
throws Exception, exception {
        Workbook workbook = getSheets("C:\\Selenium\\SelData.xlsx");
        Cell cell;
        for(int i=0; i<5; i++) {
            for(int j=0;j<5;j++) {
                cell = getCellContents(workbook, "Selenium", i, j);
                printCell(cell);
                System.out.print(" ");
            }
            System.out.println(" ");
        }
        System.out.println("Finished with File Handling Program");
        insertIntoFileExample();
        for(int i=0; i<5; i++) {
            for(int j=0;j<6;j++) {
                cell = getCellContents(workbook, "Selenium", i, j);
                printCell(cell);
                System.out.print(" ");
            }
            System.out.println(" ");
        }
        System.out.println("Finished with Insert into");
    }

    public static void insertIntoFileExample() throws IOException {
```

```java
        fileToHandle= new File("C:\\Selenium\\SelData.xlsx");

        fileInputStream = new FileInputStream(fileToHandle);

        XSSFWorkbook xssfWorkbook = new XSSFWorkbook(fileInputStream);

        XSSFSheet xssfSheet = xssfWorkbook.getSheetAt(0);

        xssfSheet.getRow(0).createCell(5).setCellValue("Test 1");

        xssfSheet.getRow(1).createCell(5).setCellValue("Test @");

        xssfSheet.getRow(2).createCell(5).setCellValue("Test 3");

        xssfSheet.getRow(3).createCell(5).setCellValue("Test 4");

        xssfSheet.getRow(4).createCell(5).setCellValue("Test 5");

        fileOutputStream = new FileOutputStream(fileToHandle);

        xssfWorkbook.write(fileOutputStream);

        fileOutputStream.close();

    }


  private static Cell getCellContents(Workbook workbook, String SheetName,
int RowId, int ColumnId) {

        Sheet sheet = workbook.getSheet(SheetName);

        Row row = sheet.getRow(RowId);

        return row.getCell(ColumnId);

    }


  private static Cell setCellContents(Workbook workbook, String SheetName,
int RowId, int ColumnId, String cellValue) throws IOException {

        Sheet sheet = workbook.getSheet(SheetName);

        Row row = sheet.getRow(RowId);

        Cell cell2 = row.createCell(ColumnId);

        cell2.setCellValue(cellValue);

        fileOutputStream = new FileOutputStream(fileToHandle);

        workbook.write(fileOutputStream);

        return cell2;

    }


   private static Workbook getSheets(String fileName) throws IOException {

        fileInputStream = new FileInputStream(fileName);
```

```java
            return WorkbookFactory.create(fileInputStream);
    }

    private static Workbook writeSheets(String fileName) throws IOException
{
        fileToHandle= new File(fileName);
        return WorkbookFactory.create(fileToHandle);
    }

    public static void printCell(Cell cell) {
        switch (cell.getCellType()) {
            case BOOLEAN:
                System.out.print(cell.getBooleanCellValue());
                break;
            case STRING:
            System.out.print(cell.getRichStringCellValue().getString());
                break;
            case NUMERIC:
                if (DateUtil.isCellDateFormatted(cell)) {
                    System.out.print(cell.getDateCellValue());
                } else {
                    System.out.print(cell.getNumericCellValue());
                }
                break;
            case FORMULA:
                System.out.print(cell.getCellFormula());
                break;
            case BLANK:
                System.out.print("");
                break;
            default:
                System.out.print("");
        }
    }
}
```

Working with property files

Another one of the key requirements for a successful implementation of the data-driven test automation is the need to handle property files. It is very important to know how to handle various types of property files to handle various automation actions, read and update data, and deliver the expected results through test automation.

We will address these with an example-driven program.Ch_9_Prog_6_Selenium_ Prop_file.java uses the Apache Commons library for property file handling. The Apache Commons library has a myriad of wonderful utilities, including file handling functions and user models. For our example, we will be using the Properties class available for handling data.

This program works as follows:

1. We open input and output file streams using `FileInputStream` and `FileOutputStream`.

2. We then use the Properties class available from the `java.utils.Properties` library.

3. We write to the properties files using a simple `FileOutputStream` class function.

4. For making this program a bit more interesting, we read the file using the `Properties` class and invoke the URLs based on the company name and run in a loop with a Driver class.

   a. This program also has a utility function to switch browsers based on a parameter passed.

   b. We can make it dynamic using the random function to pass various types of browser types to see how this program works.

The complete program is as follows:

```
import org.apache.commons.io.FileUtils;

import org.openqa.selenium.OutputType;

import org.openqa.selenium.TakesScreenshot;

import org.openqa.selenium.WebDriver;

import org.openqa.selenium.chrome.ChromeDriver;

import org.openqa.selenium.firefox.FirefoxDriver;

import org.openqa.selenium.ie.InternetExplorerDriver;

import org.openqa.selenium.safari.SafariDriver;


import java.io.*;
```

```java
import java.util.Enumeration;
import java.util.Properties;

public class Ch_9_Prog_6_Selenium_Prop_file {
    static WebDriver driver;
    static String WEBDRIVER_PATH = "C:\\Selenium\\";

    public static void main(String[] args) {
        WriteToPropertiesFile("Ch_9_Prog_6_Test_output.properties");
        ReadFromPropertiesFile("Ch_9_Prog_6_Test_output.properties");
    }

    private static void WriteToPropertiesFile(String propFileName) {
        try {
            Properties propertiesFile = new Properties();
            FileOutputStream fileOutputStream = new
FileOutputStream(propFileName);
            propertiesFile.setProperty("Novartis", "http://www.novartis.com");
            propertiesFile.setProperty("Amazon", "http://www.amazon.com");
            propertiesFile.setProperty("Apple", "http://www.apple.com");
            propertiesFile.setProperty("Facebook", "http://www.facebook.com");
            propertiesFile.setProperty("Google", "http://www.google.com");
            propertiesFile.setProperty("Microsoft", "http://www.
microsoft.com");
            propertiesFile.store(fileOutputStream, "=====Important Firms
and landing pages =====");
            fileOutputStream.close();
        } catch (FileNotFoundException e) {
            e.printStackTrace();
        } catch (IOException e) {
            e.printStackTrace();
        }
    }

    private static void ReadFromPropertiesFile(String propFileName) {
        try {
```

```
            Properties propertiesFile = new Properties();
       FileInputStream fileInputStream = new FileInputStream(propFileName);
            propertiesFile.load(fileInputStream);
          System.out.println("========== Flushing the content ======");
          System.out.println(propertiesFile.toString());
            System.out.println("========== Iterating through Key/Value
Pair " +
                  "======");
              Enumeration< String > enums = (Enumeration< String >)
propertiesFile.propertyNames();
          while (enums.hasMoreElements()) {
              String key = enums.nextElement();
              String value = propertiesFile.getProperty(key);
              System.out.println(key + " : " + value);
              setBrowser("firefox", (String) value);
              takeScreenshot(driver, key);
              closeBrowser(driver);
          }
          System.out.println("========== Random Key Search ======");
          System.out.println(propertiesFile.get("Novartis"));
          propertiesFile.clear();
      } catch (FileNotFoundException e) {
          e.printStackTrace();
      } catch (IOException e) {
          e.printStackTrace();
      }
   }

   public static WebDriver setBrowser(String browName, String URL) {
      if (browName.equalsIgnoreCase("firefox")) {
          String wdp = WEBDRIVER_PATH.concat("geckodriver.exe");
          System.out.println(wdp);
          System.setProperty("webdriver.firefox.driver", wdp);
          driver = new FirefoxDriver();
```

```java
        } else if (browName.equalsIgnoreCase("chrome")) {
            String wdp = WEBDRIVER_PATH.concat("chromedriver.exe");
            System.out.println(wdp);
            System.setProperty("webdriver.chrome.driver", wdp);
            driver = new ChromeDriver();
        } else if (browName.equalsIgnoreCase("safari")) {
            System.setProperty("webdriver.safari.driver",
                    WEBDRIVER_PATH.concat("safaridriver.exe"));
            driver = new SafariDriver();
        } else if (browName.equalsIgnoreCase("IE")) {
            System.setProperty("webdriver.IE.driver",
                    WEBDRIVER_PATH.concat("IEDriverServer.exe"));
            driver = new InternetExplorerDriver();
        }
        driver.manage().window().maximize();
        driver.get(URL);
        System.out.println("Opened Page " + URL);
        return driver;
    }


    public static void takeScreenshot(WebDriver driver, String siteName) {
       File screenShot = ((TakesScreenshot) driver).getScreenshotAs(OutputType.
FILE);
        try {
                FileUtils.copyFile(screenShot, new File("New" + siteName +
".png"));
        } catch (Exception e) {
            e.getMessage();
        }
    }

    public static void closeBrowser(WebDriver driver) {
        driver.close();
    }
}
```

Working with CSV files

Another one of the key requirements for a successful implementation of the data-driven test automation is the need to handle **Comma Separated Value (CSV)** files. It is very important to know how to handle various types of CSV files to handle various automation actions, read and update data, and deliver the expected results through test automation.

We will address these with an example-driven program.Ch_9_Prog_7_CSV_Test. java uses the Apache Commons library for CSV file handling. The Apache Commons library has a myriad of wonderful utilities, including file handling functions and user models. For our example, we will be using the CSVFormat, CSVParser, CSVPrinter and CSV Record classes available for handling data.

This program works as follows:

1. We open output file streams using FileWriter and BufferedWriter.

2. We instantiate a CSV writer capability using the CSVPrinter class by setting a default configuration and by passing the header with some details you want to maintain in the CSV file.

   ```
   new CSVPrinter(bufferedWriter, CSVFormat.DEFAULT
   .withHeader("ID", "Name", "Designation", "Company"));
   ```

3. For writing into a CSV file, we use CSVPrinter and CSVFormat, whereas we use CSVRecord and CSVParser for reading the same.

4. This example uses the classes mentioned above to both write into and read from the CSV file.

5. For making this program a bit more interesting, we read the file using the Properties class and invoke the URLs based on the company name and run in a loop with a Driver class:

   a. This program also has a utility function to switch browsers based on a parameter being passed.

   b. We can make it dynamic using the random function to pass various types of browser types to see how this program works.

The complete program is as follows:

```
import java.io.*;
import java.nio.file.Files;
import java.nio.file.Paths;
import org.apache.commons.csv.CSVFormat;
import org.apache.commons.csv.CSVParser;
import org.apache.commons.csv.CSVPrinter;
```

```java
import org.apache.commons.csv.CSVRecord;
import org.testng.annotations.Test;

import static java.nio.file.Files.newBufferedReader;

public class Ch_9_Prog_7_CSV_Test {

    @Test
    public void writeCSVFileTest() throws IOException {
        String CSV_File_Path = "C:\\Selenium\\SeleniumCSV.csv";
        FileWriter fileWriter = new FileWriter(CSV_File_Path);
        BufferedWriter bufferedWriter = new BufferedWriter(fileWriter);

        CSVPrinter csvPrinter = getCsvPrinter(bufferedWriter);
        updateCSVRecords(csvPrinter, "1", "Vas", "CEO", "Novartis");
        updateCSVRecords(csvPrinter, "2", "Jeff", "CEO", "Amazon");
        updateCSVRecords(csvPrinter, "3", "Tim", "CEO", "Apple");
        updateCSVRecords(csvPrinter, "4", "Satya", "CEO", "Microsoft");
        updateCSVRecords(csvPrinter, "5", "Sundar", "CEO", "Google");
        updateCSVRecords(csvPrinter, "6", "Mark", "CEO", "Facebook");
        csvPrinter.flush();
        csvPrinter.close();
        bufferedWriter.close();
        fileWriter.close();
    }

    private void updateCSVRecords(CSVPrinter csvPrinter, String sNo,
      String sName, String sTitle, String sComp) throws IOException {
        csvPrinter.printRecord(sNo, sName, sTitle, sComp);
    }

    private CSVPrinter getCsvPrinter(BufferedWriter bufferedWriter) throws
       IOException {
        return new CSVPrinter(bufferedWriter, CSVFormat.DEFAULT
                    .withHeader("ID", "Name", "Designation", "Company"));
    }

    @Test
    public void readCSV() throws IOException {
        String CSV_File_Path = "C:\\Selenium\\SeleniumCSV.csv";
        // read the file
```

```
        FileReader fileReader = new FileReader(CSV_File_Path);
        BufferedReader bufferedReader = new BufferedReader(fileReader);
        CSVParser csvParser = new CSVParser(fileReader, CSVFormat.DEFAULT
                .withFirstRecordAsHeader()
                .withIgnoreHeaderCase()
                .withTrim());

    for (CSVRecord csvRecord : csvParser) {
        // Accessing values by the names assigned to each column
        String id = csvRecord.get("id");
        String name = csvRecord.get("Name");
        String designation = csvRecord.get("Designation");
        String company = csvRecord.get("Company");
      System.out.println("Record No - " + csvRecord.getRecordNumber());
        System.out.println("---------------");
        System.out.println("Name : " + name);
        System.out.println("Designation : " + designation);
        System.out.println("Company : " + company);
        System.out.println("---------------\n\n");
    }
    csvParser.close();
    bufferedReader.close();
    fileReader.close();
    }
}
```

This program produces the following output:

```
[RemoteTestNG] detected TestNG version 6.13.1
Record No - 1
---------------
Name : Vas
Designation : CEO
Company : Novartis
---------------
Record No - 2
---------------
Name : Jeff
Designation : CEO
Company : Amazon
---------------
```

```
Record No - 3
---------------
Name : Tim
Designation : CEO
Company : Apple
---------------
Record No - 4
---------------
Name : Satya
Designation : CEO
Company : Microsoft
---------------
Record No - 5
---------------
Name : Sundar
Designation : CEO
Company : Google
---------------
Record No - 6
---------------
Name : Mark
Designation : CEO
Company : Facebook
---------------
PASSED: readCSV
PASSED: writeCSVFileTest

===============================================
    Default test
    Tests run: 2, Failures: 0, Skips: 0
===============================================

===============================================
Default suite
Total tests run: 2, Failures: 0, Skips: 0
===============================================
```

The CSV file is written and will have the following content, including the header specified while creating the file in the program:

```
ID,Name,Designation,Company
1,Vas,CEO,Novartis
2,Jeff,CEO,AmazonH
3,Tim,CEO,Apple
4,Satya,CEO,Microsoft
5,Sundar,CEO,Google
6,Mark,CEO,Facebook
```

Now, let us see an example on how to use databases in a Selenium program.

Working with databases

Another one of the key requirements for a successful implementation of the automation framework is the need to handle databases and use of SQL statements to navigate through. It is very important to know how to handle various types of databases to handle various automation actions, read and update data, and deliver the expected results through test automation.

We will address these with an example-driven program. `Ch_9_JDBC_ODBC_ DataBase_Connectivity_Example.java` uses the JDBC and ODBC functions from the HSQLDB library for database handling. The sample database we used for this program is a LibreOffice Base database. This is a free database that you can use in your laptop, as a replacement for Microsoft Access. Instead of the LibreOffice Base file, you can choose to use your database of choice such as MySQL, SQL*Server, MongoDB, etc. There is no restriction in using any database. We can also connect to a database available in the cloud via the Internet as well. All we need is connectivity to the database through an Internet connection, access through a database username and password, and the corresponding **Open Database Connectivity (ODBC)** driver (JDBC in case of usage of Java as a preferred programming language).

As the access to the LibreOffice Base is a bit tricky, we need to open the database file with an "`.ODB`" extension, unzip the file, open various elements embedded in the database file and connect to the database file using the ODBC/JDBC driver provided by HSQLDB libraries, perform an SQL statement, and process the results produced by the execution.

This program is more of a standard Java program than a Selenium program. Selenium WebDriver-based automation programs can use the libraries and functions available in Java to make use of the features for automation. Likewise, the libraries, drivers, and functions available in other programming languages can be leveraged for database connectivity as well. This could be direct SQL-based interactions; execution of prepared statements, batch processing, etc. like any programming language is driven in database operations.

Let us look at the example of a program.

This program works as follows:

1. We define the libraries to be used with the import statements.

2. We instantiate the variables used in the class.

   a. These include:

      i. The WebDriver for Selenium operations

      ii. JDBC driver for database connectivity and actions

      iii. Database variables for the following:

         - **Database connection:** dbConnection

         - **Database statement:** dbCommand

         - **Database Command's Result:** dbResultSet

         - **Database File Definition for unzipping the content:** dbFile

3. We then extract the ZIP files from the DBfile unzipping the DBFile by iterating through the entries available in the ODB file processed by the ZipFile class.

4. Once we have extracted all the ZIP files, we open the database file created under the name of "ooTempDatabase ":

   a. `dbFile = File.createTempFile("ooTempDatabase", "tmp");`

5. We connect to the database file using a JDBC connection through the following:

   a. `dbConnection = DriverManager.getConnection("jdbc:hsqldb:file:" + dbFile.getName(), "SA", "");`

   b. In this, the first parameter is the database connectivity file or URL, the second parameter is the user id, and the final parameter is the password to establish the connection.

6. Once the connectivity is established, we execute a database command and store the results in a result set:

   a. `dbCommand = dbConnection.createStatement();`
      `dbResultSet = dbCommand.executeQuery("select * from \"SeleniumTest\"");`

7. We then iterate the Result Set (dbResultSet) to perform the actions we want to do:

   a. In this example, we are printing the content and opening the website using the Selenium Web Driver by iterating.

The same program can be extended further by making connections to various types of databases and file types available to run different types of database statements.

The complete program is as follows:

```java
import org.apache.commons.io.FileUtils;
import org.hsqldb.jdbcDriver;
import org.openqa.selenium.OutputType;
import org.openqa.selenium.TakesScreenshot;
import org.openqa.selenium.WebDriver;
import org.openqa.selenium.chrome.ChromeDriver;
import org.openqa.selenium.firefox.FirefoxDriver;
import org.openqa.selenium.ie.InternetExplorerDriver;
import org.openqa.selenium.safari.SafariDriver;

import java.io.BufferedOutputStream;
import java.io.File;
import java.io.FileOutputStream;
import java.io.InputStream;
import java.sql.Connection;
import java.sql.DriverManager;
import java.sql.ResultSet;
import java.sql.Statement;
import java.util.ArrayList;
import java.util.Enumeration;
import java.util.List;
import java.util.zip.ZipEntry;
import java.util.zip.ZipFile;

public class Ch_9_JDBC_ODBC_DataBase_Connectivity_Example {
    static WebDriver driver;
    static jdbcDriver jdbcDriver = new jdbcDriver();
    static Connection dbConnection = null;
    static Statement dbCommand = null;
    static ResultSet dbResultSet = null;
    static ZipFile zipFile = null;
    static ZipEntry zipEntry = null;
    static Enumeration< ? extends ZipEntry > dbEnumeration = null;
```

```java
static BufferedOutputStream bufferedOutputStream = null;

static InputStream inputStream = null;

static File dbFile = null;

static int dbFileLength;

static List vectorArrayOfFiles = new ArrayList();

public static void main(String[] args) {
    try {
        zipFile = new ZipFile("C:\\SELENIUMTEST.odb");
        dbFile = File.createTempFile("ooTempDatabase", "tmp");
        dbFile.deleteOnExit();
        dbEnumeration = zipFile.entries();
        while (dbEnumeration.hasMoreElements()) {
            zipEntry = dbEnumeration.nextElement();
            if (zipEntry.getName().startsWith("database/")) {
                System.out.println("Extracting File: " + zipEntry.getName());

                byte[] buffer = new byte[1024];
                inputStream = zipFile.getInputStream(zipEntry);
                bufferedOutputStream = new BufferedOutputStream(new
FileOutputStream(dbFile.getName() + "." + zipEntry.getName().
substring(9)));
                while ((dbFileLength = inputStream.read(buffer)) >= 0)
                    bufferedOutputStream.write(buffer, 0, dbFileLength);
                bufferedOutputStream.close();
                inputStream.close();
            }
        }
        zipFile.close();
        dbConnection = DriverManager.
getConnection("jdbc:hsqldb:file:" + dbFile.getName(), "SA", "");
        dbCommand = dbConnection.createStatement();
        dbResultSet = dbCommand.executeQuery("select * from
\"SeleniumTest\"");
        while (dbResultSet.next()) {
```

```java
                System.out.println("Company Name: " + dbResultSet.
getString("CompanyName")

                        + " Web Site: " + dbResultSet.
getString("WEBSITE"));
                System.out.println("Country: " + dbResultSet.
getString("CountryOrRegion") );
                setBrowser("chrome", dbResultSet.getString("WEBSITE"));
                takeScreenshot(driver, dbResultSet.
getString("WEBSITE"));
                closeBrowser(driver);
            }
        dbResultSet.close();
            dbCommand.close();
            dbConnection.close();
        } catch (Exception e) {
            e.printStackTrace();
        }
    }

    public static WebDriver setBrowser(String browName, String URL) {
        String WEBDRIVER_PATH = "C:\\Selenium\\";
        if (browName.equalsIgnoreCase("firefox")) {
            String wdp = WEBDRIVER_PATH.concat("geckodriver.exe");
            System.out.println(wdp);
            System.setProperty("webdriver.firefox.driver", wdp);
            driver = new FirefoxDriver();
        } else if (browName.equalsIgnoreCase("chrome")) {
            String wdp = WEBDRIVER_PATH.concat("chromedriver.exe");
            System.out.println(wdp);
            System.setProperty("webdriver.chrome.driver", wdp);
            driver = new ChromeDriver();
        } else if (browName.equalsIgnoreCase("safari")) {
            System.setProperty("webdriver.safari.driver",
                    WEBDRIVER_PATH.concat("safaridriver.exe"));
            driver = new SafariDriver();
        } else if (browName.equalsIgnoreCase("IE")) {
            System.setProperty("webdriver.IE.driver",
                    WEBDRIVER_PATH.concat("IEDriverServer.exe"));
            driver = new InternetExplorerDriver();
```

```
        }
        driver.manage().window().maximize();
        driver.get(URL);
        System.out.println("Opened Page " + URL);
        return driver;
    }

    public static void takeScreenshot(WebDriver driver, String siteName) {
        File screenShot = ((TakesScreenshot) driver).getScreenshotAs
(OutputType.FILE);
        try {
            FileUtils.copyFile(screenShot, new File("New" + siteName +
".png"));
        } catch (Exception e) {
            e.getMessage();
        }
    }

    public static void closeBrowser(WebDriver driver) {
        driver.close();
    }
}
```

The input table SELENIUMTEST created using a LibreOffice Base application used for this program has the following entries:

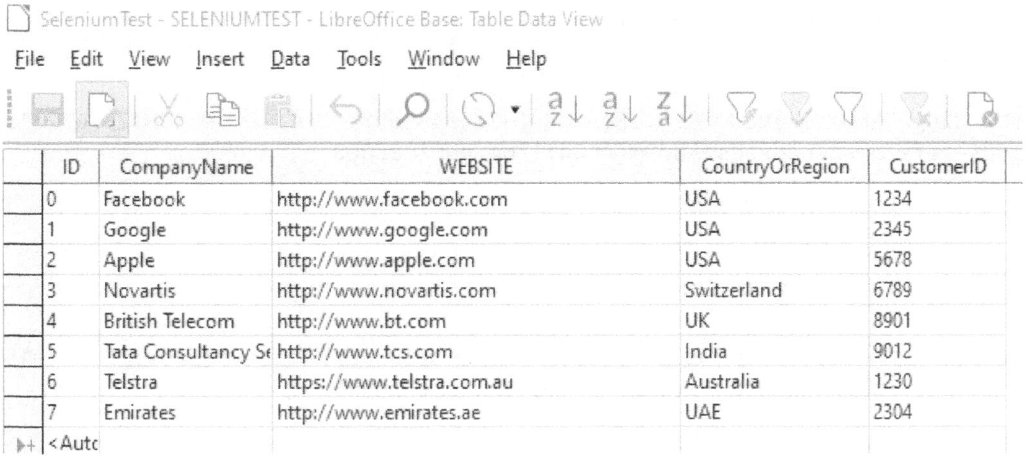

ID	CompanyName	WEBSITE	CountryOrRegion	CustomerID
0	Facebook	http://www.facebook.com	USA	1234
1	Google	http://www.google.com	USA	2345
2	Apple	http://www.apple.com	USA	5678
3	Novartis	http://www.novartis.com	Switzerland	6789
4	British Telecom	http://www.bt.com	UK	8901
5	Tata Consultancy S∈	http://www.tcs.com	India	9012
6	Telstra	https://www.telstra.com.au	Australia	1230
7	Emirates	http://www.emirates.ae	UAE	2304

Figure 9.7: SELNIUMTEST DB Content

When we execute the program, we get the following output:

```
Extracting File: database/data

Extracting File: database/properties

Extracting File: database/script

Extracting File: database/backup

Company Name: Facebook Web Site: http://www.facebook.com

Country: USA

Starting ChromeDriver 76.0.3809.68 (420c9498db8ce8fcd190a954d51297672c15
15d5-refs/branch-heads/3809@{#864}) on port 24413

Opened Page http://www.facebook.com

Company Name: Google Web Site: http://www.google.com

Country: USA

Starting ChromeDriver 76.0.3809.68 (420c9498db8ce8fcd190a954d51297672c15
15d5-refs/branch-heads/3809@{#864}) on port 41616

Opened Page http://www.google.com

Company Name: Apple Web Site: http://www.apple.com

Country: USA

Starting ChromeDriver 76.0.3809.68 (420c9498db8ce8fcd190a954d51297672c15
15d5-refs/branch-heads/3809@{#864}) on port 28598

Opened Page http://www.apple.com

Company Name: Novartis Web Site: http://www.novartis.com

Country: Switzerland

Starting ChromeDriver 76.0.3809.68 (420c9498db8ce8fcd190a954d51297672c15
15d5-refs/branch-heads/3809@{#864}) on port 36808

Opened Page http://www.novartis.com

Company Name: British Telecom Web Site: http://www.bt.com

Country: UK

Starting ChromeDriver 76.0.3809.68 (420c9498db8ce8fcd190a954d51297672c15
15d5-refs/branch-heads/3809@{#864}) on port 16984

Opened Page http://www.bt.com

Company Name: Tata Consultancy Services Web Site: http://www.tcs.com
```

```
Country: India

Starting ChromeDriver 76.0.3809.68 (420c9498db8ce8fcd190a954d51297672c15
15d5-refs/branch-heads/3809@{#864}) on port 26029

Opened Page http://www.tcs.com

Company Name: Telstra Web Site: https://www.telstra.com.au

Country: Australia

Starting ChromeDriver 76.0.3809.68 (420c9498db8ce8fcd190a954d51297672c15
15d5-refs/branch-heads/3809@{#864}) on port 13012

Opened Page https://www.telstra.com.au

Company Name: Emirates Web Site: http://www.emirates.ae

Country: UAE

Starting ChromeDriver 76.0.3809.68 (420c9498db8ce8fcd190a954d51297672c15
15d5-refs/branch-heads/3809@{#864}) on port 22581

Opened Page http://www.emirates.ae
```

The example highlighted above can be refined in multiple ways to suit the needs of test automation.

Reporting in Selenium

One of the most important aspects of any testing project is reporting. Be it manual testing or automated testing. Having worked in very large-scale testing engagements, my personal opinion is that doing a good job in testing is not good or useful if one is not able to communicate it well. Additionally, it is very important to document what is required, what is performed, what happened, what are the pieces of evidence supporting the findings, and what actions need to be taken to ensure stakeholders are informed about what is happening in the project.

Some key aspects of a good reporting capability include the following:

- A simplistic view on status.

    o **What is in scope:** How many test cases?

    o **What is covered:** How many test cases are executed?

    o **Statistics on Pass/Fail:** How many test cases are passed, how many failed and how many are remaining to be executed?

    o **Summary of logs:** What are the key logs to look at from a passed or a failed test case?

- **Detailed log on failed/debugged test cases:** Cover the screenshots, debugging data points, and status tracking to identify the root cause of failure.
- **Defect-related inputs:** To document in the defect management system with evidence what was executed, what happened, what was the expected outcome, what was the actual outcome, data used for the test cases, screenshots and other pieces of evidence (logs, files, database query outputs. etc.).

- Various projects may have different reporting requirements and hence a bit of flexibility in defining the reporting structure, dashboard, and format will be good to have.

- There are many choices to use, when it comes to reporting for Selenium automation. These include the following:

  o TestNG:

    - TestNG is one of the most commonly used unit testing and reporting framework. TestNG comes with a very comprehensive reporting that could be looked at without a need to write extensive reporting related code.

    - TestNG produces a detailed or summary report – all organized in a folder (we can define a test output folder like test-output by enabling listeners for TestNG).

      ⧗ **index.html:** This gives a drillable test reporting mechanism.

      ⧗ **emailable-report.html:** This gives a summary of test cases executed, along with any reporting logs at a higher level.

    - TestNG also allows us to extend further with the `ITestListener` interface:

      ⧗ ReportNG and other popular test reporting tools have used TestNG and extended the capability further.

  o **JUnit:** This is a simplified test reporting mechanism. JUnit was the foundation for TestNG (TestNG extended on JUnit to define custom annotations such as `@BeforeMethod` and `@AfterMethod`) or use `@BeforeClass` / `@AfterClass` to perform Pre or Post-test tasks in Junit.

  o **Extent Library:** This uses simple HTML reports and can be integrated along with JUnit and TestNG. We need to integrate the configurations with TestNG. Extent reporting has features to drilldown to finer details and work on charts and other visualization elements.

o **Allure Reporting:** This allows us to extend the reporting capabilities further by permitting us to add new steps, enable email attachments, and refine the test reporting finer.

o **PyTest:** If you are using Python, Pytest reporting is a good way to go about.

o **Maven SureFire:** This is a good tool to use if Maven is used for the Selenium Automation Project.

o There are other reporting tools such as Vigo Reports, **Automation Testing Utilities (ATU)** Reporting, ReportyNG, etc. All these reporting tools are additional wrappers on top of the testing reporting tools such as TestNG and Junit.

Selenium Test Reporting using TestNG

Now, let us see an example of using TestNG for a report generation. For running this, we will leverage TestNG and the Reporter function available in TestNG. To enable TestNG reporting, we need to do the following:

1. Download and configure the TestNG library in the classpath of the Java Project we want to use TestNG in.

2. Ensure the Listeners for the Java project is mapped to the TestNG listeners by disabling the default listeners in the IDE.

3. Using Notations in the Programs under test using the `@Test` annotation before the functions where TestNG reporting is needed. TestNG comes with multiple options for reporting. This include use of annotations such as `@BeforeSuite, @AfterSuite, @BeforeTest, @AfterTest, @BeforeGroups, @AfterGroups, @BeforeClass, @AfterClass, @BeforeMethod, @AfterMethod, @DataProvider, @Factory, @Listeners, @Parameters,` and finally `@Test`.

4. Out of the annotations mentioned, `@Test` is most important and used for the test reporting.

5. In addition to the Annotations, we could use:

   a. **Expected Exceptions:** To handle Exceptions in a better manner.

      i. `@Test(expectedExceptions = { NullPointerException.class })`

   b. Ignoring or disabling Tests using `enabledidentifies`

      i. `@Test(enabled = true)` or `@Test(enabled = false)`

   c. Enabling tests in parallel by addition of `parallel = "classes"` or `"parallel = "methods"` in the suite parameter used in `test-ng.xml`.

   d. Test method dependencies using:

i. @Test(dependsOnMethods = { "DependentTestOne", "DependentTestTwo" })

ii. In the preceding example, test specified dependsOnMethods waitsuntil the tests the completion of DependentTestOne first and then DependentTestTwo is completed.

e. **Timeout Management:**

i. This can be done by adding the time-out parameter in the testng. xml file to specify how much time is permitted for timeouts for the classes specified.

f. **Parameter Management:**

i. Using @Parameters({"Parameter-names"}), we can specify the parameters that can be passed on as inputs to the tests specified:

⧖ These parameters can be passed through the testng.xml file at runtime.

g. **DataProvider:**

i. This is used to pass the data for enabling data-driven tests that means that we can run the same class method with different inputs by invoking the @DataProvider annotation. In addition to passing the parameters via the testng.xml parameter tag, this is another important way of passing the parameters in Selenium for reporting purposes.

h. **Factory Annotation:**

i. A factory annotation permits running of sets of tests at run time with different data sets. This is done in such a way that we need not redefine the tests every time we need to change the input. TestNG has a beautiful feature to help us create dynamically during runtime and the @Factory annotation is a great way to do this.

⧖ While a data provider runs the same test method every time, a factory executes all test methods defined in a TestNG class. Therefore, it is a way to run tests on the entire class at runtime.

i. **Test Groups:**

i. One good feature about TestNG is the ability to group test cases based on a parameter and run them based on grouping – either in a suite or a class definition parameter in TestNG.

ii. @Test(groups = {"Group-Name"}) is a sample definition of how a group is used in a Test Group.

iii. We can use groups to include or exclude methods as per group definition.

iv. We can use regular expressions to select or exclude as well.

v. We can have a group of groups.

vi. All these features allow us to build dynamic suites of test cases for test execution and test reporting.

Now, let us put these examples to action for a TestNG report generated using Selenium.

For example, we are running five tests with one test having two functions in total. Depending on the exceptions thrown (either due to logic or connectivity or other reasons), we may have varying results. This TestNG suite has five programs in total – onefor successful page rendering, one for failure due to element unavailability, onefor CSV file handling, one for a Property file handling, and another for a general TestNG test class.

S.No	Program	Purpose
1	`TestNGExampleOne.java`	A simple opening of a web page using Selenium.
2	`TestNGExampleTwo.java`	Simple failing program using Selenium due to non-existent web element.
3	`Ch_9_Prog_TestNG_Reporting_Example.java`	Program for CSV file handling – A replica of the example given earlier in the section with the `System.out.println` being replaced by Reporter. log functions.
4	`Ch_9_Prog_TestNG_Reporting_Example_2.java`	Program for XLS file handling – A replica of the example given earlier in the section with the `System.out.println` being replaced by Reporter. log functions.

5	`TestNGClassTest.java`	A simple TestNG class with a simple function, including actions for all annotations.
		
		`@Test`
		`Public voidf()` `{`
		`Reporter.log("public void f()");`
		`}`

Table 9.2: TestNG examples - Code and Purpose

The two simple programs outlined are as follows:

TestNGExampleOne

```
package com.CrackingSeleniumInterviews.TestNG.examples;
import org.openqa.selenium.WebDriver;
import org.openqa.selenium.firefox.FirefoxDriver;
```

```
import org.testng.Reporter;
import org.testng.annotations.Test;


public class TestNGExampleOne {
    @Test
    Public void run() {
        // TODO Auto-generated constructor stub
        WebDriver driver = new FirefoxDriver();
        Reporter.log("The Browser is Open now");
        driver.manage().window().maximize();
        driver.get("http://news.google.com");
        Reporter.log("Opened Google News Website");
    }
}
```

TestNGExampleTwo

```
package com.CrackingSeleniumInterviews.TestNG.examples;
import org.testng.annotations.Test;
import org.openqa.selenium.By;
import org.openqa.selenium.WebDriver;
import org.openqa.selenium.firefox.FirefoxDriver;
import org.testng.Reporter;
public class TestNGExampleTwo {
    @Test
    public void run() {
        // TODO Auto-generated constructor stub
        WebDriver driver = new FirefoxDriver();
        Reporter.log("The Browser is Open now");
        driver.manage().window().maximize();
        driver.get("http://news.google.com");
        Reporter.log("Opened Google News Website");
        driver.findElement(By.partialLinkText("testfailure")).sendKeys("Test Failure");
        Reporter.log("Failing Tests Search Entered");
    }
}
```

The `TestNG.XML` file that is used to run the test case looks like the following. The XML file is a simple one and does not contain the detailed capabilities outlined above for the TestNG tool. We define all the classes we want to include in the TestNG Test under a test suite. The same XML file can be modified in multiple ways to leverage the capabilities of TestNG to suit our testing needs.

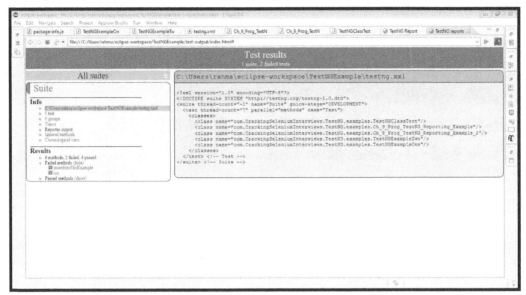

Figure 9.8: TestNG.XML file for Reporter Example

The TestNG suite can be run by first right clicking on testng.xml and then clicking on **Run** As and choosing the TestNG Suite option. This can be invoked by choosing *Alt+Shift+X* in your Windows keyboard as an alternative option. Once this action is performed, TestNG opens up the test suite and starts running the scripts.

Once executed, the testoutput folder is updated with the test results. These reports can be looked at to analyze what happened to the test cases we executed. As mentioned earlier, two key files are produced by TestNG in the testoutput folder. Index.html contains a comprehensive report that can be navigated along with hide/

show HTML features and a summary report that can be emailed (`emailable-report.html`).

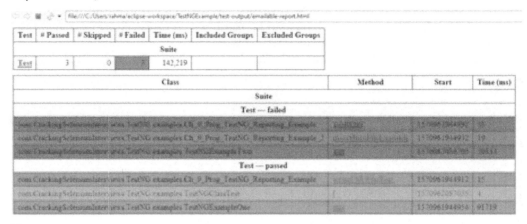

Test

com.CrackingSeleniumInterviews.TestNG.examples.Ch_9_Prog_TestNG_Reporting_Example#readCSV

Figure 9.9: *Emailable TestNG Report Example*

If we want to see the outputs logged through `Reporter.log` (which in a way is a replacement to the traditional `System.out.print` lnstatements), we can click on the Reporter output link in the TestNG report output `index.html`.

For the preceding example, the report looks like the following:

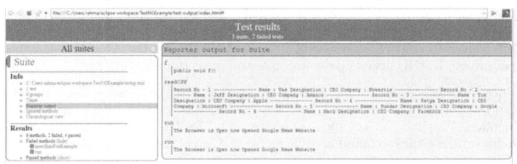

Figure 9.10: *TestNG Reporter Output*

The TestNG suite will give us a detailed summary of test cases that have failed. As you can see, the test case `TestNGExampleTwo` was written in a manner to fail, as the Web Element used for the search was non-existent. As you can see from the TestNG Suite, we have a `NoSuchElementException` in the exception. The recommended approach would be to have a good exception handling function added to the automation scripts.

Figure 9.11: Sample of a Failed Test Case Reporting in TestNG

Now, let us see how we can leverage Selenium for integration with Continuous Integration/Continuous Deployment tools such as Jenkins, Maven, etc.

Continuous Integration/Continuous Deployment /Continuous Testing with Selenium

DevOps is a very popular word these days; thanks to the growth in rapid delivery cycles and rapid code development practiced by innovative organizations. As a result, the continuous development, integration, build, deployment, and real-time testing is a very important for all innovative teams focusing on leveraging excellence through automation.

Let us see how we can leverage some of the leading tools available for CI/CD and DevOps using Selenium. One of the examples of how DevOps gets into the mix with Selenium can be seen in the following diagram:

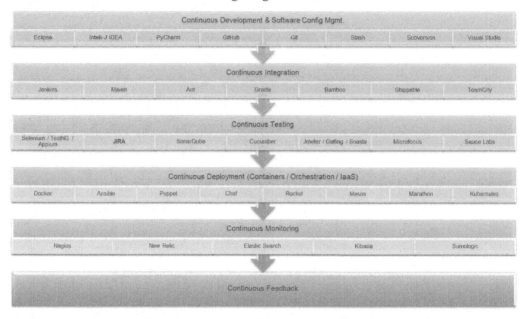

Figure 9.12: Continuous Integration/Deployment - A Reference to Selenium

The success of Selenium is largely driven by the flexibility it offers to deliver CI/CD test automation for firms requiring to test applications continuously using an automation pipeline. There are quite a few applications available to do this. However, in a simple example for representation, let us take Jenkins, TestNG, Selenium, Maven, GitHub, and JIRA for the representation of continuous testing need. All the applications are open source and free to download and use.

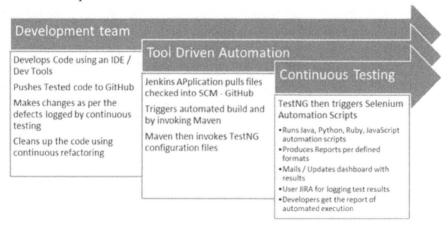

Figure 9.13: DevOps Continuous Testing

In the preceding example, we can use Jenkins to do the following:

1. Check for the new code check-ins to the software configuration management tool such as GitHub, Git, Subversion or any commercial tool.

2. Kickoff automated build and test scripts based on a trigger or at a scheduled time.

3. Kick off the build management tool Maven or any other tool such as Gradle, Ant or Bamboo to run builds automatically.

4. Run test suite defined by TestNG and produces reports, updates the test management tool such as Microfocus ALM or JIRA by updating the test status and defect status.

5. Act as a continuous feedback management tool by integrating with a tool such as Slack or connecting with a Bot monitored by the developers to update about the status of broadcasting to a developer community in an automated fashion.

All the end-to-end pipeline tools are easy to configure in the form of simple XML tags that are self-explanatory in a simple English language. This makes the process very smooth and effective overall. Maven itself runs on a POM.xml file that is driven by a Project Object Model (not page object model though) that modularizes the entire project management process by compartmentalizing it; just like we do with the Page Object Model examples we saw earlier in the chapter.

Overall, with the end-to-end automation pipeline integration, the ease of software development lifecycles improve by many notches. Selenium plays a major role by automating the test validation based on a trigger. Without this end-to-end pipeline automation, the software development lifecycle may take ages to complete.

Conclusion

In this chapter, we covered the advanced concepts used for building a test automation framework. To build a solid data-driven or a hybrid automation framework, we need to leverage advanced concepts available in the programming language of choice. We covered the key concepts such as Page Object Model, File handling, Database Handling, and how to do Reporting in Selenium. There are many concepts available across the languages available for building a Selenium-based automation framework that could be handy such as Lambda functions and regular expressions in Python to Domain-specific language using Cucumber for an implementation of a Behavior-driven Development for test automation. In the next chapter, we willbroach into another important feature of Selenium that made it so popular with automation testers today. Cross-Browser and Cross-Platform Testing is very important to validate the working of a web or a mobile application as it can be used across a myriad of choices. One of the strong points of Selenium is the ability to do this effectively. Let us see this in detail in the next chapter.

Questions

1. What is a Page Object Model?

2. What are the benefits of using a Page Object Model?

3. What is the difference between a Page Class and PageFactory class in a Page Object Model?

4. What are the differences in Page Object Models across programming languages supported by Selenium?

5. How will you handle a Properties file using Selenium? Where will you be using a Properties file?

6. How will you implement a data-driven testing framework in Selenium using an Excel-based data setup?

7. What are the benefits and disadvantages of using a Comma Separated Values file and an Excel file when it comes to data-driven testing in Selenium? Which one would you use?

8. Can you explain how a database can be accessed in a Selenium Web Driver Program? What are some of the benefits of using a database for your selenium automation?

9. Given a choice for a data setup for your automation, what would be your choice: CSV Vs XLS Vs Database? Why would you choose your choice?

10. What are the reporting choices you have for your Selenium Tests?

11. What are some of the challenges while using the basic library available in Selenium for reporting and debugging? What would be your approach?

12. What are the benefits of using TestNG with a Selenium program?

13. What are some of the features available in TestNG that can be used for running different types of tests while using a tool such as Maven or Jenkins?

14. What are some of the CI/CD tools you can use with Selenium for running a DevOps Model?

15. What are some of the monitoring tools that you can use for a Selenium-based DevOps Model?

16. What are some of the Deployment tools for Continuous Deployment that can be used along with Selenium?

Cross-Browser Test Automation

"Software testers succeed where others fail."

– Anonymous

So far, we have covered Selenium test automation to be run linearly or sequentially or in a single system or instance. One of the greatest advantages and power of Selenium is its ability to run tests in parallel and thus against multiple browsers, operating systems, and combinations thereof. This chapter covers advanced Selenium Concepts to perform Cross-Browser Test Automation using the Selenium Grid, use of browser emulators, running multiple tests across browsers, leveraging commercial tools for test automation using selenium, state management, and reporting.

Structure

Cross-browser testing is a multi-faceted phenomenon that delivers a powerful report and we need to cover key aspects of cross-browser testing. These include coverage on the following topics:

- What is cross-browser testing and why is it important?
- How can we run cross-browser testing using the Selenium Grid?
- How can we leverage emulators to run testing against various configurations?
- How can we leverage commercial tools to deliver cross-browser testing?

Objectives

In this chapter, we willexplore the various aspects of test automation to evaluate what are some good tips to follow, what to automate, when to automate, what is the right approach, what are some suggested approaches,and what are the different ways in which we can automate efficiently? This chapter will focus more on the theoretical and concept-based understanding of test automation.

Cross-browser testing and why is it important?

The original objective of *PhillipeHanrigou* when he created the Selenium Grid was to allow the execution of selenium scripts across operating systems and a myriad of browsers and versions – all at once and in parallel. This is important because we cannot rely on the validation of a web application with a localized and customized version of Selenium Web Driver. This model is neither scalable nor sustainable. This is because we cannot expect all the users to use a setup similar to the setup a developer has.

The examples given in this book may produce different results and behaviors when executed in different browsers and configurations as the setup may differ. Some programs may not work, as a configuration in Linux could be different from the one in Windows. Forexample, how the file folders are referred to in Unix/Linux vs. Windows operating system. Likewise, the browser versions and the web driver implementations may vary across the browsers and operating systems. Hence, it is important to validate critical web applications in a myriad of browsers and platforms by analyzing the user configurations (like a market research).

It is also important to ensure that the application developed works across the most important configuration ones. The management team using a risk-based approach if needed can decide on the long tail of configurations. There are well over 2000+ configurations with the popular operating systems, browsers, and mobile and desktop versions. A web application if built can be accessed via any one of these configurations and may need to work well in any of the heavily used configurations. Use of automated cross-browser testing will help us take care of the need to configure and test in multiple combinations. It also depends on how the infrastructure is used.

Based on the complexity timelines, budget and project needs, and the project team needs to make a choice on whether it will be:

- Fully in house and tested in real physical combinations
- Or an in-house device farm can be used by the testing team
- Alternatively, virtual test device farms or testing services (provided by vendors such as browser stack or **crossbrowsertesting.com**).

In addition, how many browsers and versions can a machine hold? What about memory consumptions, if tests are run in parallel? What about the handling of asynchronous responses? Are these behaviors similar to the actual end-user behavior? These are some of the dilemmas the tester faces while running automated scripts. There is no silver bullet solution to this challenge. With good cross-browser testing, we can smoothly address these challenges.

Additionally, if a website or an application with responsive web design approach needs to be tested, the appearance and user experience of the application in various devices, various form factors, browsers, and configurations need to be tested extensively. This is an arduous challenge for web application developers. For testers, the challenge is multi-fold. Being the last line of defense for code quality, testers have a significant role to play. When it comes to automation, Selenium plays a significant role in addressing this issue with the cross-browser testing and use of multi-platform test setup leveraging Selenium Grid and other advanced concepts.

We also need to focus on accessibility of testing requirements as well as the users could be having different challenges for accessibility and some of the stern acts by governments enforces mandatory support for all types of users with the ADA act, etc. This would mean an application needs to be supported for voice, content, navigation, colour, and form factors to ensure the application is accessible by all types of users.

To do effective cross-browser testing, one needs to have a strategy for carrying out the testing. This includes:

1. **Decide whom are you building for:** Who are your users, and what are their preferences when it comes to platform, gadgets, technology, and browser?

2. **Decide what is your target platform:** What are the prominent browsers and platforms would you be automating for:

   a. This can be decided by doing market research by looking at the browser market share using sites such as NetMarketShare (**https:// www.netmarketshare.com/browser-market-share.aspx**).

   b. If your website were already live, use Usage Analytics through Google Analytics or other market metrics analysis tools to decide what would be your prominent platforms and combinations to test.

3. **Decide on how you will test:** What are your testing approaches when it comes to actual devices, emulators, virtual machines, remote device farms, etc.

   a. It is generally best to test the actual applications using some physical devices and platforms. The top platforms can be chosen based on analysis done for the target platform as mentioned above.

   b. It is always good to decide two or three combinations to test your applications.

    c. Emulators can be very handy and plenty of tools are available for the same.

    d. **Virtual Machines:** These can be used when testing against multiple platforms and combinations is a challenge. With virtual machines, this can be addressed. However, having in-house virtual machines could be a decision to be made based on budgetary constraints.

    e. **Device Farms:** This is the most preferred option by many of the upcoming companies and popular mobile apps. The need to test against 1000s of combination for each build can be an arduous task to complete. With device farm usage and automation scripts, the tests can be done very quickly in a concurrent manner. This is a costly affair but the benefit gained is the ability to test your applications very quickly.

4. **Decide on what tools to use to test:** This is a very important decision to be made as the success of the test automation program largely depends on this specific decision.

5. **Decide on how much to test:** This is very important as one could be boiling the ocean with an infinitesimal number of test cases and infinite permutations of *Device + OS + Browser + Screen Factor Setting + User Preferences.*

Once the strategy and approach are ready, we can move into the next phase of our cross-browser testing with planning. One of the approaches could be how we can address some of the common challenges we face for browser testing such as the HTML and CSS problems seen in various browsers due to differences in the implementations of various protocols, JavaScript browser behavior challenges, accessibility, and page rendering challenges.

For example, when the browser war between Netscape and Microsoft Internet Explorer was at its peak, the browsers had different HTML elements for a different browser such as IFRAME, etc. If an application is developed predominantly for a particular browser and some of the non-standard tags are used, they may not work in different browsers or show a different browser behavior. These challenges need to be considered and taken care of.

Similarly, some of the tags used in HTML or CSS may work differently in different browsers (especially older browsers). The need to check these aspects becomes tricky and challenging at times. Similarly, we have a responsive design and screen layout related issues. While deciding the cross-browser testing approach, we need to be cognizant of these challenges and decide how we want to tackle these challenges.

Some of the good commercial cross-browser testing services include LambdaTest, SauceLabs, **CrossbrowserTesting.com**, BrowserStack, and TestingBot among hundreds of other services available.

Let us see how we can run a cross-browser testing script using the Selenium Grid.

Running Cross-Browser Testing – With Selenium Grid

Let us leverage the learning we had so far aboutthe Selenium Grid. For references on how to setup the Selenium Grid, please refer to *Chapter 4 Understanding Selenium Tools* in this book. This program runs a command to open a web page, get the title, and print the text content of what appears on the page. The way it is executed is by connecting to a hub that assigns this to a node connected to it, based on the capabilities and options chosen and executes the same.

```java
Packagecom.CrackingSeleniumInterviewExamples.CrossBrowser;

Importjava.net.MalformedURLException;
import java.net.URL;

import org.openqa.selenium.By;
import org.openqa.selenium.Platform;
import org.openqa.selenium.UnexpectedAlertBehaviour;
import org.openqa.selenium.WebDriver;
import org.openqa.selenium.chrome.ChromeOptions;
import org.openqa.selenium.remote.CapabilityType;
import org.openqa.selenium.remote.RemoteWebDriver;

public class Ch_10_Prog_1_Grid_Example{

    public static void main(String[]args)throwsMalformedURLException{
            WebDriverdriver;
System.setProperty("webdriver.chrome.driver",
"C:\\Selenium\\chromedriver.exe");
ChromeOptionschromeOptions=newChromeOptions();
chromeOptions.setCapability(CapabilityType.PLATFORM_NAME,Platform.WINDOWS);
chromeOptions.setCapability(CapabilityType.UNEXPECTED_ALERT_BEHAVIOUR,Unexpecte
dAlertBehaviour.ACCEPT);
chromeOptions.setCapability(CapabilityType.ACCEPT_SSL_CERTS,true);

        driver=newRemoteWebDriver(newURL("http://192.168.0.100:4444/wd/hub"),chro
meOptions);
            driver.get("http://www.bing.com");
            System.out.println("Checking the Program ...");
            System.out.println(driver.findElement(By.tagName("title")));

    System.out.println(driver.findElement(By.tagName("body")).getText());
            driver.quit();
        }
    }
```

Figure 10.1: Ch_10_Prog_1_Grid_Example.java

"// FOR TRACKING THE COMMENT TO BE DELETED IN COPY EDITING Changed //"

What you will see when this program gets executed is that this program connects to the hub using the RemoteWebDriver command and opens the URL **http://www.**

bing.com in the node assigned. The hub and the node logs will appear as shown in the following screenshot:

Selenium GRID – Hub Console output for a connection with capabilities and options registered:

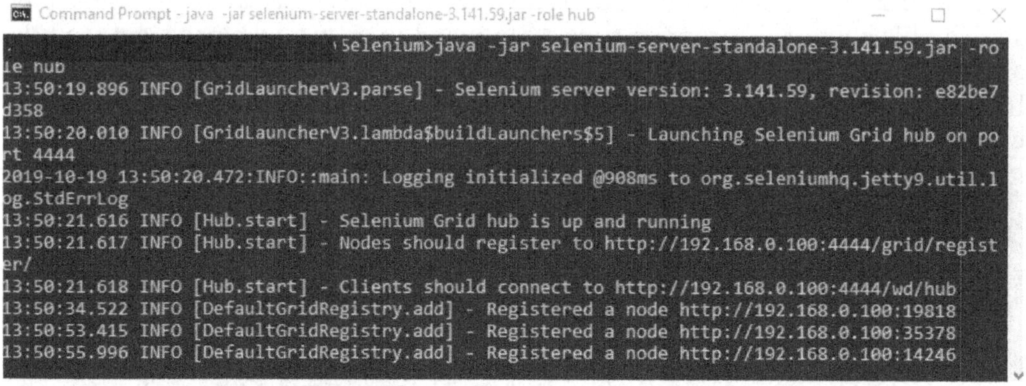

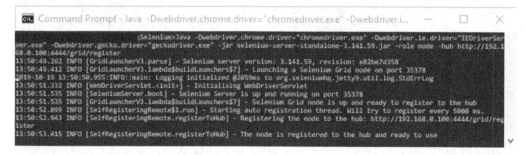

Figure 10.2: Starting of Selenium GRID - Hub

Selenium GRID – Node Console output for a connection with capabilities and options registered:

The following screenshot displays what we willsee when we start a Selenium Grid node that gets registered to a Selenium Hub on the IP Address/URL and port specified:

Figure 10.3: Starting of the Selenium GRID - Node

As you can see, the session is attached, the program is executed, and then the session gets disconnected. We get the following screenshot as the output. As we can see, the search engine is invoked:

Figure 10.4: Grid Program Output

The console output comes out like the following:

```
Oct 28, 2019 5:38:46 PM
org.openqa.selenium.remote.ProtocolHandshakecreateSession
INFO: Detected dialect: W3C
Checking the Program ...
[[RemoteWebDriver: chrome on XP (8c032318c0c0072cc6d957a621f04f77)] -> tag
name: title]
Bing
Bing
Languages:???????????????????????????????????????????????????????
AllImagesVideosMapsNews
Sign in
A night on the (ghost) town
Trending news
```

Figure 10.5: Grid Program Output

Now, if we want to extend this further and run a program in a truly cross-browser manner, we need toleverage the Selenium Grid to run the same program against multiple browsers. Let us see how this can be done with an example.

Now, let us see a code snippet for a Grid using Python.

Selenium Grid-based Example – Python Code

The following example does a similar job to the Java example we read just now in the earlier section. We will not go into details of the program. The key section to focus on is given in the following table:

```python
import datetime

import time

import unittest
```

```python
from selenium import webdriver
from selenium.webdriver.common.desired_capabilities import
DesiredCapabilities

class SeleniumPythonGridExample(unittest.TestCase):

defsetUp(self):
        print("Driver Getting Initiated")
self.driver = webdriver.Remote(
command_executor='http://192.168.0.100:4444/wd/hub',
desired_capabilities=DesiredCapabilities.CHROME
        )
        print("Driver Initiation Success")
self.driver.get('https://www.bing.com')
        print("driver.get() success")

deftest_something(self):
        print("Testing the URL")
        if not "Bing" in self.driver.title:
raise Exception("Unable to load Bing page!")
        print("Sending Search String")
elem = self.driver.find_element_by_name("q")
elem.send_keys("Selenium")
elem.submit()
        print("Submitted Search String")
        print(self.driver.title)
dt_format = '%Y%m%d_%H%M%S'
cdt = datetime.datetime.fromtimestamp(time.time()).strftime(dt_format)
        picture = 'selGridPyExample' + cdt + '.png'
self.driver.save_screenshot(picture)

deftearDown(self):
        print("Quitting the Driver")
self.driver.quit()
```

```
if __name__ == "__main__":
```

```
unittest.main(verbosity=1)
```

The following is the code snippet to focus on that invokes the `RemoteWebDriver` class to connect to the Grid and pass the desired capabilities. The `RemoteWebDriver` establishes a session as per the capabilities specified to run the test through a node connected to the grid.

```
self.driver = webdriver.Remote(
```

```
command_executor='http://192.168.0.100:4444/wd/hub',
```

```
desired_capabilities=DesiredCapabilities.CHROME
```

```
        )
```

Let us see how to run a Page Object Model-based program using the Selenium Grid.

Selenium grid-based cross-browser testing

Now, let us see a program that leverages the Selenium Grid for testing the precedingexample. This example (SeleniumGrid_CB_example_2.java) uses various functions defined to run the same test in two different browsers (Firefox and Chrome). Let us see what each function does.

S.No	Function/Code Snippet	Purpose
1	`setUpGridTest()`	Invokes the Grid Setup class `SetupGrid` `SetupForCBTesting` by passing the parameters such as operating system, browser, and URL to test and the Grid details (IP address or URL).
2	`bingUrlTest()`	Performs comparison on the URL to be correct.
3	`bingSearch` `ButtonTest()`	Performs a check on whether the Search icon is displayed and enabled.
4	`bingTitleTest()`	Performs check on the Title text.
5	`bingSearchBox()`	Performs a check on whether the search text box is displayed and enabled.
6	`closeBrowser()`	Closes the open browser with a `driver.close()` function call.
7	Constructor `SetupGridSetupFor` `CBTesting in the` `Class SetupGridSetup` `ForCBTesting`	Receives parameters to establish a connection to a Selenium Hub through a node as per the parameters passed. By default (unless specified), 5 Firefox and 5 Chrome Browsers along with an Internet Explorer browser is permitted per node. We can run up to 11 instances connected to a node to perform tests.

Table 10.1: SeleniumGrid_CB_Example_2.java - Function and Purpose reference

The complete program is as follows:

```java
Packagecom.CrackingSeleniumInterviewExamples.CrossBrowser;

importjava.net.MalformedURLException;

import org.openqa.selenium.By;
import org.openqa.selenium.WebDriver;
import org.openqa.selenium.WebElement;
import org.testng.Assert;

public class SeleniumGrid_CB_example_2 {
    publicstaticWebDriverwebDriver = null;

    public static void main(String[] args) throwsMalformedURLException {
        System.out.println("Testing the Crossbrowser options ... Firefox");
        setUpGridTest("WIN10", "firefox", "https://www.bing.com",
"http://192.168.43.155:4444");
        System.out.println("Testing the Crossbrowser options ...
Chrome");
        setUpGridTest("WIN10", "chrome", "https://www.bing.com",
"http://192.168.43.155:4444");
        System.out.println("Completed the test");
    }

    public static void setUpGridTest(String os, String browser,
String url, String node) throwsMalformedURLException {
        SetupGridSetupForCBTestingsetupGrid =
newSetupGridSetupForCBTesting(os, browser, url, node);
        System.out.println("Creating a new Web Driver instance for
" + os+ " " + browser + " " + url + " at " + node);
        webDriver = setupGrid.getDriver();
        bingUrlTest();

        bingSearchButtonTest();
        bingTitleTest();
        bingSearchBox();
        closeBrowser();
```

```java
                System.out.println("Closed the Web Driver instance at " +
os + " " + browser + " " + url + " at " + node);
        }

        public static void bingUrlTest() {
                Assert.assertTrue(webDriver.getCurrentUrl().contains("www.
bing.com"));
                System.out.println("bingUrlTest is success " + webDriver.
getCurrentUrl());
        }

        public static void bingSearchButtonTest() {
                WebElementsearchButtonElement = webDriver.findElement(By.
name("go"));
                Assert.assertTrue(searchButtonElement.isDisplayed());
                Assert.assertTrue(searchButtonElement.isEnabled());

        }

        public static void bingTitleTest() {
                Assert.assertTrue(webDriver.getTitle().
contentEquals("Bing"));
                System.out.println("bingTitleTest is success " + webDriver.
getTitle());
        }

        public static void bingSearchBox() {
                WebElementsearchElement = webDriver.findElement(By.
name("q"));
                Assert.assertTrue(searchElement.isDisplayed());
                Assert.assertTrue(searchElement.isEnabled());
                System.out.println("bingSearchBoxTest is success " +
searchElement.isEnabled());
        }

        public static void closeBrowser() {
                webDriver.close();
        }
}
```

The `SetupGridSetupForCBTesting` class is used for setting up the node for Grid testing. We pass the parameters such as the WebDriver reference, the browser name (Chrome, Firefox, etc.), URL to invoke, the node details, and the operating system of the browser where the tests will be run:

Packagecom.CrackingSeleniumInterviewExamples.CrossBrowser;

Importjava.net.MalformedURLException;

import java.net.URL;

importjava.util.concurrent.TimeUnit;

import org.openqa.selenium.Platform;

import org.openqa.selenium.UnexpectedAlertBehaviour;

import org.openqa.selenium.WebDriver;

import org.openqa.selenium.chrome.ChromeOptions;

import org.openqa.selenium.firefox.FirefoxOptions;

import org.openqa.selenium.ie.InternetExplorerOptions;

import org.openqa.selenium.remote.CapabilityType;

import org.openqa.selenium.remote.RemoteWebDriver;

```java
public class SetupGridSetupForCBTesting {
    privateWebDriverwebDriver = null;
    private String browserName = null;
    private String baseUrl = null;
    private String operatingSystem = null;
    private String nodeDetails = null;

    publicSetupGridSetupForCBTesting(String  osName,  String  browser,
String urldetails, String nodedetails)
            throwsMalformedURLException {
        this.browserName = browser;
        this.operatingSystem = osName;
        // This config is used for IE and Firefox settings primarily
        this.baseUrl = urldetails;
        this.nodeDetails = nodedetails;
        if (browser.equalsIgnoreCase("chrome")) {
            ChromeOptions = newChromeOptions();
```

```
                        chromeOptions.setCapability(CapabilityType.PLATFORM_
NAME, Platform.WINDOWS);
                        chromeOptions.setCapability(CapabilityType.
UNEXPECTED_ALERT_BEHAVIOUR, UnexpectedAlertBehaviour.ACCEPT);
                        chromeOptions.setCapability(CapabilityType.ACCEPT_
SSL_CERTS, true);
                        this.webDriver = newRemoteWebDriver(new
URL(nodeDetails + "/wd/hub"), chromeOptions);
            } elseif (browser.equalsIgnoreCase("firefox")) {
                        FirefoxOptionsfirefoxOptions = newFirefoxOptions();
                        this.webDriver = newRemoteWebDriver(new
URL(nodeDetails + "/wd/hub"), firefoxOptions);
            } else {
                        InternetExplorerOptionsieOption =
newInternetExplorerOptions();
                        this.webDriver = newRemoteWebDriver(new
URL(nodeDetails + "/wd/hub"), ieOption);
            }
            this.webDriver.manage().timeouts().implicitlyWait(60,
TimeUnit.SECONDS);
            this.webDriver.manage().window().maximize();
            this.webDriver.get(baseUrl);
    }


    public String getOs() {
            returnthis.operatingSystem;
    }


    public String getBrowser() {
            return this.browserName;
    }


    public String getBaseUrl() {
            return this.baseUrl;
    }
```

```
public String getNode() {

        return this.nodeDetails;

}


PublicWebDrivergetDriver() {

        return this.webDriver;

}

}
```

When we execute this program, we get the following output:

```
Problems  @ Javadoc  Declaration  Console ⊠  Progress                                    ■ ✖ ✖ | ▣ ▣ ▣ ▣ ▣
<terminated> SeleniumGrid_CB_example_2 [Java Application] C:\Program Files\Java\jdk-12.0.2\bin\javaw.exe (21-Oct-2019, 6:45:58 pm)
Testing the Crossbrowser options ... Firefox
Oct 21, 2019 6:47:02 PM org.openqa.selenium.remote.ProtocolHandshake createSession
INFO: Detected dialect: W3C
Creating a new Web Driver instance for WIN10 firefox https://www.bing.com at http://192.168.43.155:4444
bingUrlTest is success https://www.bing.com/
bingSearchButtonTest is success
bingTitleTest is success Bing
bingSearchBoxTest is success true
Closed the Web Driver instance at WIN10 firefox https://www.bing.com at http://192.168.43.155:4444
Testing the Crossbrowser options ... Chrome
Oct 21, 2019 6:48:29 PM org.openqa.selenium.remote.ProtocolHandshake createSession
INFO: Detected dialect: W3C
Creating a new Web Driver instance for WIN10 chrome https://www.bing.com at http://192.168.43.155:4444
bingUrlTest is success https://www.bing.com/
bingSearchButtonTest is success
bingTitleTest is success Bing
bingSearchBoxTest is success true
Closed the Web Driver instance at WIN10 chrome https://www.bing.com at http://192.168.43.155:4444
Completed the test
```

Figure 10.6: Selenium Grid-based Cross-Browser Testing Example

One more way to run these tests in parallel would be to use TestNG and use the parallel execution threads to make it more impactful.

Use of emulators for cross-browser test verification

Browsers such as Chrome and Firefox have a lot of tools available for the developers to help test the web application in a very comprehensive manner. One such feature is available in the emulation capabilities provided. The following JavaScript program runs an emulation of Chrome on four different devices (iPhone 5, iPad Mini, Nexus 5X, and Galaxy S5). The emulation is implemented using the setMobileEmulation() option available in the setChromeOption() functions using the Builder class used for creating the instance of the Chrome browser in JavaScript.

The rest of the program is straightforward with the use of the variable and constant definition, library requirement definition, screenshots capturing, and console logging for debugging purposes. The program is almost similar to the earlier examples – we are searching for "selenium" at the Bing Search engine:

```javascript
'use strict';
const {Builder, By, Key, until} = require('..');
const {Options} = require('../chrome');
(async function() {
  let driver;
  var browsers = ["iPhone 5", "iPad Mini", "Nexus 5X", "Galaxy S5"];
  var i=0;
  var fs = require('fs')
  try {
    for (i = 0; i < browsers.length; i++) {
    var filename = "Chrome_Browser_Emulation_";
    filename = filename.concat(browsers[i],".png");
    console.log(filename);
    driver = await new Builder().forBrowser('chrome')
                    .setChromeOptions(new Options()
                    .setMobileEmulation({deviceName: browsers[i]}))
                    .build();
        await driver.get('https://www.bing.com');
        await driver.findElement(By.name('q'))
                    .sendKeys('webdriver', Key.RETURN);
      await driver.wait(until.titleIs('webdriver - Bing'), 1000);
        await driver.takeScreenshot().then(
          function (ScreenShotImage, err) {
            fs.writeFile(filename, ScreenShotImage, 'base64', function (error) {
                if (error != null)
                    console.log("Error occured during screenshot" + error);
              });
          }
        );
  await driver.close();
    }
  } finally {
    await driver && driver.quit();
  }
})().then(_ => console.log('SUCCESS'), err => console.error('ERROR: ' + err));
```

Figure 10.7: Ch_10_Prog_3_Chrome_MobileEmulation_Ex_Bing.js

When we execute the program, we get the following output captured using the screenshot function written in the program:

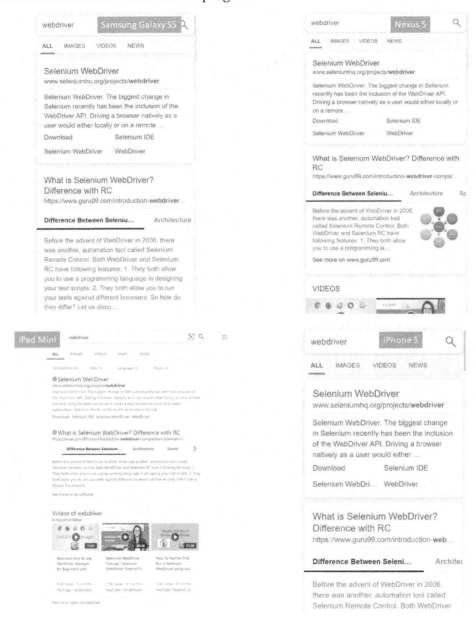

Figure 10.8: *Mobile Emulation across devices*

We get the following output on the console as well:

```
Command Prompt
Chrome_Browser_Emulation_iPhone 5.png

DevTools listening on ws://127.0.0.1:57233/devtools/browser/355cb3da-35b6-4b34-942e-8fdd6840aa06
Chrome_Browser_Emulation_iPad Mini.png

DevTools listening on ws://127.0.0.1:57284/devtools/browser/2b755597-2038-49f9-9b73-89ebdcbcb8d0
Chrome_Browser_Emulation_Nexus 5X.png

DevTools listening on ws://127.0.0.1:57338/devtools/browser/7afd563f-3d2f-4bb8-91d6-cbaaa60a480b
Chrome_Browser_Emulation_Galaxy S5.png

DevTools listening on ws://127.0.0.1:57368/devtools/browser/8760061f-1a10-4b7d-8355-8eee3852b1db
SUCCESS
```

Figure 10.9: Mobile Emulator Program Test Execution - Console Output

Now, let us check some of the commercial options available for cross-browser testing along with examples.

Use of commercial tools and services for cross-browser testing

As mentioned earlier in the chapter, there are a lot of well-established commercial services available for cross-browser testing. Some of the leading providers include BrowserStack, SauceLabs, and Crossbrowser Testing to name a few. They also offer a free trial service to test the capabilities they provide before using the services on a full-fledged scale. The offering covers cross-browser testing across mobile apps and browsers across operating systems. There is emulation or real-device options provided as well. The availability of screenshots, evidence capture, and examples make it easier for automation engineers to automate and validate the results in a rapid fashion. There are services to perform live testing and capture screenshots of the web or mobile apps across platforms instantaneously. Doing the same work in a restricted infrastructure will result in a lot of time and effort for the project teams. This can be looked at as an option.

For the examples I am going to share, we will look at BrowserStack service that is one of the leading commercial services for cross-browser testing.

For performing a cross-browser testing using commercial platforms such as BrowserStack, all we need is a registered account. Once we register, we will get a USERNAME and access key known by AUTOMATE_KEY. We can use these two core inputs to perform automate using BrowserStack.

The following program invokes the BrowserStack Grid using the RemoteWeb Driver() class. For the testing purposes, we will establish the configuration using the `DesiredCapabilities()` class. This class allows us to establish the testing capabilities we need to run the program. For this example, we are choosing to run the test on a real Samsung Galaxy S10 device running Android 9.0 version. The output from the test execution will be passed back to the calling program. In this case, we are running it from an IDE and the output will be captured at a console:

```java
package com.CrossBrowser.Selenium.TestExamples;

import java.net.URL;

import org.openqa.selenium.By;
import org.openqa.selenium.WebDriver;
import org.openqa.selenium.WebElement;
import org.openqa.selenium.remote.DesiredCapabilities;
import org.openqa.selenium.remote.RemoteWebDriver;

public class BrowserStackExample {

        public static final String USERNAME = "YOUR_BROWSER_STACK_USERNAME";
        public static final String AUTOMATE_KEY = " YOUR_BROWSER_STACK_
AUTOMATE_KEY";
        public static final String URL = "https://" + USERNAME + ":" +
AUTOMATE_KEY + "@hub-cloud.browserstack.com/wd/hub";

        public static void main(String[] args) throws Exception {

                DesiredCapabilities caps = new DesiredCapabilities();
                caps.setCapability("browserName", "android");
                caps.setCapability("device", "Samsung Galaxy S10");
                caps.setCapability("realMobile", "true");
                caps.setCapability("os_version", "9.0");
                caps.setCapability("name", "Bstack-[Java] Sample Test - Bing");

                WebDriver driver = new RemoteWebDriver(new URL(URL), caps);
                driver.get("https://www.bing.com");
                WebElement element = driver.findElement(By.name("q"));

                element.sendKeys("Selenium");
                element.submit();

                System.out.println(driver.getTitle());
```

```
            System.out.println(driver.getCurrentUrl());

            System.out.println(driver.getPageSource());

            driver.quit();


        }

}
```

When we execute this program, we get three outputs: Result title, URL, and the HTML content of the page. The console output will be similar to the following screenshot:

Figure 10.10: *Cross-Browser Testing - Browser Stack Example-1 Bing Output*

Cross-browser testing – Example-2

Let us see how we can use these commercial platforms for using complex test cases. To showcase this, let us take a page object model and see how this gets executed. This program uses a Page Object Model created for the site **https://rahmankalilur. wixsite.com/crackingselenium**. All the elements in this page are generated on a Page Object Model. The calling program "Ch_10_Wix_CrackingSelenium_ BrowserStackExample" invokes the test using two configurations by invoking the grid set up in the BrowserStack platform:

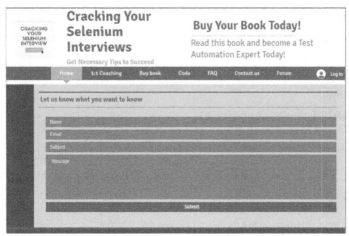

Figure 10.11: *CrackingSelenium Website - Landing Page - POM Example*

This example takes the landing page of the site mentioned above and fills out the form in an automated fashion. The other pages on the website can be picked up for automation using various concepts we have learnt so far.

Now, let us see the Page Object Model we used for testing this.

Ch_10_Wix_CrackingSelenium_Website_POM_HomePage.java:

```java
package com.CrossBrowser.Selenium.TestExamples;

import java.util.Map;

import org.openqa.selenium.WebDriver;
import org.openqa.selenium.WebElement;
import org.openqa.selenium.support.CacheLookup;
import org.openqa.selenium.support.FindBy;
import org.openqa.selenium.support.PageFactory;
import org.openqa.selenium.support.ui.ExpectedCondition;
import org.openqa.selenium.support.ui.Select;
import org.openqa.selenium.support.ui.WebDriverWait;

public class Ch_10_Wix_CrackingSelenium_Website_POM_HomePage  {
    private Map<String, String> data;
    private WebDriver driver;
    private int timeout = 15;

    @FindBy(id = "DrpDwnMn02linkElement")
    @CacheLookup
    private WebElementbuyBook;

    @FindBy(id = "DrpDwnMn01linkElement")
    @CacheLookup
    private WebElement coaching11;

    @FindBy(id = "DrpDwnMn03linkElement")
    @CacheLookup
    private WebElement code;

    @FindBy(id = "DrpDwnMn05linkElement")
    @CacheLookup
```

```java
    private WebElementcontactUs;

    @FindBy(id = "comp-jwf1bc1bdropdownMenuMobile")
    @CacheLookup
    private WebElementcrackingYourSeleniumInterviewsgetNecessaryTips;

    @FindBy(id = "DrpDwnMn04linkElement")
    @CacheLookup
    private WebElementfaq;

    @FindBy(id = "DrpDwnMn06linkElement")
    @CacheLookup
    private WebElement forum;

    @FindBy(id = "DrpDwnMn00linkElement")
    @CacheLookup
    private WebElement home;

    @FindBy(id = "comp-jwf1bc1buser")
    @CacheLookup
    private WebElementkalilurRahman;

    @FindBy(id = "comp-jxad7hnvinput")
    @CacheLookup
    private WebElement letUsKnowWhatYouWant1;

    @FindBy(id = "comp-jxad7ho5input")
    @CacheLookup
    private WebElement letUsKnowWhatYouWant2;

    @FindBy(id = "comp-jxad7hoeinput")
    @CacheLookup
    private WebElement letUsKnowWhatYouWant3;

    @FindBy(id = "comp-jxad7hoptextarea")
    @CacheLookup
    private WebElement letUsKnowWhatYouWant4;

    @FindBy(id = "comp-jwf1bc1bmenuItem3")
```

```java
@CacheLookup
private WebElementlogOut;

@FindBy(id = "WPht6link")
@CacheLookup
private WebElement maskwpht6imgsvgFillFffStrokeFff;

@FindBy(id = "DrpDwnMn0__more__linkElement")
@CacheLookup
private WebElement more;

@FindBy(id = "comp-jwf1bc1bmenuItem2")
@CacheLookup
private WebElementmyAccount;

@FindBy(id = "comp-jwf1bc1bmenuItem1")
@CacheLookup
private WebElementmyBookings;

private final String pageLoadedText = "Most of the developers prefer
selenium over any other commercial tool available ";

private final String pageUrl = "/crackingselenium";

@FindBy(id = "comp-jwf1bc1bmenuItem0")
@CacheLookup
private WebElement profile;

@FindBy(id = "StBttn0link")
@CacheLookup
private WebElement readMore1;

@FindBy(id = "StBttn1link")
@CacheLookup
private WebElement readMore2;

@FindBy(id = "comp-jxad7hoylink")
@CacheLookup
private WebElement submit;
```

```java
@FindBy(id = "top")
@CacheLookup
private WebElementthisSiteWasDesignedWithThe;

@FindBy(id = "LnkBr01imagelink")
@CacheLookup
private WebElementtwitterClean;

@FindBy(id = "LnkBr00imagelink")
@CacheLookup
private WebElementwfacebook;

public Ch_10_Wix_CrackingSelenium_Website_POM_HomePage () {
}

public Ch_10_Wix_CrackingSelenium_Website_POM_HomePage (WebDriver driver) {
    this();
this.driver = driver;
}

public Ch_10_Wix_CrackingSelenium_Website_POM_HomePage (WebDriver
driver, Map<String, String> data) {
    this(driver);
this.data = data;
}

public Ch_10_Wix_CrackingSelenium_Website_POM_HomePage (WebDriver
driver, Map<String, String> data, int timeout) {
    this(driver, data);
this.timeout = timeout;
}

/**
 * Click on Buy Book Link.
 *
 * @return the Ch_10_Wix_CrackingSelenium_Website_POM_HomePage
class instance.
 */
```

```
    public Ch_10_Wix_CrackingSelenium_Website_POM_HomePage
clickBuyBookLink() {
buyBook.click();

        return this;

    }

    /**
     * Click on 11 Coaching Link.
     *
     * @return the Ch_10_Wix_CrackingSelenium_Website_POM_HomePage
class instance.
     */
    public Ch_10_Wix_CrackingSelenium_Website_POM_HomePage
clickCoachingLink11() {
        coaching11.click();

        return this;

    }

    /**
     * Click on Code Link.
     *
     * @return the Ch_10_Wix_CrackingSelenium_Website_POM_HomePage
class instance.
     */
    public Ch_10_Wix_CrackingSelenium_Website_POM_HomePage
clickCodeLink() {
code.click();

        return this;

    }

    /**
     * Click on Contact Us Link.
     *
     * @return the Ch_10_Wix_CrackingSelenium_Website_POM_HomePage
class instance.
     */
    public Ch_10_Wix_CrackingSelenium_Website_POM_HomePage
```

```
clickContactUsLink() {
contactUs.click();
        return this;
    }

    /**
     * Click on Faq Link.
     *
     * @return the Ch_10_Wix_CrackingSelenium_Website_POM_HomePage
class instance.
     */
    public Ch_10_Wix_CrackingSelenium_Website_POM_HomePage
clickFaqLink() {
faq.click();
        return this;
    }

    /**
     * Click on Forum Link.
     *
     * @return the Ch_10_Wix_CrackingSelenium_Website_POM_HomePage  class
instance.
     */
  public Ch_10_Wix_CrackingSelenium_Website_POM_HomePage clickForumLink()
{
forum.click();
        return this;
    }

    /**
     * Click on Home Link.
     *
     * @return the Ch_10_Wix_CrackingSelenium_Website_POM_HomePage
class instance.
     */
    public Ch_10_Wix_CrackingSelenium_Website_POM_HomePage  clickHomeLink() {
```

```
home.click();

        return this;

    }

    /**

     * Click on KalilurRahman Button.

     *

     * @return the Ch_10_Wix_CrackingSelenium_Website_POM_HomePage
class instance.

     */

    public Ch_10_Wix_CrackingSelenium_Website_POM_HomePage
clickKalilurRahmanButton() {

kalilurRahman.click();

        return this;

    }

    /**

     * Click on Log Out Link.

     *

     * @return the Ch_10_Wix_CrackingSelenium_Website_POM_HomePage
class instance.

     */

    public Ch_10_Wix_CrackingSelenium_Website_POM_HomePage
clickLogOutLink() {

logOut.click();

        return this;

    }

    /**

     * Click on Maskwpht6imgsvg Fill Fff Stroke FffStrokewidth 0 Link.

     *

     * @return the Ch_10_Wix_CrackingSelenium_Website_POM_HomePage
class instance.

     */

    public Ch_10_Wix_CrackingSelenium_Website_POM_HomePage
clickMaskwpht6imgsvgFillFffStrokeFffLink() {

        maskwpht6imgsvgFillFffStrokeFff.click();
```

```
        return this;
    }

    /**
     * Click on More Link.
     *
     * @return the Ch_10_Wix_CrackingSelenium_Website_POM_HomePage
class instance.
     */
    public Ch_10_Wix_CrackingSelenium_Website_POM_HomePage
clickMoreLink() {
more.click();
        return this;
    }


    /**
     * Click on My Account Link.
     *
     * @return the Ch_10_Wix_CrackingSelenium_Website_POM_HomePage
class instance.
     */
    public Ch_10_Wix_CrackingSelenium_Website_POM_HomePage
clickMyAccountLink() {
myAccount.click();
        return this;
    }

    /**
     * Click on My Bookings Link.
     *
     * @return the Ch_10_Wix_CrackingSelenium_Website_POM_HomePage  class
instance.
     */
    public Ch_10_Wix_CrackingSelenium_Website_POM_HomePage
clickMyBookingsLink() {
myBookings.click();
```

```
        return this;

    }


    /**
      * Click on Profile Link.
      *
      * @return the Ch_10_Wix_CrackingSelenium_Website_POM_HomePage
class instance.
      */
    public Ch_10_Wix_CrackingSelenium_Website_POM_HomePage
clickProfileLink() {
profile.click();
        return this;

    }


    /**
      * Click on Read More Link.
      *
      * @return the Ch_10_Wix_CrackingSelenium_Website_POM_HomePage
class instance.
      */
    public Ch_10_Wix_CrackingSelenium_Website_POM_HomePage
clickReadMore1Link() {
        readMore1.click();
        return this;

    }

    /**
      * Click on Read More Link.
      *
      * @return the Ch_10_Wix_CrackingSelenium_Website_POM_HomePage  class
instance.
      */
    public Ch_10_Wix_CrackingSelenium_Website_POM_HomePage
clickReadMore2Link() {
        readMore2.click();
```

```
            return this;

        }


    /**

     * Click on Submit Button.

     *

     * @return the Ch_10_Wix_CrackingSelenium_Website_POM_HomePage  class
instance.

        */

    public Ch_10_Wix_CrackingSelenium_Website_POM_HomePage
clickSubmitButton() {

submit.click();

System.out.println("Clicked Submit Button");

            return this;

        }


    /**

     * Click on This Site Was Designed With The .Com Website Builder.
Create Your Website Today.start Now Link.

     *

     * @return the Ch_10_Wix_CrackingSelenium_Website_POM_HomePage
class instance.

        */

    public Ch_10_Wix_CrackingSelenium_Website_POM_HomePage
clickThisSiteWasDesignedWithTheLink() {

thisSiteWasDesignedWithThe.click();

            return this;

        }


    /**

     * Click on Twitter Clean Link.

     *

     * @return the Ch_10_Wix_CrackingSelenium_Website_POM_HomePage
class instance.

        */
```

```
    public Ch_10_Wix_CrackingSelenium_Website_POM_HomePage
clickTwitterCleanLink() {
twitterClean.click();

        return this;

    }


    /**

     * Click on Wfacebook Link.

     *

     * @return the Ch_10_Wix_CrackingSelenium_Website_POM_HomePage
class instance.

     */
    public Ch_10_Wix_CrackingSelenium_Website_POM_HomePage
clickWfacebookLink() {
wfacebook.click();

        return this;

    }


    /**

     * Fill every fields in the page.

     *

     * @return the Ch_10_Wix_CrackingSelenium_Website_POM_HomePage  class
instance.

     */
    public Ch_10_Wix_CrackingSelenium_Website_POM_HomePage  fill() {
    setCrackingYourSeleniumInterviewsgetNecessaryTipsDropDownListField();

        setLetUsKnowWhatYouWant1EmailField();

        setLetUsKnowWhatYouWant2EmailField();

        setLetUsKnowWhatYouWant3TextField();

        setLetUsKnowWhatYouWant4TextareaField();

        return this;

    }

    /**

     * Fill every fields in the page and submit it to target page.
```

```
     *
     * @return the Ch_10_Wix_CrackingSelenium_Website_POM_HomePage  class
instance.
     */

   public Ch_10_Wix_CrackingSelenium_Website_POM_HomePage  fillAndSubmit()
{

        fill();

        return submit();

    }


    /**

     * Set default value to Cracking Your Selenium Interviewsget Necessary
Tips To Succeedbuy Your Book Today Drop Down List field.
     *

     * @return the Ch_10_Wix_CrackingSelenium_Website_POM_HomePage
class instance.
     */

    public Ch_10_Wix_CrackingSelenium_Website_POM_HomePage
setCrackingYourSeleniumInterviewsgetNecessaryTipsDropDownListField() {

        return setCrackingYourSeleniumInterviewsgetNecessaryTipsDrop
DownListField(data.get("CRACKING_YOUR_SELENIUM_INTERVIEWSGET_NECESSARY_
TIPS"));

    }


    /**

     * Set value to Cracking Your Selenium Interviewsget Necessary Tips
To Succeedbuy Your Book Today Drop Down List field.
     *

     * @return the Ch_10_Wix_CrackingSelenium_Website_POM_HomePage
class instance.
     */

    public Ch_10_Wix_CrackingSelenium_Website_POM_HomePage
setCrackingYourSeleniumInterviewsgetNecessaryTipsDropDownListField
(String crackingYourSeleniumInterviewsgetNecessaryTipsValue) {

        new Select(crackingYour SeleniumInterviewsgetNecessaryTips).
selectByVisibleText(crackingYourSeleniumInterviewsgetNecessaryTips
Value);

        return this;
```

```
    }

    /**
     * Set default value to Let Us Know What You Want To Know Email field.
     *
     * @return the Ch_10_Wix_CrackingSelenium_Website_POM_HomePage
class instance.
     */
    public Ch_10_Wix_CrackingSelenium_Website_POM_HomePage
setLetUsKnowWhatYouWant1EmailField() {
        return setLetUsKnowWhatYouWant1EmailField(data.get("LET_US_KNOW_
WHAT_YOU_WANT_1"));
    }

    /**
     * Set value to Let Us Know What You Want To Know Email field.
     *
     * @return the Ch_10_Wix_CrackingSelenium_Website_POM_HomePage  class
instance.
     */
    public Ch_10_Wix_CrackingSelenium_Website_POM_HomePage
setLetUsKnowWhatYouWant1EmailField(String letUsKnowWhatYouWant1Value) {
        letUsKnowWhatYouWant1.sendKeys(letUsKnowWhatYouWant1Value);
System.out.println("Set Values for letUsKnowWhatYouWant1"  +
letUsKnowWhatYouWant1.getText());
        return this;
    }


    /**
     * Set default value to Let Us Know What You Want To Know Email field.
     *
     * @return the Ch_10_Wix_CrackingSelenium_Website_POM_HomePage
class instance.
     */
    public Ch_10_Wix_CrackingSelenium_Website_POM_HomePage
setLetUsKnowWhatYouWant2EmailField() {
```

```
        return setLetUsKnowWhatYouWant2EmailField(data.get("LET_US_KNOW_
WHAT_YOU_WANT_2"));
    }

    /**
     * Set value to Let Us Know What You Want To Know Email field.
     *
     * @return the Ch_10_Wix_CrackingSelenium_Website_POM_HomePage
class instance.
     */
    public Ch_10_Wix_CrackingSelenium_Website_POM_HomePage
setLetUsKnowWhatYouWant2EmailField(String letUsKnowWhatYouWant2Value) {

        letUsKnowWhatYouWant2.sendKeys(letUsKnowWhatYouWant2Value);

System.out.println("Set Values for letUsKnowWhatYouWant2"  +
letUsKnowWhatYouWant2.getText());

        return this;
    }


    /**
     * Set default value to Let Us Know What You Want To Know Text field.
     *
     * @return the Ch_10_Wix_CrackingSelenium_Website_POM_HomePage
class instance.
     */
    public Ch_10_Wix_CrackingSelenium_Website_POM_HomePage
setLetUsKnowWhatYouWant3TextField() {

        return setLetUsKnowWhatYouWant3TextField(data.get("LET_US_KNOW_
WHAT_YOU_WANT_3"));
    }

    /**
     * Set value to Let Us Know What You Want To Know Text field.
     *
     * @return the Ch_10_Wix_CrackingSelenium_Website_POM_HomePage
class instance.
     */
    public Ch_10_Wix_CrackingSelenium_Website_POM_HomePage
```

```
setLetUsKnowWhatYouWant3TextField(String letUsKnowWhatYouWant3Value) {

        letUsKnowWhatYouWant3.sendKeys(letUsKnowWhatYouWant3Value);

System.out.println("Set Values for letUsKnowWhatYouWant3"  +
letUsKnowWhatYouWant3.getText());

        return this;

    }


    /**

     * Set default value to Let Us Know What You Want To Know Textarea
field.

     *

     * @return the Ch_10_Wix_CrackingSelenium_Website_POM_HomePage
class instance.

     */

    public Ch_10_Wix_CrackingSelenium_Website_POM_HomePage
setLetUsKnowWhatYouWant4TextareaField() {

        return setLetUsKnowWhatYouWant4TextareaField(data.get("LET_US_
KNOW_WHAT_YOU_WANT_4"));

    }


    /**

     * Set value to Let Us Know What You Want To Know Textarea field.

     *

     * @return the Ch_10_Wix_CrackingSelenium_Website_POM_HomePage
class instance.

     */

    public Ch_10_Wix_CrackingSelenium_Website_POM_HomePage
setLetUsKnowWhatYouWant4TextareaField(String letUsKnowWhatYouWant4Value)
{

        letUsKnowWhatYouWant4.sendKeys(letUsKnowWhatYouWant4Value);

System.out.println("Set Values for letUsKnowWhatYouWant4"  +
letUsKnowWhatYouWant4.getText());

        return this;

    }


    /**
```

```
     * Submit the form to target page.
     *
     * @return the Ch_10_Wix_CrackingSelenium_Website_POM_HomePage
class instance.
     */
    public Ch_10_Wix_CrackingSelenium_Website_POM_HomePage  submit() {
clickKalilurRahmanButton();
        Ch_10_Wix_CrackingSelenium_Website_POM_HomePage  target = new
Ch_10_Wix_CrackingSelenium_Website_POM_HomePage (driver, data, timeout);
PageFactory.initElements(driver, target);
        return target;
    }


    /**
     * Unset default value from Cracking Your Selenium Interviewsget
Necessary Tips To Succeedbuy Your Book Today Drop Down List field.
     *
     * @return the Ch_10_Wix_CrackingSelenium_Website_POM_HomePage
class instance.
     */
    public Ch_10_Wix_CrackingSelenium_Website_POM_HomePage
unsetCrackingYourSeleniumInterviewsgetNecessaryTipsDropDownListField() {
        return unsetCrackingYourSeleniumInterviewsgetNecessaryTipsDrop
DownListField(data.get("CRACKING_YOUR_SELENIUM_INTERVIEWSGET_NECESSARY_
TIPS"));
    }


    /**
     * Unset value from Cracking Your Selenium Interviewsget Necessary
Tips To Succeedbuy Your Book Today Drop Down List field.
     *
     * @return the Ch_10_Wix_CrackingSelenium_Website_POM_HomePage  class
instance.
     */
    public Ch_10_Wix_CrackingSelenium_Website_POM_HomePage
unsetCrackingYourSeleniumInterviewsgetNecessaryTipsDropDownListField
```

```
(String crackingYourSeleniumInterviewsgetNecessaryTipsValue) {

        new Select(crackingYourSeleniumInterviewsgetNecessaryTips).
deselectByVisibleText(crackingYourSeleniumInterviewsgetNecessaryTips
Value);

        return this;

    }


    /**
     * Verify that the page loaded completely.
     *
     * @return the Ch_10_Wix_CrackingSelenium_Website_POM_HomePage
class instance.
     */
    public Ch_10_Wix_CrackingSelenium_Website_POM_HomePage  verifyPage
Loaded() {

        (new WebDriverWait(driver, timeout)).until(new ExpectedCondition
<Boolean>() {

            public Boolean apply(WebDriver d) {

                return d.getPageSource().contains(pageLoadedText);

            }

        });

        return this;

    }


    /**
     * Verify that current page URL matches the expected URL.
     *
     * @return the Ch_10_Wix_CrackingSelenium_Website_POM_HomePage
class instance.
     */
    public Ch_10_Wix_CrackingSelenium_Website_POM_HomePage
verifyPageUrl() {

        (new WebDriverWait(driver, timeout)).until(new
ExpectedCondition<Boolean>() {

            public Boolean apply(WebDriver d) {

                return d.getCurrentUrl().contains(pageUrl);
```

```
            }
        });
        return this;
    }
}
```

Let us take the first example – The runner program.

Ch_10_Wix_CrackingSelenium_BrowserStackExample.java:

```java
package com.CrossBrowser.Selenium.TestExamples;

import java.net.MalformedURLException;
import java.net.URL;

import org.openqa.selenium.WebDriver;
import org.openqa.selenium.remote.DesiredCapabilities;
import org.openqa.selenium.remote.RemoteWebDriver;
import org.openqa.selenium.support.PageFactory;

public class Ch_10_Wix_CrackingSelenium_BrowserStackExample {

    public static final String USERNAME = "YOUR_BROWSER_STACK_USERNAME";
    public static final String AUTOMATE_KEY = " YOUR_BROWSER_STACK_
AUTOMATE_KEY";
    public static final String URL = "https://" + USERNAME + ":" +
AUTOMATE_KEY + "@hub-cloud.browserstack.com/wd/hub";

    public static void main(String[] args) throws Exception {
        DesiredCapabilities caps = setBrowserStackSettings();
        System.out.println("Test -1 IPad ");
        runTestsInBrowserStack(caps);
        caps = setBrowserStackSettingsDynamic("android","Samsung
Galaxy S10","true","9.0", "Android - BStack Sample Test");
        System.out.println("Test -2 Samsung Galaxy S10 ");
        runTestsInBrowserStack(caps);
        caps = setBrowserStackSettingsDynamic("android","Samsung
Galaxy Tab S4","true","8.1", "Android - BStack Sample Test Galaxy Tab");
        System.out.println("Test -3 Samsung Galaxy Tab S4 ");
```

```
                runTestsInBrowserStack(caps);

        }


        private static void runTestsInBrowserStack(DesiredCapabilities
caps) throws MalformedURLException {
                WebDriver = new RemoteWebDriver(new URL(URL), caps);
                System.out.println("===========Browser  Session  Started  -
========");
                webDriver.get("http://rahmankalilur.wixsite.com/
crackingselenium");
                Ch_10_Wix_CrackingSelenium_Website_POM_HomePage
checkPOMandSubmit = PageFactory.initElements(webDriver,
                        Ch_10_Wix_CrackingSelenium_Website_POM_
HomePage.class);
                System.out.println("=====Initiated POM=====");
                System.out.println("=====Application Started=====");
                System.out.println("=====Data Entry starts=====");
                enterDataInBrowser(checkPOMandSubmit);
                System.out.println("=====Data Entered");
                // webDriver.close();
                System.out.println("=====Application ended=");
                webDriver.quit();
        }


        private static void enterDataInBrowser(Ch_10_Wix_CrackingSelenium_
Website_POM_HomePage checkPOMandSubmit) {
                // Call the method
                checkPOMandSubmit.setLetUsKnowWhatYouWant1EmailField
("Selenium User");
                System.out.println("Entered checkPOMandSubmit.setLetUs
KnowWhatYouWant1EmailField(Selenium User)");
                checkPOMandSubmit.setLetUsKnowWhatYouWant2EmailField
("Selenium.User@seleniuminterviews.com");
                System.out.println("Entered checkPOMandSubmit.setLetUsKnow
WhatYouWant2EmailField(Selenium.User@seleniuminterviews.com");
                checkPOMandSubmit.setLetUsKnowWhatYouWant3TextField
("Selenium is such a brilliant Tool");
                System.out.println("Entered checkPOMandSubmit.setLetUsKnow
WhatYouWant3TextField(Selenium is such a brilliant Tool)");
                checkPOMandSubmit
```

```
.setLetUsKnowWhatYouWant4TextareaField("Selenium \n Selenium \n Selenium
\n Great \n Great \n");
            System.out.println("Entered setLetUsKnowWhatYouWant
4TextareaField(Selenium \\n Selenium \\n Selenium \\n Great \\n Great
\\n)");
            checkPOMandSubmit.clickSubmitButton();
            System.out.println("Entered checkPOMandSubmit.clickSubmit
Button()");
        }

    private static DesiredCapabilitiessetBrowserStackSettings() {
            DesiredCapabilities caps = new DesiredCapabilities();
            caps.setCapability("browserName", "iPad");
            caps.setCapability("device", "iPad Pro 12.9 2018");
            caps.setCapability("realMobile", "true");
            caps.setCapability("os_version", "13");
            caps.setCapability("name", "Bstack-[Java] Sample Test");
            return caps;
        }


    private  static  DesiredCapabilitiessetBrowserStackSettingsDynamic
(String  capBrow,  String  capDev,  String  capMob,  String  capOS,  String
capTestName) {
            DesiredCapabilities caps = new DesiredCapabilities();
            caps.setCapability("browserName", capBrow);
            caps.setCapability("device", capDev);
            caps.setCapability("realMobile", capMob);
            caps.setCapability("os_version", capOS);
            caps.setCapability("name", capTestName);
            return caps;
        }

}
```

When we execute this program, we get the following output:

Figure 10.12: *Cross Browser - Browser Stack - Program Output*

One of the end outputs that comes off as an email comes across as follows. As you can see, the data sent in the form is shared accurately via email to the email id associated with the website:

Figure 10.13: *POM Program Example Output - BrowserStack POM*

Now, let us see some additional examples in Ruby and JavaScript to use against BrowserStack platform.

Cross-browser testing – Example 3

Let us see an example in Ruby. This program runs a Selenium test of the Lycos Search engine on an Apple Macintosh Machine running a Safari Browser:

```ruby
require 'rubygems'
require 'selenium-webdriver'

# Input capabilities
caps = Selenium::WebDriver::Remote::Capabilities.new
# Following Commented lines can be used for a mobile device testing
#caps[:browserName] = 'iPhone'
#caps['device'] = 'iPhone 8 Plus'
#caps['realMobile'] = 'true'
#caps['os_version'] = '11'
#caps['name'] = 'Bstack-[Ruby] Sample Test'
#Let us use capabilities for testing in a Mac Device
caps['browser'] = 'Safari'
caps['browser_version'] = '12.1'
caps['os'] = 'OS X'
caps['os_version'] = 'Mojave'
caps['resolution'] = '1920x1080'
caps['name'] = 'Bstack-[Ruby] Sample Test - MAC iOS 12.1 test'
driver = Selenium::WebDriver.for(:remote,
  :url => "http://BROWSER_STACK_USER_ID:BROWSER_STACK_SESSION_KEY@hub-
cloud.browserstack.com/wd/hub",
  :desired_capabilities => caps)
driver.navigate.to "http://www.lycos.com"
element = driver.find_element(:name, 'q')
element.send_keys "Selenium"
element.submit
puts driver.title
puts driver.page_source
driver.quit
```

Figure 10.14: BrowserStackRuby.rb

As you can see, the only configuration we need to make is on the capabilities. If we need to run the same test against multiple browsers, we can leverage the TestNG or any other framework that can be used to pass a comprehensive set of parameters if you are running the test locally. BrowserStack provides similar settings as well wherein you can run hundreds of tests in parallel for various configurations you want to use:

```
Command Prompt
Lycos.com
<html lang="en"><head>
<meta charset="utf-8">
<meta http-equiv="X-UA-Compatible" content="IE=edge">
<meta name="viewport" content="width=device-width, initial-scale=1">
<!-- The above 3 meta tags *must* come first in the head; any other head content must come *after* these tags -->
<meta name="description" content="Lycos, Inc., is a web search engine and web portal established in 1994, spun out of Carnegie Mellon University.
 a network of email, webhosting, social networking, and entertainment websites.">
<meta name="author" content="">
<link href="https://ly.lygo.com/static/lycos/img/favicon.ico" rel="icon" type="image/png">
<title>Lycos.com</title>
<link href="//fonts.googleapis.com/css?family=Lato:400,300,300italic,400italic,700,700italic" rel="stylesheet" type="text/css">
<link rel="stylesheet" type="text/css" href="/css/in/fonts.css">
<link rel="stylesheet" type="text/css" href="https://ly.lygo.com/static/lycos/css/in/font-awesome.css">
<!-- Bootstrap core CSS -->

<link href="https://ly.lygo.com/static/lycos/css/in/bootstrap.css" rel="stylesheet">

<!-- IE10 viewport hack for Surface/desktop Windows 8 bug -->
<link href="https://ly.lygo.com/static/lycos/css/in/ie10-viewport-bug-workaround.css" rel="stylesheet">


<!-- HTML5 shim and Respond.js for IE8 support of HTML5 elements and media queries -->
<!--[if lt IE 9]>
    <script src="https://oss.maxcdn.com/html5shiv/3.7.3/html5shiv.min.js"></script>
    <script src="https://oss.maxcdn.com/respond/1.4.2/respond.min.js"></script>
  <![endif]-->
```

Figure 10.15: *BrowserStack - Ruby Example – Cross-browser testing - Lycos*

Let us see one more example using Node.JS and JavaScript.

Cross-browser testing – Example 4:

```
varwebdriver = require('selenium-webdriver');

// Input capabilities
var capabilities = {
 'browserName' : 'Edge',
 'browser_version' : '18.0',
 'os' : 'Windows',
 'os_version' : '10',
 'resolution' : '1280x1024',
'browserstack.user' : 'BROWSER_STACK_USER_ID',
'browserstack.key' : 'BROWSER_STACK_SESSION_KEY',
 'name' : 'Bstack-[Node] Sample Test'
}

var driver = new webdriver.Builder().
usingServer('http://hub-cloud.browserstack.com/wd/hub').
withCapabilities(capabilities).
build();

driver.get('http://www.lycos.com').then(function(){
driver.findElement(webdriver.By.name('q')).sendKeys('webdriver\n').then(function()
{
driver.getTitle().then(function(title) {
console.log(title);
console.log(driver.getCurrentUrl());
console.log(driver.getSession());
console.log(driver.takeScreenshot());
driver.quit();
    });
  });
});
```

Figure 10.16: *BrowserStackJSLycos_new.js*

When we execute the program, we get the following output:

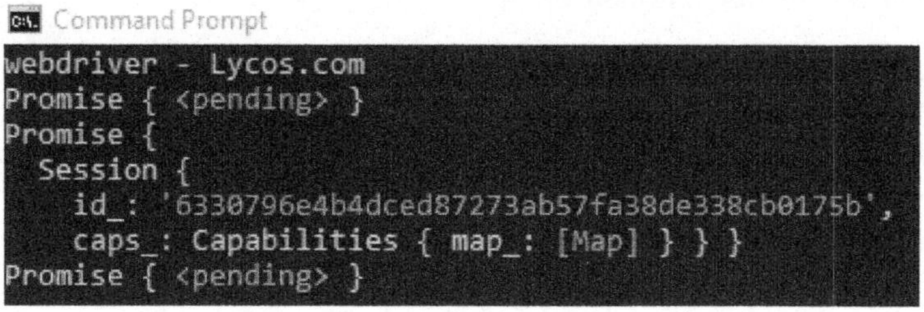

Figure 10.17: BrowserStack JavaScript Example - Output

We get the webpage title printed along with the session id that is readily available for the other two log items using the `getCurrentUrl()` and `takeScreenshot()` functions, we get a Promise { `<pending>` } as the main function is `async`. As a promise in JavaScript is a data structure that needs to be either resolved, rejected or pending, a call back function needs to be implemented using a `.then()` function as highlighted in `driver.getTitle()`. This example also highlights the importance of asynchronous functions. This is because an `async` function in JavaScript needs to resolve a promise with a returned value. For Selenium developers planning to use JavaScript for automation, the promise concept must be learnt well. As per the Mozilla Developer Network definition, a promise object represents the eventual completion or failure of an asynchronous operation and its resulting value. We can use the following functions on a promise object:

- **Promise.all():** This returns a single promise function that resolves all the promises passed as a reference or an iteratable promise.

- **Promise.allSettled():** This returns a promise after all the promises are either resolved or rejected.

- **Promise.prototype.catch():** This returns a promise and deals only with rejected promises.

- **Promise.prototype.finally():** This provides a way to execute code when the promises are fulfilled or rejected successfully. This is akin to finally in a try-catch-finally in Java.

- **Promise.prototype.then():** This is the most widely used function returning a promise by taking two arguments – one a callback function for success and another for failure cases of `Promise()`.

- **Promise.race():** This returns a promise that fulfils or rejects as soon as the promises in an iterable promises completes.

- **Promise.reject():** This returns a promise object that is rejected with a reason.

- **Promise.resolve():** This returns an object that is resolved with a particularly given value.

BrowserStack also provides multiple options to do cross-browser testing and is one of the wonderful options to consider.

Other commercial platforms to consider

One key aspect to consider which platform to choose for your cross-browser testing depends on the organizational needs, the ability of the platform to support the requirements and more importantly, the commercial aspects and flexibility to implement the solution quickly, along with scalability, security to name a few:

Platform / Product / Solution	URL	Features
SauceLabs	www.saucelabs.com	One of the first global solution providers Provides solution across platforms. Offers Private, Public and Hybrid Options. Good support and training options.
CrossBrowser Testing by SmartBear	https:// crossbrowsertesting. com	The solution from a leading Software Testing Tool Vendor. One of the sophisticated and leading tools. Comprehensive Options.
Browsershots	www.browsershots. org	A good tool for getting screenshots across browsers to validate your website. No features available for programming and automation.
LambdaTest	www.lambdatest.com	Similar to BrowserStack, CrossBrowserTesting or SauceLabs – Provides similar options and different commercial choices.
TestingWhiz	https://www.testing-whiz.com	Like SmartBear, TestingWhiz is primarily a testing tool company that provides automated cross-browser services capability.
Testing Bot	https://testingbot.com	Another choice available for cross-browser testing.

Table 10.2: List of Leading Cross-Browser Testing Services

There are many more platforms available that could be considered for cross-browser testing. At the end of the day, the choice should be purely business-driven than a technical capability driven.

Two major highlights from this observation are
1. Selenium is at the base of all these leading cloud-based cross-browser testing services
2. The power of Selenium as a tool of choice for test automation is unquestionable.

Conclusion

We covered all the essentials of automation using Selenium so far. In this chapter, we covered one of the most important and top features of Selenium which is cross-browser testing. Without cross-browser testing capabilities, Selenium would not have achieved the popularity and status it is having now. In this chapter, we covered how to do Selenium cross-browser testing using Grid, how to use mobile device emulation using the browser development tools, and how to leverage commercially available tools and platform by running some examples with BrowserStack. In the next chapter, we will cover a good number of tips and tricks to follow while doing automation, pitfalls to avoid, various tools that we can consider, recommendations on strategy and how test automation can benefit through script less automation, visual regression automation, use of artificial intelligence and contribute to DevOps mode of delivery.

Questions

1. What do you mean by cross-browser testing?

2. Why is cross-browser testing important?

3. What are some of the options available to perform cross-browser testing?

4. How will you perform cross-browser testing with a parallel execution across browsers in a Selenium Grid?

5. What are the restrictions of using a Selenium Grid when you need to test an application across 1000s of combinations?

6. What are some of the benefits of using mobile emulators for cross-browser test verifications?

7. What are some of the commercial options available for cross-browser testing?

8. What are some of the typical challenges faced in cross-browser testing? How will you overcome them?

9. Can you use TestNG and other frameworks to do cross-browser testing? How and why?

10. Given a choice, what type of cross-browser test automation would you choose? Explain why:

    a. Fully in-house using a Grid

    b. Hybrid model using emulators and cloud-based test automation

    c. Hybrid in-house model with Grid and device farms

    d. Fully cloud model with real devices and testing platform

Tips and Tricks for Test Automation

> *"Good programmers write code for humans first and computers next."*
>
> – *Anonymous*

In the 10 chapters of this book, we have covered all the essential elements of Selenium for test automation. In this chapter, we will focus on how to do test automation efficiently. What are some of the good tips to follow for test automation programs? What are some tricks to be followed by the test automation team? This section covers Generic Test Automation Topics. (i.e.) Why test automation instead of manual testing, differences between testing and checking for assurance, automating useless test cases vs designing test cases before automation, removal of uncertainty by having clean test automation, automating stable functionality vs unstable functionality, myths about 100% test automation, partial automation vs. end-to-end automation, inverted pyramid of test automation, 100% test automation vs 100% better benefit through test automation, tools and techniques to leverage, risk-based test automation approaches, etc. We will cover test automation coverage for DevOps and AI-based application development as well.

Structure

We willlook at the following concepts to test the test automation knowledge and include content as a reference and tips to the following. These include coverage on the following topics:

- When and What to Automate?
    a. What are the differences between Manual Vs Automated Testing?
    b. Benefits of Automating Stable Vs Unstable Applications
    c. Strategizing right vs automating fast
    d. Automating all vs automating right
    e. Record and Hard-coding Vs Intelligent Automation
    f. 100% Automation Myth Vs Beneficial Automation

- Tips to Automate better
    a. Automation Tools and Methods
    b. Script-less Test Automation
    c. Automating the Test Automation Process
    d. AI in Test Automation
    e. Visual Regression Automation
    f. Test Automation for DevOps

Objectives

In this chapter, we willexplore the various aspects of test automation to evaluate what are some good tips to follow, what to automate, when to automate, what is the right approach, what are some suggested approaches,what are the different ways in which we can automate efficiently? This chapter will focus more on the theoretical and concept-based understanding of test automation.

When and what to automate?

Let us analyze why we need to automate, what we can automate, how we can automate, when to automate, and why to automate and not automate elaborately. Firstly, let us understand why we should automate by comparing the manual and automation testing. We broached on this topic briefly in the first two chapters but this chapter will focus more on an advanced and informed analysis of the reasons.

Manual Vs Automated Testing – Some comparison

Let us compare the manual and automated testing in a simple table as follows:

Manual Testing	Automated Testing
Manual Testing need not be consistent. As different testers may follow different approaches and perform actions in an inconsistent manner.	Automated testing is driven by logic and automated testing will always be consistent and repeatable in nature.
Repeatability is a challenge	The automated script will be behaving in exactly the same way in a consistent manner, every time the script is executed. There will be no change in how a script is executed.
Manual Testing can be time-consuming	Automated testing can be used to reduce time.
Parallel test execution would mandate more resources and more cost	We can write once and run multiple times in parallel in different environments at the same time.
Investment is on human resources and the effort spent is not reclaimable	Investment is on the tools and building of the script. The returns will be based on the number of times a script is executed.
There can be human errors	These are consistent and repeatable and there will be noerrors in the process. The script can fail due to many reasons but will not have an error.
Not feasible to run all test cases for a complex application with thousands or millions of test scenarios	If implemented efficiently, automated testing gives good coverage and the ability to run thousands of test cases in a very short amount of time.
Mundane test execution tasks can be demotivating for talented testers	Automated testing of mundane tasks, especially in regression testing can be done seamlessly using automated testing.
Useful when exploratory testing or skilled validation of functionalities are needed	Not very useful in rapidly changing the UI or deep domain knowledge-centric test scripts that are done efficiently by skilled manual testers.
Customer experience can be a question mark – especially when skilled tester churn happens	Since it is repeatable and person agnostic, the experience is always the same.

No coding skills needed for testing	Coding may be required to do test automation.
If a step is missed or a screenshot is missed out, rework risks increase	With automated test cases, human errors and rework as a result can be reduced.
A lot of administrative tasks are required after testing	All non-value adding admin tasks can be done quickly with automated steps.
If a step is missed or a screenshot is missed out, rework risks increase	With automated test cases, human errors and rework as a result can be reduced.
Time and complexity increases based on the number of verification points and test cases	Time and complexity increase issuesthat can be reduced by cross-platform parallel test execution.

Table 11.1: Comparison between Manual and Automated Testing

Inverting the test automation pyramid

Traditionally, test automation is done at the user interface level when the amount of testing, test automation, cost of testing and time needed are all on the higher side. Almost all organizations fall into this big trap of doing the most important things at the last moment, resulting in delays, poorer quality, and cost and schedule over runs in addition to getting poor customer feedback. What is meant by inverting the test automation pyramid is to do more automation inthe earlier phases so that the incremental feature validation and automation requirements reduce, as the product quality gets better through the software development life cycle. Let us see this in the following image:

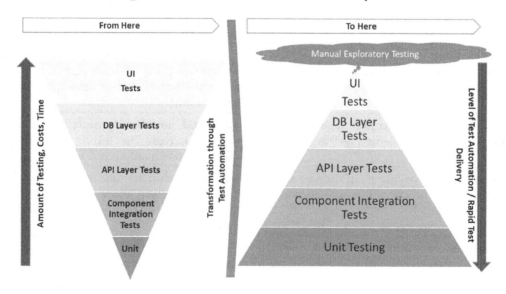

Figure 11.1: Inversion of Test Automation Pyramid

What we are suggesting is to have more automation in theearlier phases such as unit testing where script-less automation or rapid testing is feasible and fixing a defect in the earlier phases is a lot cheaper than fixing a defect at later stages. Ideally, the test automation at the UI level should be minimal if we do a good job of validating the functionalities, interfaces, APIs, and integration touch points earlier in the SDLC using various test automation methods and frameworks. Use of automation tools to validate a build, validate an action, validate an API, validate an interface, validate a Micro service, validate data integrity, and validate responses can go a long way. This means we can tiethe system components together in a modular and progressive manner. The ease of automation, effort involved in automation, and the ability to fix the issues are all favorable for an excellent SDLC. The later we start this activity, the longer, inefficient and costlier the entire process will become. The benefit of inverting the pyramid is like flipping the nominator and the denominator and the value could be a lot smaller when the numerator is big when it is flipped. The tautology is very much applicable for the inverted test pyramid – for both testing and test automation.

Test automation strategy

Let us see some tips we can leverage to understand the benefits of automating stable vs unstable applications, strategizing right vs automating fast, and automating all vs automating right in the following sections.

Strategizing right vs automating fast

When it comes to strategizing a test automation project, some of the key questions to ask about test automation before we get started is depicted in the following table:

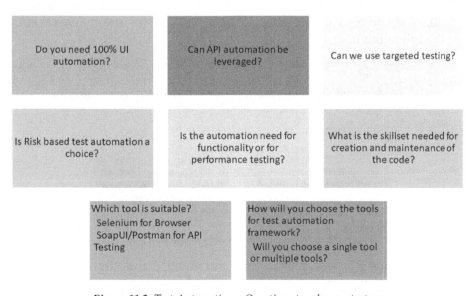

Figure 11.2: Test Automation – Questions to ask as a strategy

In addition to the questions in the preceding table, some additional points to ponder include:

- It is always a good idea to automate primarily around the functional logic and in the zone of implementation of business logic as the checks will be critical here.
    - o Other checks and balances may be less important and a paretor's 80-20 rule may be applicable.
    - o A tester can consider the risk-based testing approach here to decide what is important for automation and testing.
- Efficient test automation projects will focus on minimizing the impact on the automation framework due to moving parts or by minimizing the impact of end-to-end automation by modularizing it.
    - o Hence, an automation framework that is abstract, extensible and easy to maintain is very important to have.
    - o Having a mechanism to address the user interface changes easily is very important and most of the maintenance for test automation arises due to the dynamic nature of the user interface changes.
    - o With the added complexity of asynchronous JavaScript and other dynamic features, the automation of the UI becomes even more complex.
    - o This is an area handled very efficiently by excellent test automation tools and frameworks built using Selenium.
- One more focus area will be to address the challenge of unwanted automation or obese automation. To address this, it is wise to ask some of the following questions before we choose the script or test case for automation as shown in the following image:

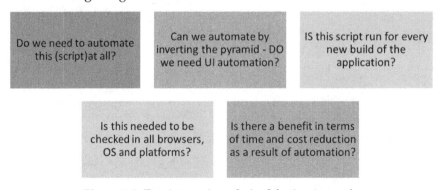

Figure 11.3: Test Automation – Script Selection Approach

Once we have chosen a tool, picked up a framework, and strategized test scripts to automate, it becomes important to decide what is the purposeful automation objective we can attain.

Benefits of automating a stable application versus an unstable application

One of the challenges faced by automation developers is to decide when to automate? What is the golden period for test automation? Is automating early an option? What about automating progressive and unstable application features and functionalities? Wouldn't manual testing be a more suitable option than automation? Doing automation on an unstable application or a feature will result in a significant maintenance effort of the automation scripts and the benefits we are likely to gain via test automation will go for a toss. This means that we choose an automation window that is likely to help rapid automation with minimal to negligible maintenance effort. How do we do that?

We can consider picking up test cases for automation once the scripts have passed through at least a system test cycle and once the majority of the bugs have been fixed with almost all the features delivered. While there is a risk of bug fixes resulting in code changes and impact to test automation, this 'Golden Window' for test automation is likely to deliver the maximum benefit. This is because the scripts that are likely to be a part of the regression suite in future cycles will be run no matter what the new functionality scope is and will give the ROI needed to make a successful automation project. Hence, the automation priority should be on automating the regression suite test cases during the golden window for test automation.

In addition to picking up the automation suite, scenario analysis on the impact of failure (business) and the likelihood of failure (technical) of the regression test suite needs to be performed. Based on the priority and ranking, the automation team can focus on the most value-adding regression test cases and finish them first. This is very useful when the team is faced with resource, cost, and timeline challenges.

It is also important to build various types of regression suites to be executed for various types of testing needs. A core regression pack can be automated for the execution of scenarios for all changes. An extended regression pack (can be further segmented based on the product and functionality features as well) can be used in case of comprehensive regression test needs. Additionally, a smoke test regression suite can be built for the execution of test cases post a build deployment in test environments. The benefit of smoke test regression suite automation is that we can identify build issues immediately, fix them, and not wait for a long time to find issues with the build. Smoke test automation is a very good candidate for getting immediate benefits.

Some of the areas to avoid automation, as it will result in an unstable test automation suite are as follows:

- **Web pages with a lot of dynamic content and DOM elements:** This will result in massive maintenance if not automated well. It is good to have simple objects built in a modular fashion. A page with more than 1000+ objects will be an automation nightmare.

- **Web pages and mobile apps with too much asynchronous content:** This will result in a lot of asynchronous waits and threads causing the automation scripts to fail. It is advised to go for partial, feature-based automation in-lieu of comprehensive automation.

- **Pages/Apps with multiple technology interfaces:** Assume you are trying to automate an application end-to-end that covers a gamut of technology – for example, a web page that has embedded frames/apps with say Adobe Flash, etc. it technically becomes impossible to automate and handle different behaviors. It is better to avoid them.

- **Pages with Alerts/Popups/Modal Windows:** Unless you know the features and functionalities very well, it is advised to avoid spending too much time on these issues, especially if the alerts/popups and content are dynamic.

- **Pages with unpredictable results:** Better to avoid automation of these. An example could be a page that is produced dynamically using an AI program.

- **Pages like CAPTCHA and RECAPTCHA that needs human intelligence:** Difficult to pass the Turing test with an automation program and it is better to avoid them.

- Other pages to avoid include:
  a. Native OS applications on a mobile platform
  b. Pages with multi-level complex workflows
  c. Apps and content that are single-use
  d. Test cases for pages/apps with static content (nothing changes)

Given the current understanding, let us see how can we automate right? Is automation of all test cases the way forward or is it automating intelligently better?

Automating all vs automating right

As a test automation engineer/architect, it is very important to perform a cost-benefit analysis of the automation, portfolio analysis for test automation selection, script rationalization and selection, and modularization to name some of the essential tasks to be performed by the automation team. If there is a value in doing the test automation, if there is a good team available to support you in the journey and right frameworks designed with simple maintenance tasks in future, you are all set for a good test automation journey.

It is important to not forget that sometimes partial automation such as micro automation of APIs and Services can deliver maximum value than large-scale end-to-end automation due to the number of uses it would have, including theability to do load testing. Not every automation needs to be end-to-end automation!

If test automation passes, it may not mean tests are passing. Test automation scripts need to be validated now and then as well. It also highlights that a test automation script that fails now and then could be more trustable than a test that never fails at all.

While it is a good practice to catch the exceptions and exit gracefully after the automated test execution, it is not necessary to boil the ocean to capture every single exception and not focus on the main job in hand – to validate the functionality of the test script using test automation. A good test automation engineer does not hold on to poor automation code but is very open to refactoring of the code and is never afraid to throw away poorly written automation code.

In addition, an automation tool is an enabler. Just having a tool does not make the automation program a success. Need to have a well-defined test automation strategy, framework, and execution plan to make a program success.

Like AI is augmenting human intelligence, automation scripts can never replace good manual testers, they augment the manual testing. Automation is not a record-and-playback or a linear and simple hard coded program. They are pragmatic software code and they need to be tested just like an application. You need to test the test automation code. It could be done manually or one can use an automated program to test the automated script as well (to reduce complexity and time).

The proof of the pudding is in the level of maintenance consumed by the automation programs. The lesser the maintenance, the better the outcome. The second value adds the number of defects found in regression because of the automation scripts. The third value adds the synthetic test data created because of running the test automation scripts. This way an automation script can be used by the testing team as a data generation tool as well.

Now, let us see some of the good tips and tricks to consider whiledoing test automation as a practitioner.

Some tips and tricks to follow whiledoing test automation

Some tips for strategizing right include having a sold test automation process as follows:

- Analysis & Design ▪ Scripting & Config ▪ Definition of Parameters ▪ Mgmt. of Params ▪ Scenario Collection ▪ Validations ▪ Testing of Scripts ▪ Script Execution ▪ Review of Results ▪ Result Communication
- It is also important to take care of the following earlier by the project/ program management team.
- Get executive buy-ins and support.

- o Have a champion sponsor for automation to help you through the valleys, peaks and downhills.

- Automation is a disciplined profession. Have objectives set clearly. This is very important.

- Have good collaboration and cooperation with other stakeholders.

- Learn from mistakes of self and others. Always learn from others and external learning – Both from failures and leading practices.

- Have a good team building between automation engineers, testers, developers, business analysts, and the project teams.

- Celebrate simple wins and successes.

- Have a good tooling strategy:
    - o Have an internal and external advocate/evangelist for the test automation tool/framework.
    - o Even test automation tools have bugs and restrictions so beware of the same and factor in during your test automation strategy.
    - o The automation test suite needs to be flexible and capable of letting users select automation pack based on options and configurations.
        - ▪ This makes the test suite efficient and permits the scripts to run faster.
    - o It is important to spend the time of training on the tools and learn about the usability and features of an automation tool.
    - o Exploratory test automation is a good choice to consider.

- Focus on most valuable tests but have the automation scripts ready before the software product or application under test is shipped for production use.

- Always Avoid Never-Ending Maintenance of automation scripts.
    - o See if you can do partial automation for complex areas that cannot be automated and run a modular approach for your automation.
        - ▪ For example, if you do not have a page object model defined in a lightweight manner, every change to the DOM/POM will result in massive maintenance.
        - ▪ This needs to be closely looked at.

- Never underestimate the need for test automation support on a long-term basis. It is not written once and run infinitely. A good automation project should factor in continuous test automation support.

- Automating exactly the way a manual test script is executed is also a giant no-no.
    - o The reason is that manual steps could be long-wounded and may not be an efficient way to go about doing the testing.

- o With the automated testing, we can take advantage of the efficient processes, direct DB access, etc.
- Avoiding primitive programming practices (such as hardcoding and in a procedural manner with no modularity, etc.) is an important aspect.
  - o It is always good to use good programming practices and functions, methods available for test automation.
- Writing a tool dependent automation code could be a bad behavior.
  - o Being locked down to one tool without having thedynamic capability to move the test automation framework across tools and platform is not a good idea.
  - o Having good agility is a good thing to have.
- Having a **SMART** goal (**Specific, Measurable, Achievable, Realistic and Time-Bound**) for test automation is essential.
  - o Having unrealistic goals of 100% automation, real-time, in-sprint 100% zero-touch automation, etc. are some bad examples. Having good goals is essential for the success of an automation project.
- Having a person agnostic and tool agnostic test automation framework, the methodology is the key.
  - o Being too much dependent on a particular tool or a specialist could be dangerous to long-term success of an automation program.
- It is also important to use an inverted test pyramid-based approach to do automation:
  - o This means that it is good to do less automation at the user interface level and more automation at levels beneath the UI such as API, Database, Micro Services, and Unit test level.
  - o The more rapid and stable the test automation is at the unit and service level, end-to-end test automation at the UI level becomes much more reliable, efficient and quick, in addition to being easy to create and maintain.
- It is also advisable to use a Page Object Model to ensure that the test automation scripts are scalable.
  - o This effectively means that we create at least one class per unique page of the web application.
  - o The next task will be to generalize and deduce commonality across objects, pages and use abstraction to improve ease of maintenance.
  - o Good abstraction will be at keywords, actions and objects, and identifiers in the web application.
  - o The more the abstraction of the test automation functions, the better it would be to maintain the automation.

Now that we have a good number of tips to consider, let us check on some of the pitfalls to avoid whiledoing a test automation project.

Pitfalls to avoid whiledoing a test automation project

There are plenty of examples of how successful and not so successful test automation projects have run. Similarly, projects that have positively started on a strong foot have gone pear-shaped and ended up as failures. Using the learning available, let us see some of the pitfalls to avoid while doing a test automation project. For example, let us take the following image that gives the typical progress of a test automation project in an organization with limited resources and is a bit skeptical about test automation:

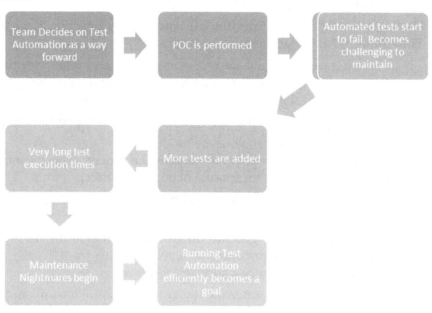

Figure 11.4: Atypical example of a challenging test automation project

As per the preceding example, the test automation program runs longer to execute and the benefits forecasted, to begin with, is eroded. Meaningful feedback and defect finding capability diminishes. This can cause an erosion in the value to add the test automation suite. Maintenance increase will eat away the benefits delivered via test automation execution effort savings. This needs to be closely managed.

Some other challenges include simple, single-use, and localized test automation where a small set of testers develop and use the test automation capabilities in a simple manner. What it means is that it could be a personal project and not a project or enterprise-wide. An automation initiative should also have an end objective, just like what happened with Selenium. Have the big picture while developing a framework or an automation project.

Myths about test automation – 100% automation vs automating right

There is a lot of hearsay and snake-oil selling type of myths floated about what test automation is, what it can and cannot deliver, etc. Let us look atsome of the myths of test automation in a tabular manner:

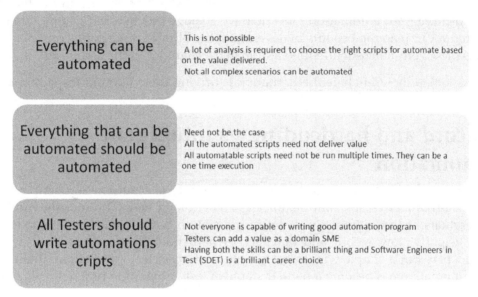

Figure 11.5: *Test Automation Myths*

The myths are endless but the three myths outlined are the top myths we hear time and again when it comes to automation. As a practitioner, it becomes important for an automation specialist/expert/project manager to ensure that the stakeholders understand the myth by explaining the reality and rationale to decide on the best and SMART goals for the automation project to work towards.

We covered the key aspects of test automation so far, including the tips, myths, and pitfalls. Now, let us look at some tips on how to automate the automation.

Automating the test automation

The benefits of automation are reaped when the automation is executed and the benefits of automated labor are reaped by cost and labor avoidance. To do effective automation, we need to automate the automation execution itself. This can be done in multiple ways such as using a tool-based automation scheduler, custom automation execution framework, building a custom scheduler, writing a trigger or workflow-based automation to kick-start the test automation scripts. We could also use robotic process automation tools to run some automated processes to kick-start the scripts. It could be run with a simple Excel-based VBA macro as well.

The real benefit of test automation is reaped when we run a zero-touch, scheduled automated run that runs when everyone sleeps and produces automated results, creates the logs, updates test execution in a test management tools, logs the defects with necessary details, etc. Some of the tools outlined earlier have a solid integration with the test management, test automation, defect tracking, deployment and requirements management tools to do all this on a real zero-touch automation basis. It is very important to leverage the tools available to take it further. Some of the new age AI-driven test automation tools help,we achieve this in a self-healing manner. Selenium can reap the benefits by leveraging the libraries and extensions available to do these zero-touch-unattended automated executions of the scripts automated.

Let us look at how intelligent automation is driving innovation in test automation in the next section.

Record and hardcoding vs intelligent automation

Ever since the first record and playback of simple test automation scripts from the mainframe days, test automation has come a long way. Through the multiple generations of test automation, a lot of innovation has driven test automation to new heights. Now, record and playback or hardcoded automation is not even a child's play but a simple way to get people to start on test automation. Intelligent test automation has become a regular staple of test automation professionals across the globe.

Record and playback or standard test automation is the program that only 'DOES' certain activities that they are programmed or scripted to do. By intelligent test automation, we refer to the automation programs that 'THINK', 'ADAPT', and 'LEARN' using Artificial Intelligence and Machine Learning to do self-healing of the scripts. Human intelligence is augmented by these thinking and learning test automation scripts. With the use of techniques such as Robotic Process Automation, Structured Data Interaction, Natural Language Processing, Machine Learning, Natural Language Generation, Deep Learning, Semantics and Ontology, Sentiment Analysis, and other advanced techniques such as Autonomic automation, use of Smart APIs, it is easy to perform intelligent automation. Tools can predict what user behavior is before they intend to perform a certain action, based on the machine learning models and data available. All the advanced tools such as test.ai, testim. ai and few other tools such as Functionize and Applitools Visual Eye perform these tasks.

However, all this cutting-edge stuff is being tried out in some big organizations but not more than 10% of the organization. Just like COBOL is one of the tour-de-force to reckon with even after 60 years, scripted test, automation is here to stay and Selenium will have a future. However, these advanced tools will change the way test automation works.

Now, let us do a recap and understand some of the test automation methods and tools that are available for the automation engineers in the next section.

Automation tools and methods

In the first two chapters, we covered various generations of test automation, various methods of test automation to follow and a reference to some of the tools to consider, in addition to Selenium. As a recap, let us look at what are the tools and methods we can look at.

Some of the ways we can automate are as follows:

1. **Linear Test Automation:**
   a. Use of record and playback-based code or a simple procedural code
2. **Structured Test Automation:**
   a. A simple structured control block-based test automation with the use of constructs such as 'IF-THEN-ELSE', 'WHILE', 'FOR', 'SWITCH', condition-based control structures. Something like a VBA-based automation.
3. **Data-driven Test Automation:**
   a. Use of data in a spreadsheet, control files or a database. Testing logic is driven by the data given such as a login id, location, data type, etc.
4. **Keyword Driven Test Automation:**
   a. Use of various keywords to derive the test automation logic.
5. **Hybrid Test Automation:**
   a. Use of one or more of the automation type such as a combination of Data and Keyword Driven or Data-Driven automation using an automation tool giving only Structured programming constructs (such as an automation IDE).
6. **Behavior Driven Development(BDD-based Automation):**
   a. Use of simple user behavior actions using a language such as Gherkin and tools such as Cucumber or RSpec to generate automation code.
7. **Model-Based Test Automation:**
   a. Use of Domain/Functional Model to perform Test Automation.
8. **Intelligent Test Automation:**
   a. Automation framework that performs DO-CHECK-LEARN-ADAPT-THINK-CHANGE type of test automation maintenance.
9. **AI-Driven Automation:**
   a. Taking intelligent test automation to the next level using AI/ML/DL/NLP/NLG, etc.

10. Visual Automation

    a. Automation-based on the UI content present

As far as tools available, we have covered all of them in detail in earlier chapters. Now, let us understand another topic that is picking up a lot of interest in the tester's community in the next section – Visual Regression.

Use of Visual Regression in test automation

Visual regression is a technique focusing at the UI level to check whetherthe UI components and behaviors are predictable. It checks for the screenshots for predictable behavior; and in case of deviations from expected behavior, the tool can give hints on what is changing. The regression tool is very good for checking the style element changes in a CSS in a web application. This is very useful for testing stable UI apps with predictable behavior and it works well for testing of web applications. Sometimes, Visual CSS regression testing or comparison of visual differences of a website is also considered a Visual regression. In some cases, Visual regression can be used to do A/B testing to choose the right visual elements to be rolled out to the users.

Visual regression testing can also check for comparison of various web pages side by side for various web browsers on different platforms, OSes and versions with different screen configurations as well. This gives a way for the testers to validate the actual behavior of the application against the expected behavior. The aim is to check for visual flawlessness in terms of HTML, CSS, and JavaScript changes in your application in terms of visual aesthetics, user experience, and functional behavior.

Visual regression testing can be a good choice to check for cross-browser testing and there are plenty of tools available for doing automated visual regression testing. Some of the tools include:

- **Applitools:** This integrates with other tools such as SmartBear CrossBrowser Testing and allows you to map with Selenium, Appium and other frameworks.
- **Selenium:** With the headless browser testing options and the ability to take screenshots, Selenium can be a very powerful visual regression tool. Many programming skills is needed though. Some of the successful tools leverage Selenium as a base for their visual regression testing capabilities. Some of the Selenium-based tools include:
  - o **Selenium Visual Diff / Gemini/WebDriver CSS:** Use JavaScript on Selenium
  - o **Visual Ception:** Use PHP on Selenium
  - o **Huxley / Needle:** Use Python on Selenium
  - o **Wraith-Selenium:** Use Ruby on Selenium

- **Phantom CSS:** This excellent tool uses various JavaScript frameworks to perform visual regression testing. A strong JavaScript programming capability is needed for using PhantomCSS

    o **Wraith:** Uses Ruby with PhantomCSS

    o **dpdxt:** Uses PHP with PhantomCSS

    o **Grunt & Snap and Compare:** Uses JavaScript with PhantomCSS

Visual Regression is getting very popular and is getting help with advanced tools that permit script-less automation, leveraging **Artificial Intelligence (AI)**. Now, let us understand what we mean by script-less test automation in the next section

Script-less test automation

Script-less test automation refers to automating tests without the need to do programming. The example would be to automate say a web application without a need to write a Selenium of a QTP code to do the end-to-end automation. This could be done through a tool using workflow or using behavior-driven test design tools (BDD) such as Cucumber with the help of a script-less automation tool such as Tricentis Tosca or Worksoft Certify to generate test automation. This is very useful for the team as the business domain experts can help automate the test suite as early as the application requirements evolve. The components can be created quickly and they are in a position to be reused as the scope grows progressively. The ability to modularize the test cases also helps in easy maintenance of the automated test scripts.

Let us see some benefits of the script-less test automation scripts.

- These scripts-less test automation suites record the user interactions in a web or mobile application and generate the scripts automatically. The tools can also read the requirements and test case documents and generate test automation suites using Natural Language Processing and AI and Machine Learning.

- The script-less test automation suite can reduce the overall effort of automation. However, it is advisable for a good test automation engineer or a domain/business specialist to validate the output produced to ensure it is fit for purpose, to refactor and make the code relevant for the scope in hand. This is because a script-less automation framework is not 100% code free. There will be a need to customize it. The automation testers who are in charge of the script-less test automation framework need to be good in programming to ensure a good product is built. A script-less framework is not a simple record and playback as well.

- Some of the top tools include:

Applitools Eyes using Visual AI	Cucumber using BDD
Ghost Inspector that uses Automated UI Testing	Katalon Studio – Generates Test Automation scripts based on user actions
MABL uses AI to generate cross-browser scripts, auto-healing test scripts, visual test and diagnostics capabilities	Sauce Labs permits you to run across multiple browsers and platforms
CrossBrowserTesting – Cloud-Based Platform / Tool	SmartBearTestComplete
Tricentis Tosca	Worksoft Certify
Testim.IO	Test.AI
TestCraft	Ranorex Studio
Leapwork	QARA Test
Functionize	BrowserStack
Lambda Test	AppAchchi
Provar	Monkey Test It
Eggplant	Screenster
Optima	TestArchitect
CloudQA – TruRT	Endtest
SoftwareTesting.AI	Appvance

Table 11.2: List of Script-less and Visual Regression Automation Tools

Reference to script-less automation leads us to the next important topic in test automation that is thebuzzword these days – Artificial Intelligence. These days, AI is a key tool to propel the efficiency, efficacy, and productivity of the test automation projects. Plenty of tools and techniques are available for the same. It also adds its layer of complexity. Let us check it out in the next section.

Use of Artificial Intelligence (AI) in test automation

AI has come a long way since its inception. Let us see some of the key benefits of using AI in testing. AI has been a hyped term in the industry for some time now. When it comes to automation, AI has been hyped and quoted for various reasons such as

- Automated Defect Detection, Automated Exploratory Testing, Test Coverage Heat map
- Self-Healing Test Automation, Predictive Modeling, Self-Adjusting Regression, Defect and Execution Pattern Recognition

- Risk and Coverage Optimization, Test Diagnostics for Prescriptive and Predictive Analysis of Test Planning
- Deep Learning for efficiency, Automated Root-Cause Analysis for failures, User Behavior

  And
- Sentiment Analysis

To name a few. Now, let us see some of the key benefits of AI in test automation:

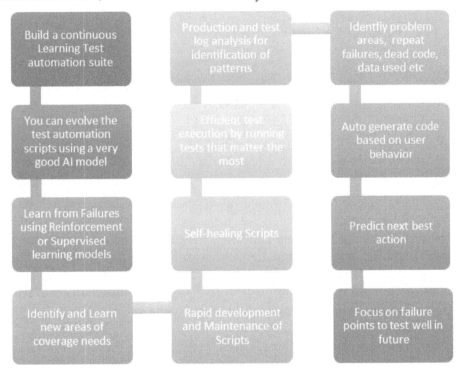

Figure 11.6: Benefits of AI in Test Automation

Now, let us see how an AI tool gets its script designed. Most of the tools capture the user actions either by capturing it through an agent running in the user desktop or through a spider/crawler mode to emulate user actions. One of the simpler representations is seen in the following figure:

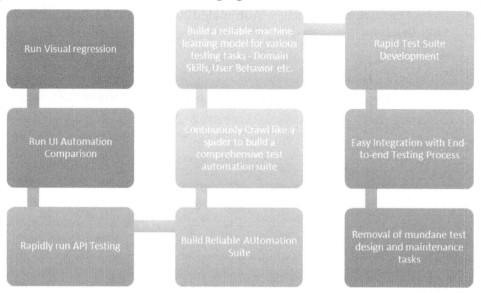

Figure 11.7: *Test Automation Design Process using AI Tools*

Once the scripts are designed and captured, the organizations can use the AI/ML techniques to build the models and algorithms for the use of AI in testing. The main aim of the enterprises to use of AI in the automation of testing is to optimize resources, effort, costs associated with testing while increasing the quality and coverage of the product being tested with an optimal number of test cases.

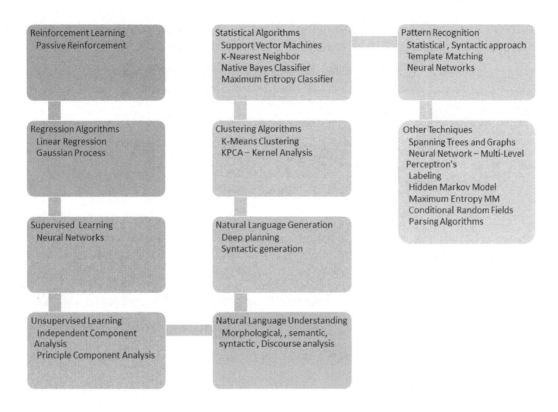

Figure 11.8: AI Algorithms and implementation approaches

Out of the techniques mentioned above, the following are some of the top techniques used for test automation using AI:

- Monte Carlo Simulation Tree
- Support Vector Machines
- Search Tree/Deep Neural Networks
- Bayesian Classification
- Probabilistic Models

We have understood some of the available techniques for AI/ML. Using various techniques and options available, let us see how an AI-based system can be built using test automation. The following image is one of the examples of how an automation application can be used for test automation using AI.

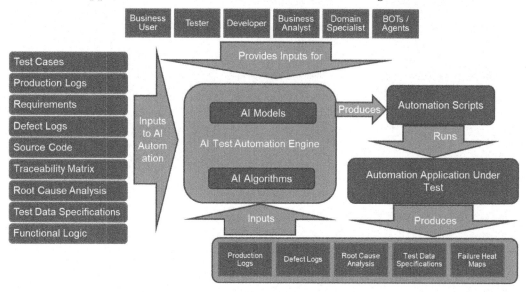

Figure 11.9: AI-based Test Engine - Example

There are multiple ways to implement AI for test automation, based on the needs, skills and tools applicable to a particular business problem and domain. Let us take an example of how AI was used for test automation is a very popular game.

Example

One of the examples of AI in testing can be looked at in the Gaming Industry. The popular game **Candy Crush Saga** was tested with the use of an AI engine for continuous Feedback Loop mechanism. The testing team used AI-driven BOTS to perform testing. All the outputs were fed through in a continuous feedback loop into a Deep Artificial Neural Network built for testing of the billions of permutations across various levels. The testing team used **Monte Carlo Tree Search (MCTS)** and bots built by a Hybrid Test team (150-200 + Testers) with unique skills across the domain, technology and testing ran test automation scripts. The testing team used Data Scientists for Domain Knowledge, Fun (using historic info and User Behavior, Game Balancing). Test automation scripts looked for Regular Crash Testing through automation, and leveraged automated scripts to do performance testing and regression testing. The team also leveraged AI upgrades for the AI Bot for regular testing.

The key take away from this is to let AI do exhaustive testing through automation and advantage humans to perform qualitative and cognitive aspects. The automated scripts need to Be Creative and Business/Customer-Centric and the automation should be done at the earliest for automation with a long-term focus.

Another key focus area in the industry is to use test automation for rapid quality delivery using Agile and DevOps projects. Let us see how we can leverage test automation for DevOps Engagements.

Test Automation for DevOps Projects

There is a standard question from testers about AI Testing, DevOps and other new Software Engineering evolution. *"Will Automation / AI / DevOps remove the need for Manual Testers?"* A simple answer is *"No"*.Automation, AI, or DevOps is not going to replace Manual Testing as a discipline. Firms implementing test automation or AI-based testing or continuous testing through DevOps have a vision for better product quality workable by brilliant testing.

Test automation for DevOps or use of AI for test automation is an enabler for the following:

- Reduction in IT Budgets
- Efficient end-to-end delivery
- Lean delivery framework
- Working end-to-end automation framework

Successful businesses today are driven to deliver features quickly using various techniques. With a design thinking and customer-centric, focus with a strong sense of urgency and a need to succeed in the market quickly. Availability of brilliant tools and innovation aided by software engineering techniques make it possible. All the successful firms of today are driven by technology, as it has become a backbone, enabler and catalyst all in one. Many tech giants are capable of running millions of test cases in an automated fashion in a span of minutes not seconds, using continuous testing and delivery. For example, the Microsoft team does 82,000 deployments per day, with over 28,000 work items created per day and over 2.4 million code commits per month. How can one test so many changes quickly while making sure the product is of highest quality as billions of people use them across the globe? To do this, we need to have effective habits of DevOps.

Test automation within zero-touch-end-to-end delivery is essentials. Most of the projects are moving towards AI/ML driven delivery. We have tools that allow a developer to auto complete the entire chunks of code. Even for testing, we can use Cucumber through Gherkin; generate a fully automatable Selenium code that reduces automation code development effort for the automation engineer. DevOps Governance and delivery model is also important, as we need to avoid manual-errors and stove-piped communication due to distributed teams and vendors that can be removed with a good DevOps practice.

In addition, it is important to adopt a *'Test-First'* delivery method driven by ATDD or BDD or any such test-driven method to fail fast and fail often to fail early and fix the issues earlier, as shown in the inverted test pyramid. DevOps permits us and there are many benefits in moving towards such a model:

- Rapid , progressive, and useful product feature development
- Cost reduction in end-to-end delivery through intelligent automation
- Reduction of manual errors and de-duplication
- Streamlined governance and rapid go-to-market
- Early and rapid defect identification
- Agile and cohesive team focused on quality deliverables

Implementing a successful test automation project for AI/ML or DevOps projects is very tricky in organizations having a legacy and monolithic systems and processes. An appetite for a strong culture change is critical for successful DevOps and continuous delivery. Top leadership team needs to sponsor this.

From a testing standpoint, test automation and DevOps can address some of the following challenges, with the current change in landscape of the tech infrastructure:

- When it comes to Quality Engineering/Test Environments, the DevOps life cycle makes it very simple with real-time, on-demand provisioning done in a span of minutes and not months and years.
- With the DevOps Model, we can reduce the overall test effort in terms of cost and life cycle with automation completion of tasks from design to deployment and support.

NIST – A standards body reported in 2002 that the Cost of Poor Quality (in the US alone) was **$59.5** Billion per year with this value increasing annually. COPQ is the biggest waste of money in large established organizations running legacy systems. By some evaluations, the average cost of a production bug is at least **$14,000 to $15,000.** In some cases, the cost of a production bug can outweigh the benefits delivered by the feature change that resulted in the bug fix or a feature fix that caused it. Given the new customer base of fivevaried generations, having a poor COPQ will result in poorer customer experience and the organization agility will be impacted. DevOps can be a super catalyst here.

The skeptics questioning the effectiveness of test automation may have some data to support their argument but failed test automation projects are due to poor strategy, design, planning and execution. The tech giants delivering brilliant services have reached their position purely based on their capabilities and skills, leveraging the power of DevOps.

Some key factors to implement for successful test automation practice for DevOps or an AI-based project is as follows:

- Cohesive, one team mentality between teams
- Implementation and use of tools that take away the manual effort

- Continuous delivery phases:
  - o Superior, automated configuration management approach
  - o Continuous improvements across phases
  - o Continuous automation
  - o Continuous integration
  - o Continuous testing
  - o Continuous monitoring

Having a solid governance model and strategy for tools and processes to implement DevOps and leveraging the power of Test Automation will help the organizations achieve its objectives.

Putting together all the learning, what are some of the recommendations a Selenium automation tester should follow? Let us get some tips and leading practices for implementation.

Selenium automation leading practices/ recommendations

There are many learning and tips that a Selenium automation engineer can follow. Some of the top tips to follow are given in the following image:

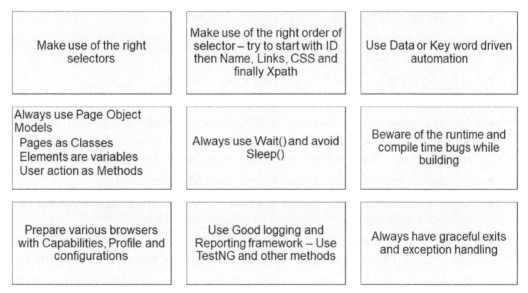

Figure 11.10: Selenium Automation – Top Tips to consider

Additional tips to pursue include:

- Always automate most frequent and repeated test cases
- Automate scripts that are easy to automate
- Automate scripts that are stable and predictable in behavior
- Automate low value-adding and tedious test cases for a manual tester
- Automate scripts that takes a lot of manual effort but easy to automate using scripts
- Automate scripts that are run in multiple platforms and browsers
- Automate frequently used business functionalities
- UI automation focus alone is not very good
- See if script-less, model-based or BDD-based test automation is possible
- Use test patterns using design patterns and architectural principles
- Use a test automation framework for your testing
- Always make the framework portable across platforms and if possible, tools
- Have a good nomenclature for naming
- Use assertions and screenshots for validations
- Have a very good explanation for the programs in the form of comments
- Have a good reporting mechanism
- Always keep the scripts to run independently
- Focus on data-driven, keyword-focused or hybrid automation. Do not keep the tests run linearly
- Have a very good quality test data for automation
- Test more and test often
- Always factor efforts by other stakeholders into your automation estimate such as business analysts, developers, end-users, tool specialists, compliance specialists, etc. The teams doing automation sometimes overlook this.
- The tool is important but it is not a one-size-fit-all solution.
- Good automation script needs to have a very good manual test case as a reference. Garbage in – Garbage out is applicable here.
- If GUI automation can be avoided with API or micro services automation, go ahead with it and avoid boiling the ocean with extensive GUI automation.
- Beware of Assert vs. Verify usage – Assert breaks the test whereas verify continues. You may want to consider this.
- Build your library of functions and methods as it could be very handy for your application

It is advisable to understand the challenges and document the learning one may have while implementing the project and share it with the wider community.

Conclusion

We covered all the essentials of automation using Selenium until *Chapter 10*. In this chapter, we covered a good number of tips and tricks to follow while doing automation, pitfalls to avoid, various tools that we can consider, recommendations on strategy and how test automation can benefit through script-less automation, visual regression automation, use of artificial intelligence, and contribute to DevOps mode of delivery. As mentioned in the chapter, test automation is a discipline and it takes a lot of good practice to become a solid expert. If you learn from the mistakes made by self and others, implement the leading practices, follow a disciplined strategy and approach, use the tips and tricks for your test automation, you are all set for a very successful career. In the next chapter, we willcover one more important aspect of getting a dream job you deserve. How to ace interviews? What are some tips and preparation one needs to do to perform well? Well begun is half done they say, to do well in the interview, you need to prepare well. We will coverthis and other aspects in the next chapter.

Questions

1. What are some top tips to consider while using Selenium for Test Automation?

2. What are some tips to consider while choosing test automation?

3. What are the top myths attributed to test automation?

4. What does Visual Regression mean? How is it useful?

5. What is the script less Automation? What are the benefits?

6. What are some of the benefits of manual testing over test automation? Where is manual testing more reliable than automation?

7. How will you use AI in test automation?

8. How can test automation help DevOps delivery model?

9. What do you mean by purposeful test automation?

10. What do you mean by Intelligent Test automation?

11. What is a self-healing test automation code? Can you give some examples?

12. Is 100% test automation possible? What is your take on the same?

CHAPTER 12
Interview Tips

> *"Choose a job you love, and you will never have to work a day in your life."*
>
> *—Confucius*

Interviews cause a lot of anxiety and fear in the minds of interviewees. Regardless of readiness for interviews, mastery of the subject and an impeccable profile, even a top candidate can have a nightmare and a difficulty sleeping the night before. On the other hand, some candidates take interviews in a very light manner with zero or no preparation. Both are situations that could be avoided. Interviews can be handled well with very good preparation, by energizing the mind and body, with a very confident and positive mindset, realistic expectation of the outcome and curiosity to learn and make course corrections. This chapter introduces the audience to a set of tips to practice and follow to create better outcomes.

Structure

- Interview strategy, approach and planning
- interview preparation
- types of interview & approaches
- interview process

- virtual interviews
- Conclusion

Objective

After studying this chapter, you will be able to understand the preparatory steps essential for an automation interview. What are the important preparatory steps? How to answer? What are some good behaviours to exhibit? What are some behaviours to avoid? What do the interviewers look for? How to show good soft skills? How to answer non-technical questions? How to answer in video/Skype interviews? How to be better groomed?

Interview strategy, approach and planning

Remember the quotes *"Rome was not built in a day"* by John Heywood and *"Well begun is half-done"* by Aristotle. If you want to succeed in your interviews, you need to plan well. Although there would be a lot of preparation and groundwork, you need to have a strategy, an approach to handle the interview and a plan to execute your strategy and approach. If you want to get into the work that would make you feel good about it and satisfied, while being paid really well, you need to work hard to earn it.

As a first step, prepare a mind map or an outline highlighting your strategy for the interview. It is important to understand and ask questions to yourself such as what do you want to achieve, will the job help you in the long run? What does the job-offering firm expect? Are the expectations and views aligned? Are you qualified for the job? What are the essentials the hiring team is looking at? What are your strengths and weaknesses? What should be the approach while addressing your weaknesses, technical areas and the whole process of the interview itself?

Some of the approaches would include analysis and research about the job/role, the company offering the job and the job division type. If the company is a small-scale, start-up or an emerging one, you may want to check about the financial capability of the firm. In the case of start-ups, check the early as well as the advanced stage of the firm, including whether is it bootstrapped or angel-funded or seed-funded etc. Once you have analysed the firm, try to find out about your interviewer, if you can. You may the interviewer's professional profile on social media websites, especially LinkedIn, to understand his or her background. This would help you learn something about the interviewer and whether he or she is a technically orientedprofessional or a general management professional.

Since the next approach would be your preparation, you should focus on your readiness in terms of technical skills. This book covers one aspect of the Selenium's technical skills. If there are other technical skills needed as an addendum, you need to prepare well on those topics as well. You also need to remember, what the interviewer sees in a resume is what they typically get. This is very important and what is in your resume/CV and your skills highlighted and exemplified should match. A good interviewer can easily identify a lie in the CV and hence it is important to make sure you chisel your CV/profile to reflect your true self.

In addition to your technical skills, you need to identify what are the skills that can be transferred to the new company. This would highlight your value to the hiring companyfor the long-term prospects. In many cases, a seasoned interviewer and firms may look for a person with outstanding transferable skills and decent technical skills than some with outstanding technical skills. Techies normally overlook the importance of soft skills but this is also very important. The soft skills the firms will be looking for may vary from firm to firm. The roles and function fitment the team is looking for could be evaluated in a behavioural interview or a human resources style interview for soft skills and situational leadership . Some of the key soft skills to be aware of include communication skills, influencing capability, team camaraderie, entrepreneurial risk-taking skills, integrity, creative talent, flexibility and adaptablity to new changes (especially in technology), awareness of external changes (in the industry, technology etc.), awareness about the organization, leadership skills (for senior roles), empathy, delegation skills, relationship skills, , team-building skills, project and program management skills.

The next thing to focus on will be to practice the technical interview questions. Reading this book is one of them but not the only source. Look at all the options available, prepare voraciously. Over-preparation or practising is never a bad thing. This will put you in better shape and readiness over your competitors in an interview. The next approach should focus on practising the competency-based interview questions. Prepare a list of standard questions that are likely to be asked. Use your friends, roommates, colleagues, family or anyone (with understanding/ skills) willing to help to ask you questions. This will help you in preparing your answers. Do not memorize them though. A role-playapproach or a method with your acquaintances, such as friends, family, colleague, roommate, partner etc., can also help you motivate your skills and abilities with the job opportunity.

Have a dry-run of the audio, Skype or video interviews. In the case of video interviews, if you are not able to test the mode of interview platform, try a platform that is similar and accessible by you. You need to ensure the phone or the audio in your laptop or a desktop is tested and validated. For a video interview, ensure that your audio and camera are tested. In addition, it is always good to check the video lighting, colour, angle of the video, background appearance etc. beforehand to avoid any potentially uncomfortable experience.

If you put all the aforementioned points into a mind-map and execute them impeccably, success will most likely follow. Let us summarize all these into a pictorial format as per *Figure 12.1.*

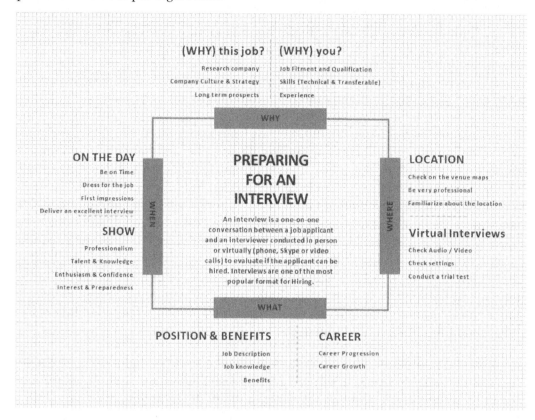

Figure 12.1: *Pictorial representation of how to prepare for an interview*

Interview preparation

One of the most important aspects of handling the interview is preparing for the interview. Abraham Lincoln quoted famously *"Give me six hours to chop down a tree and I will spend the first four sharpening the axe."* There is no such thing as over-preparation whereas under preparation can be a killer of ambitions. Interview preparation is a very methodical approach and one needs to plan well. It is one of the most important parts of an interview, which needs to be well structured and follow a methodical approach, done in a disciplined manner. Unless a person is a superstar, every interview could be a challenging exam that may turn out to be a tough one to crack. The preparation needs to be more for big and well-known market-leading technology firms and start-ups.

Key points to prepare for the interview

The first point to be prepare for is, do you know yourself very well? Do you know what the prospective recruiter knows about you? Are they aligned? Are you clear about what do you want and what do you want to achieve? There could be a lot of reasons you can look at to know about yourselves. Some of the questions to prepare for include:

Why are you looking for a job change?Be very clear about it. Is it change of role, change of supervisor, change of company, better salary, better opportunity, personal reasons such as work location, to be closer to home or campus or a near and dear, fresher out of college, applying in-campus, laid-off and looking for a job, looking for a job after post-graduation, looking for a job after a work gap (to attend to familial needs/birth of a child, education, failed entrepreneurship), change of function etc. You may need to have a convincing reason for your application. No answer maybe 100% perfect or correct. However, you may need to have a solid, believable and convincing storyline to tell.

- Why are you interested in the firm you are applying for? – This is where your research about the firm can be handy. Be very realistic and reasonable. Do not go overboard with fancy superlatives and stories. The persons(s) on the other side of the interview table may know far better than the superlatives. At the same time, your research needs to be of very good quality and approximately close to the reality (especially if you are mentioning numbers, rankings etc.)

- Do you know your strengths and your weaknesses? – This is a definite question to be asked by almost all the interviewers. Answering such a question would give you an opportunity to tell your story and be very honest about it. The interviewer to frame probing questions could use what you tell here. Hence, it is prudent to be very honest. Many candidates highlight mostly strengths and take a humble-bragging route for weaknesses. All humans have weaknesses and it is good to be honest and highlight what you are doing to overcome the same.

- Does the things mentioned in your resume match with your personality?– Good interviewers can easily figure out a lie/fake information against a genuine point. Many interviewers focus on what you have in your resume. Do not put anything in your resume that you are not sure of answering well.

- Ensure your online presence/digital trail is good – It is good to understand and have clarity on your online posts, as at times, interviewer(s) may ask about them as well. This is relevant, especially if you have contributed to GitHub, Quora, LinkedIn, Stack Overflow and similar forums of popularity.

Logistics and firm/company research preparation

While preparing for an interview, a personneeds to analyse the job roles he or she is applying for. It is important to understand the logistics for the process such as pre-interview tasks, online tests, coding challenges and approaches, which could be followed during interviews, including the types of interviews, the number of rounds, interview methods (telephonic, Skype/video, face-to-face etc.) etc. Additionally, logistics for in-person or virtual interviews need to be taken care of by the candidates as well. One of the most important aspects of the interview is to analyse the company profile and the job description (JD).

Some systematic approaches you should consider while preparing for a job interview are:

- Always review the JD given in the job posting.
- Since most of the time, a lot of informationis succinctly given in a job description, you should always consider thinking about the following points –

    o Can you prepare a mind-map or a point-by-point map of what a company or a firm is looking for? Does yourresume/CV/experience correspond well to the needs of the JD? The more matches you have, the better it will be for you in terms of acknowledgement of your application

    o A one size fits all resume or a /CV may not fit the requirements of the organizations.

    o Can you prepare your CV/resume with relevant JD skills to get a better ranking through an automated tracking system (ATS)?

    o Can you avoid over-engineering or overdoingyour resume, as lying in a resume/CV is considered a big crime.

    o Can youfocus on the critical responsibilities of the firm, understand its needs and pitch a convincing, honest story around thecompany's key needs.

- Apply for the roles/jobs that you qualify for. Do not try a blue ocean strategy for a straight forward technology job or a role with a specific need. For example, an engineer can't apply for the role of a cardiothoracic surgeon etc.

- Be focused in your job search and prepare a super solid resume/CV that can get through advanced the ATS used by the firms.

- Prepare your CV in such an intelligent way that it highlights your strengths on the ATS system.

- Get your networks into action and see if you can get referrals.

Know about the firm you are applying for

- You can perform research on what the firmdoes for a living
- You can perform research on the company's mission, vision and strategy
- You can complete your research on the company's vision and aspirations, including its interest in technology and industries
- You can perform research on the position you are applying for
- You can try to understand the levels/bands/designations and comparison against the position you are applying for
- You can also try to understand the organizational type (flat vs hierarchical) and rewards and recognition
- You can try to understand about power styles and intra-team political situations
- You can try to get an understanding of how the career growth will likely shape up later
- You may also perform research on the campus you are requested to visit in case of an in-person interview
- You can try to get inputs from your friends or ask for details from your hiring coordinator to familiarize yourself
- In the case of travel, ensure you have enough travel time planned, including traffic jams, weather-related etc. If you can afford to reach ahead of time, it is a good investment, especially when you are aiming to get into an important role. It is better to be early than to give the impression that you are not very serious or lackadaisical.
- You can analyse the technology set up in the case of a video or audio interview
- If possible, try to run a mock session with your close friend to test the setup.

Technical/functional Preparation

Technical and functional interviews are meant to determine the skills and capabilities of a candidate and they mostly decidethe outcome of the interview process. Hence, the preparation for technical and functional interviews is absolutely critical. In addition to looking at online resources available and speaking to the candidates orthe current and past employees can be a good tip to follow. This way, you will get to know the crux of the details you need to focus on to prepare for the interview.

Some systematic approaches for your preparation include:

- Prepare a set of questions and try answering them
  - o Try mirror-imagingtechnique; speak to a person over a Skype to practice for the interview. This will give you a real-life experience.

- Understand how the interview process will be executed
  - o How many interview rounds
  - o Interviewer profiles
  - o Types of questions to prepare for

- Prepare for a starting elevator pitch
  - o What would be your opening gambit? How will you introduce yourself? Nine out of 10 times the first question will be to help you speak first. This is a great opportunity and equally dangerous if not executed well, as first impressions may carry a lot of weight in the minds of interviewers.

- Understand the question well before answering it
  - o Be specific and to the point
  - o Be very positive and confident
  - o Appear knowledgeable
  - o Highlight yourself
  - o Focus on your diction and flow
  - o Collect your thoughts
  - o Try to be yourself and be the same person reflected in the resume
  - o Keep in mind that you are being watched
  - o Always close your conversation on a very positive, upbeat note

Appearance/grooming preparation

In a Greek and Latin proverbs, Erasmus famously quoted *"Clothes Maketh a man"*. To get a first-mover advantage via a good first impression, one needs to appear professional and successful. To appear professional and confident, one needs to ensure that his or her grooming and appearance areas per the job needs. He or she should not worry about being overdressed for a job. Being well groomed and pleasant makes a clear statement that you are serious about the job role that you have applied for and that you are very professional about the approach you choose.

Personal appearance and grooming

Personal appearances can be a key factor in deciding the outcome of the interview. Regardless of what the skills are of a candidate, the first impressions count. Let us see how we can address this

  - o If you can afford, get advice from a professional grooming professional trained to get grooming tips relevant for your persona.

o If you can't afford, some important tips for grooming to consider include –

- Be clear on what you wear – clothing is always important, including shoes, watches, ties, glasses, tops, heels etc.
- Remember that it is always better to dress-up well and dress up more than the level demands. No one is rejected for dressing up

o Check on your jewels, it is better to be professional

o Check your perfumes and deodorant –

- Ensure there is no odour and there is an optimal use of a deodorant or a perfume

Body Language

As per a quote, 70% of the communication happens in a non-verbal mode and it is essential to have a very positive body language. The skilled interviewers can easily figure out if you are good, confident and know the subject or a novice who is lying, just by observing the body language.

- Always have a very positive and confident posture
- You need to showcase that you are full of energy and have a good body language
- Avoid giving wrong body language messages such as leg fiddling, tapping
- Avoid fidgeting hands or fidgeting of a pen if you have one
- Have good eye contact – not too much or not too less. Avoid looking at your foot, doors or the ceiling
- Do not sit cross-armed or too tense. Use hands for positive and open gestures to showcase your honesty and openness.
- Do not slump into the chair as it may sound you are either arrogant or not interested in the job offer.

First meeting/contact with the interviewer

- Before you meet the interviewers, if you know whom you will be meeting or speaking to, complete your research onthem.

  o Look at the LinkedIn profiles, professional and social media information readily available, work and cultural styles and leadership styles

  o If the interviewer is a technical stalwart, understand the contributions, literature done by him or her and try to be cognizant and careful whilst broaching on these topics.

- Give a very warm *"Hello. Good Morning/Afternoon"* regards and a very firm shake hand to the interviewers

- Smile and greet. It is always good to smile and avoid looking very serious, nervous or tensed
- Good interviewers can easily identify liars and mental state of the interviewee by monitoring the body language

Types of interview & approaches

There are different types of interviewers and interviewsbased on the approach adopted by the interviewers. Different firms follow various techniques and the human resources (HR) or people & operations interviews follow a certain format. Typically, HR or leadership team interviews focus on behavioural interview approach and the hiring team normally focuses on the technical and functional skills needed for the role. This section provides tips, including some approaches to address various types of interviews

Interview approaches

In continuation to the previous paragraph, interviewers can follow different types of approaches. The approach chosen depends on the recommendations followed by a firm or the interviewer's personal preference. To make it look dynamic, some of the interviewers may change the approach, if they want to come across as an unpredictable person. As a candidate, it is good to be aware of various types of interviews and how to handle each of them to be successful.

- **Traditional and timeline-basedresume**
    - o Traditional approach primarily focuses on the resume
    - o Typically followed by most of the technical talent recruiters
    - o Focused more on the employment history, projects done, tools and skills mentioned in the profile
    - o Focused on academic data and certifications (for fresh graduates) and discussion around key achievements
    - o Typically starts with an ice-breaker introduction or a query about travel, weather, office etc., and an introduction, followed by a "Can you please introduce yourself?" question
    - o There will be a focus to know about the strengths, weaknesses, aspirations and ambitions of a candidate and a focus on how the career progression had been so far.
    - o If you have any extra-curricular hobbies including technical ones such as contribution to GitHub or any Open Source development projects or forums, include the same in the resume and discuss about that during the interview process.

o   Do not display yourself in such a way that you will answer immediately as soon as the questions are asked.

- It is better to be rational and instantaneous and come across as a person with no knowledge than being an imposter.

- While answering a question, try to find neutral and positive messages that you can send across and imbibe positivity vibes in your responses

- When in doubt always paraphrase or rephrase what you just heard. This would help you to stick on to the topics related to the questions asked.

o   Keep a check on your answers. If you are taking too much time while answering the questions, the interviewer may feel that you do not know the subject or that you may not be interested.

o   Don't answer the question before the question is asked completely or don't cut the interviewer or jump halfway in-between a question or a response.

- Wait for the completion of question or the statements.

- **Behaviour-based interviews**

o   Behavioural approach will focus mostly on the exploration of behavioural skills

o   Interviewers at leadership level or H/people & organization level conducting a functional interview post a technical interview

o   Behavioural interviews focus more on the storytelling aspect and behaviours showcased in a situation.

o   The focus will be on gathering information from various situations, responses, outcomes, emulated behaviours, contributions and lessons learnt.

o   The aim is to provide input to the interviewer with experiential, concrete and solid information in an objective manner. The interviewee should avoid a flip-flopping story or a contradicting message or superfluous information.

o   An opportunity for the interviewees to highlight themselves at a personal level:

- If you are a good storyteller, this phase will be a very smooth one. Things to keep in mind include telling a story based on the situation and not spilling out a regurgitated narrative memorized during your rehearsal.

- It is important to appear very authentic.

- If you do not know a subject or get a difficult question from an area that is not your expertise, it is better to say you do not have enough/any experience in the area/subject instead of giving a wrong answer or posing to give an answer that could put you totally out of the picture.

- It is also important to have a good story to tell.

  o It should be not superficial or unbelievable but more authentic and relatable one:

  - It is important to not get carried away by giving out too many details like names, brands, titles etc., as it could breach confidentiality at times.

- Interviewers use a STAR technique or a CAR technique during a behavioural interview to evaluate candidates. Both the techniques follow a structured approach for evaluation of the candidates:

STAR Interview Technique	CAR Interview Technique
• S-Situation ==>What was the Situation?	• C-Context ==>What was the context?
• T-Task==>What was the task taken?	• A-Action ==> What was the action taken?
• A-Action ==>What was the action taken?	
• R-Result ==>What was the result/Outcome?	• R-Result==> What was the result/outcome?

- Some of the questions asked during a behavioural interview include:

  o How one maintains a good working relationship with teammates (social, introverted, aggressive etc.)

  o A situation where one led a team

  o What approach should acandidate follow in conflicts/difficult situations?

  - A request to share an example of a conflict handled.

  - A request to share an example of a technology-oriented challenge or a conflict handled.

  o Situations where one used innovation and creativity to solve a problem or adding value

  o Experiences of failure and lessons learnt

  o Saying "No" to an ask and standing firmly on the same and the outcome and approach followed

  o Situations where one compromised on a decision for a better outcome to the project/firm o   Examples of negotiation and influencing techniques used to achieve goals with integrity

o   Examples of leadership skills and communication skills used to improve situations

o   Questions about leadership/management skills used and recommendations

o   Approach to people management

   ▪   How do you motivate and inspire the team?

   ▪   What is your approach to teamwork?

   ▪   How do you constructively pass difficult feedback to the team or team members?

   ▪   How do you receive negative or constructive feedback?

o   Approach to delivering on-time and on-commitment to work

o   Approach to stakeholder management

o   An example where the candidate exceeded the expectations by going above and beyond for a customer

o   A question on what the previous managers, colleagues, co-workers, team members would say about the candidate

o   An example of how an ad-hoc priority impacted the work schedule and how the candidate handled the situation

o   And, millions of other questions

Interview process

The interview process may be a very smooth and wonderful experience or could be a long-drawn and draining experience. It all depends on how serious the hiring team is about the role they are hiring for, the interest levels of the interviewer, hiring manager, recruitment team, agencies facilitating the mapping and interviews and the candidate. The experience and the challenges the candidates go through can be very demanding and tiring and could make or break their ambitions. If the candidate is very well prepared and understands the process of the interview, it could be an excellent experience throughout.

Good questions to ask by the candidates

It's always a good idea to ask some good questions to show your interest, research and willingness to contribute. A well-prepared candidate will be doing a fantastic job here, if he/she has done good research about the company and shows his or her brilliance during the interview process.

Some of the good ones to ask would be on:

- Clarifications on the vision and mission of the company
- Strategic focus of the company including corporate social responsibility
- Culture of the company
- Employee growth and organizational development approach
- Typical career progression model
- Professional aspiration and growth-related concerns

It's also important to avoid asking questions that could act as deterrents such as:

- Query about salary in a technical interview. This could be a permissible discussion during an HR salary negotiation stage.
- Checking on what an interviewer is looking for. This is an uncomfortable question and shows you are underprepared.
- Checking on chances. This shows you are not confident and conveys a wrong message.
- Asking or checking on how you performed in the interview. This shows nervousness. If you did well, you need to be very confident.
- Questions that could challenge the authority of the interviewer

In case, you are visiting the office premises for an interview:

- Look at the company site and see the office setup, workplace environment and interact with people to get an understanding of the company's work culture
- Interact with other employees and people attending the interview along with you to get an understanding
- Check if you can get details about the roles and responsibilities, in case if you are confident of getting selected and making a decision that is suitable to you
- Try to understand the benefits offered as much as possible, either through the information available on the company's site or through the HR interview process

After the interview is over

Sometimes the most important tasks take place after the interview is over. Sometimes the long-wait and not so pleasant experience takes place after the interviews. The end-to-end process gets prolonged here. The need to be very poised and dignified is a lot more after the interview is over, for the candidate. The candidate needs to showcase a more proactive approach after the interview is over. Some of the key tasks to take care includes:

- Send a "thank you" note to your recruitment coordinator, in a formal manner for the support rendered to you, regardless of the outcome. Ideally, this should be done on the same day or within a day if you are travelling. Remember, they played a key role in getting you the interview.

- Assess the interview. Try to replay and assess what went well, what didn't go well, what could've been better, what you can do to improve for the future interviews.

- After some time, if you are confident or unsure about the interview, check with your contacts and the interviewers as a follow-up and keep in touch with them.

  o You can send an email stating your interest in the role and would love feedback (either positive or negative) available.

  o If you do not get any response, check again after a few days (or a week) to see if there is an update.

  o If you still did not get a response, you can choose to move on.

- Try to continue your job search, if you are not confident about the outcome.

  o Ensure tokeep moving on positively.

What are some reasons why people are not hired?

There are many reasons why one does not get hired and the prime reason will be the fact that the candidate didn't do a good job during the interview and another candidate did a better job. It is a fact that most companies interview multiple candidates, including internal candidates for a single role. The priorities of the company could be varying. A focus on diversity could also play a role at times. The process of hiring is very long winded in big companies and some of the companies could have multiple rounds of interviews. One of the companies I interviewed for had seven rounds of interviews including a face-to-face.

There could be so many additional reasons. Some of them could be:

- Focus on money as a primary objective for a career growth

- Coming across as too underprepared and performing very poorly in the interview

- Coming across as lacklustre with no focus on career or not being goals oriented

- Showing up in an inappropriate appearance for an interview:

  o Remember there is no harm in dressing up

- Showing no interest in the role or interview

- Poor academic or career records (it is a major matter for fresher recruitment by big MNC firms)

- Expecting super-fast track when not qualified – by being over-ambitious in an irrational manner

- Not maintaining eye-contact by looking very fidgeting, not confident or uncomfortable

- Poor communication skills with grammatical error or diction, use of clutch and filler words like '" like", "but", "you know", "Uhm…", "mph…", "and", etc."

  o If you have some issues with stammering or any other difficulties, please inform the interviewer about it during your introduction, stating how you are addressing them. It is better to showcase your courage and fight to address this challenge rather than a surprise to the interviewer. As not all interviewers are alike or diversity sensitized, it is better to brief them in advance.

- Coming across as pompous, arrogant and aggressive

- Lack of confidence and showing nervousness through a poor body language and postures

What are some reasons why people are hired?

A major reason for the selection of a candidate is purely based on fitment; and that the candidate aced the interview(s). Reasons include a killer resume/CV, job-relevant experience, communication skills, good emotional intelligence and long-term potential, very good technical skills and transferrable soft skills, drive and energy, problem solving skills, cultural fit, good team working/managing/collaboration skills, ability to work with others, influencing and negotiating skills to name a few.

What are the things not to do during an interview?

It is always easy to get carried away during an interview mainly due to excitement, lack of preparation or the pressure of the situation. It is very important for a candidate to keep certain do's and don'ts to do better.

Some of the points to keep in mind during a behavioural interview include:

- Long-winded, beating around the bush and elongated answers could become a part of a rambling conversation. Remember the quote from Einstein *"If you can't explain it simply, you don't understand it enough"*. Use the STAR or a CAR technique mentioned earlier to explain in a succinct, precise and concise manner. Time is limited and the interviewer (and you) may lose out the opportunity to understand better.

- Do not share personal or confidential information. It could be your previous firms, college, family or projects you worked on. Ensure you mask the data and give a relevant answer. Transparency does not mean sharing of confidential or trivial data for the interview.

- Never berate or belittle your previous bosses or firms. It puts your integrity and discretion ability at risk. You may come across as a non-trust-worthy person.

- Avoid usage of unprofessional, friendly slangs and filler words. "Buddy, gonna, wassup, dude, kewl, ki, and, like, you know" etc., are not going to paint you as a professional.

- Do not show your nervousness or lack of confidence. Watch your body language and ensure that you are in a comfortable position to maintain good posture, eye-contact and confidence.

- Embark on topics, experience or projects not relevant to the job being interviewed for. What happened a few years back in an irrelevant area may not be relevant for the interview.

- Dinosaurs are good for the museum and not relevant in today's world.

- If you are planning to become an entrepreneur (have your own start-up etc.), have plans for higher-studies or plans to go on a world tour, you need not disclose unless asked by the interviewers.

How to make a good decision, when offers are made?

Good candidates perform well and are always in demand. Good companies will try to onboard good candidates as early as possible. This means that solid candidates will get many good offers to choose from. However, at times, this puts the hiring managers, candidates and the recruitment agencies at risk. It is very important to keep in mind that a professional relationship needs to be kept in mind and it is very important to maintain a very good professional image.

Some of the points to keep in mind while making a decision on the offer include:

- If you are getting too many offers, you need to rank the offers based on various parameters, including what is important to you .

- Evaluate the pros and cons, cost vs. benefits, short term vs. long term fitment of the offers against that of your objectives.

- See if you can collect additional info informally or get questions clarified formally.

- Do not disclose offers from competitor firms to negotiate a better offer as they are confidential. Without breaching the confidence, use the analysis done in an objective manner to decide.

- Once you have decided to accept an offer, do not let other offers waiting. Thank them formally and give a simple rationale by being polite with them (You may need a job at this firm later, who knows!)

- Give your feedback, complete a survey, if you are done with the process.

- Once you understand and accept an offer, do not renege or keep on interviewing to look for better offers

- Once you've decided, do not back-track. If you renege or keep on trying for a better package, your trustworthiness could go for a toss – as the recruiters are very well connected.

Virtual interviews

Given the progress in technologies and the need to interview candidates around the clock, especially using global specialists to evaluate and to avoid expenses and longer times for conducting the interviews, virtual interviews are becoming a de-facto mode of interview type by many organizations. The virtual interviews make up the first few rounds of the selection process. Once the screening goes well, the interview stage moves to a face-to-face mode. Virtual interviews include a telephonic, Skype, a video interview mode, or a combination of a few of these types.

Handling telephonic interviews

One of the key challenges (or advantages) of a telephonic interview is that it's difficult to read the body language, gauge confidence level, integrity of the candidate (from not looking up the answers) etc. Voice quality of the candidate plays a key role in determining the outcome of the interview as well. Some of the key aspects to keep in mind for a telephonic interview include:

- Be very clear in speaking up.

- Try a test call from where you will take your interview with a friend in an almost similar setup.

- Make sure you sort out any technical or audio setup issues from your end before the interview.

- Record your interview call and review how the voice comes across.
    - Check for clarity, tonality, pace, diction and grammar.
    - Check for filler words like "um"," like", "and", "you know".
    - Check for nonstandard responses such as "yeah", "yea", "yup", "no", "gotcha" etc.
    - Be clear and respond with a reason where feasible.

- Try avoiding timewasters such as "can you hear me now", "sorry, I missed a word, can you repeat", "Sorry, can't hear you" etc. While these technical challenges are not fully unavoidable, with better preparation/readiness such thingscanbe avoided.

Handling Skype telephonic/video interviews

A Skype or a video interview is a good way to address some of the disadvantages of a telephonic interview wherein the body language, responsiveness, honesty in answering can be checked. It also poses some challenges to handle in terms of technology. Nevertheless, this is where good preparation and checking the setup will help.

- All aspects of grooming are applicable for a Skype call.
- All aspects of handling telephonic interviews are applicable for a Skype audio or a video call.
- All aspects of body language and first contact are relevant for a Skype call.
- Just like telephonic call, be very clear whilespeaking up.
    - o Try a test call from where you will take your interview with a friend in an almost similar setup.
    - o Make sure you sort out any technical or audio setup issues from your end before the interview
- As far as eye-contact is concerned, try to scan around the camera and focus in the middle. Try to look away now and then, just like a normal interview.
- Always dress up as you do for an in-person interview.
- In case of use of hand gestures, ensure this gets covered by the webcam or cameras so that the interviewers can see the gestures.
- Do not show any signs of nervousness in the telephonic or video calls.

Behaviours to adopt and avoid

To ace interviews, the candidates should practice and develop or build certain behaviours. They may need to avoid certain behaviours to emerge successful. While some of these suggestions may sound simple and primitive, the point is, they are indeed simple. Following certain simple behaviours will help the candidates emerge successful. These are as follows:

- **Be disciplined**
    - o Being disciplined gives a jumpstart to your strategic approach and planning.
    - o Be a disciplined and properly skilled speaker.
    - o Be a very clear writer (emails, resume, CV, cover letter, social media content etc.)

o Be very presentable. Be well dressed, groomed, and presentable. Get professional help if required.

o Practise having courteous and professional behaviour. Behave properly even when no one is watching.

o Put the effort needed relentlessly. You need to persevere to succeed.

o Proofread everything you produce such asCVs, resumes, cover letter etc. Do you want to get ignored because of a spelling error, in spite of being a rock star and the best in the industry?

o Procrastination could invent something but may not get you a job. Do not put preparation until the last minute. It's a recipe for chaos.

- **Practice, practice, and practice**

  o Remember, "No Pain, No Gain" and "practice makes one perfect". Keep on sharpening your axe. It could be your CV/resume, LinkedIn or social media profiles, your technical skills, soft skills, networking skills, communication skills.

  o Keep a goal of doing 1% improvement a day/week. It could improve you by 3678% (1% daily) or 67% (1% weekly) in a year.

  o Learn vociferously. Be active on LinkedIn, Stack Overflow, GitHub, Quora and all other useful and relevant forums.

  o Keep on preparing for the interviews.Prepare for mock-interviews and answers to questions. You can do this even if you are not applying for any jobs to ensure you are relevant.

  o Understand your limits and plan as per your restrictions.

  o Be a realist and a continuous learner –

    ▪ Develop an appetite for handling disappointments.

    ▪ Not everyone is good at handling bad news and it is better to be prepared than going on a downward spiral.

  o Divide and conquer – Split a bigger plan into bite-sized tasks so that you can focus on one task at a time.

- **Mirror play and practice**

  o Be affirmative and play a mirroring role to assure yourself that you are a star and exhibit confidence.

  o Be smiling and courteous and try to be more open and extroverted to get better in a social and professional setting.

  o Enjoy the company of people who groom you, grow you, motivate you and build you and avoid negative ones.

- **Avoid**
  - o Being nervous
  - o Preparing at the lost minute
  - o Overselling and understating
  - o Including skills and work that you don't have any experience or expertise – Reading a few pages on the Internet does not make you a subject matter expert.
  - o Being late to the interviews
  - o Being Rude or discourteous
    - ▪ For example,questioning the credentials of the interview panel or performing a reverse interview due to overconfidence. It's good to showcase your intelligence but you need to manage it within a limit.
  - o Asking too many questions about money on offer
  - o Being very closed or introverted
  - o Taking the interviewers for granted

Conclusion

To succeed in the interviews, it is important for the candidate to have a concrete strategy for the overall process, an approach to address the needs of the process and a structured planning to get the favourable outcomes. This includes a meticulous interview preparation in a disciplined manner, being ready with an approach to handle various types of interviews and a game-plan for each of them, a fully rehearsed or planned execution during the interview to address the interview process and how to deal with technology-centric virtual interviews.

Good interviewers are well trained in identifying good candidates versus average ones and to come across as a good candidate to good interviewers, the candidate needs to do a disciplined and meticulous preparation. Reading this book is a good example of preparing well for the interviews. Although the constructs may largely remain the same, the technology and behavioural questions may differ a bit. Having a good understanding of the process, a clear thinking and approach to execute well during the interview process may go a long way. This is a repeatable process.

As an example, simple things such as not appearing as hung-over, or arriving late or appearing in a sleepy mode, or being in a rush, or wearing unprofessional attire or wearing uncomfortable dresses or shoes can make one very uncomfortable and make the experience a not so welcoming one for the interviewers as well. All these can be avoided by preparationand planning well in advance.

The candidates need to keep in mind that an interview is not a one-way interrogation but an equal-partnership exploration of fitment and an open discussion to find out the best for both a good and enjoyable job at a comfortable pay for the candidate ora well-fitted, skilled and productive employee for the organization. Having a relaxed and happy approach will help the candidates in a very positive way.

Interviews are like examinations. To pass the exams with distinction a person needs to do an extraordinary preparation. He or sheshould be able to solve complex problems within the timelines specified in an intelligent manner. If one does not deliver the expected solution (in the minds of the interviewers), the result is an obvious failure. Hence, understanding the question (or the needs of the organization in this case) is very important.

Questions

1. What is the importance of preparation for an interview?

2. What are some of the soft skill behaviours recommended to exhibit during an interview?

3. What are some reasons for rejecting candidates?

4. What are some of the different types of interviews followed?

5. What is the importance of body language in interviews?

6. What would be your approach while doing a research on the company?

7. What is your approach to a virtual interview?

8. How would you handle a telephonic interview vs. Skype call vs. Skype/video conference interview?

9. What is the importance of interview practice? How would you practice to prepare?

10. What behaviours one need to avoid at the time of interview process?

11. How would you handle the situations when job offers are made?

12. What are some recommended tasks you can perform immediately after your interview?

13. What are some good questions to ask during the interview?

14. What is the importance of appearance and grooming?

15. How would you make a good first impression?

Made in the USA
Monee, IL
20 May 2020